The Spirit of the Sword

THE SPIRIT OF THE SWORD

Iaido, Kendo, and Test Cutting
with the Japanese Sword

NAKAMURA TAISABURO

Translated by Gavin J. Poffley

BLUE SNAKE BOOKS
BERKELEY, CALIFORNIA

Published by Blue Snake Books,
   an imprint of North Atlantic Books
Huichin, unceded Ohlone land
aka Berkeley, California

Cover photo from the film *Eien naru budo*
   (Budo: The Art of Killing)
Cover and book design by Brad Greene

Printed in the United States of America

All photographs and illustrations are taken from the original Japanese edition. Every effort has been made to locate the holders of copyright. If you have any information, please contact North Atlantic Books.

The Spirit of the Sword: Iaido, Kendo, and Test Cutting with the Japanese Sword is sponsored and published by North Atlantic Books, an educational nonprofit based in the unceded Ohlone land Huichin (aka Berkeley, CA) that collaborates with partners to develop cross-cultural perspectives; nurture holistic views of art, science, the humanities, and healing; and seed personal and global transformation by publishing work on the relationship of body, spirit, and nature.

North Atlantic Books' publications are distributed to the US trade and internationally by Penguin Random House Publishers Services. For further information, visit our website at www.northatlanticbooks.com.

PLEASE NOTE: The creators and publishers of this book are not and will not be responsible, in any way whatsoever, for any improper use made by anyone of the information contained in this book. All use of the aforementioned information must be made in accordance with what is permitted by law, and any damage liable to be caused as a result thereof will be the exclusive responsibility of the user. In addition, he or she must adhere strictly to the safety rules contained in the book, both in training and in actual implementation of the information presented herein. This book is intended for use in conjunction with ongoing lessons and personal training with an authorized expert. It is not a substitute for formal training. It is the sole responsibility of every person planning to train in the techniques described in this book to consult a licensed physician in order to obtain complete medical information on his or her personal ability and limitations. The instructions and advice printed in this book are not in any way intended as a substitute for medical, mental, or emotional counseling with a licensed physician or health-care provider.

Library of Congress Cataloging-in-Publication Data

Nakamura, Taisaburo, 1912–2003
   [Nihonto tameshigiri no shinzui. English]
   The spirit of the sword : iaido, kendo, and test cutting with the Japanese sword / Nakamura Taisaburo ; translated by Gavin J. Poffley.
      p. cm.
   Summary: "A complete translation of Nakamura Taisaburo's book on the essence of test cutting and Japanese swordsmanship. Includes photographs, technical information, analysis, and stories from the author's life"—Provided by publisher.
   ISBN 978-1-58394-542-1
1. Iaido. 2. Kendo. I. Poffley, Gavin J. II. Title.
   GV1150.2.N3413 2013
   796.86—dc2   2012026042

5 6 7 8 9 SHERIDAN 24 23 22 21

TABLE OF CONTENTS

From the film *Eien naru budo (Budo: The Art of Killing)*

IMPORTANT EVENTS IN THE LIFE OF NAKAMURA TAISABURO

Martial Arts Ranks and Awards

Chief Instructor of the All-Japan Toyama Ryu Iaido Federation
(Zen Nihon Toyama ryu Iaido Renmei So Shihan)
Head of the All-Japan Battojutsu Federation
(Zen Nihon Battojutsu Renmei)
Nakamura ryu battojutsu shodai soke
(first-generation headmaster)
Battojutsu hanshi ninth dan
Iaido hanshi ninth dan
Jukendo hanshi eighth dan
Kendo kyoshi seventh dan

JANUARY 24, 1912

Born in the Futsukamachi district of Kamiyama city in Yamagata prefecture as the fourth son of Nakamura Shichigoro.

1923

Drops out of the Kamiyama primary school after four years and leaves his hometown for Yokohama. Is involved in the shipping trade at the home of Mr. Nagasawa Otojiro in Namamugi in Yokohama's Tsurumi ward until 1932.

1927

Enrolls in the Yokohama Namamugi Youth Training Center (later renamed as the Youth School). While studying at the center enters the Genbukan judo and kendo dojo, training under the dojo head Sho Genji sensei in both arts. By 1932 has achieved a third dan in kendo and a third dan in judo.

The author in 1932 as a kendo third dan

The author heads out on campaign in 1933, aged twenty-one.

1934 in Manchuria's Rehe province. At this time the author was a light machine gun operator.

1930

Is awarded a medal by the chief officer in charge of the Imperial Army's Kofu recruitment area (the conscription area covering Yamanashi prefecture and part of Kanagawa prefecture).

Is awarded the same honor again in the following year.

1932

Graduates from the Namamugi Youth Training Center.

1933

In January, volunteers for active military service and is enrolled in the Thirty-Second Yamagata Infantry Regiment's reserve corps. During service in this regiment is dispatched to the Manchurian incident and participates in the Rehe campaign. While part of the Kawabara Volunteer Corps takes a bullet in the left side of his chest at the battle for the ancient northern gate of China's Great Wall but carried on fighting. (A depiction of the March 10 occupation of the Great Wall can be found on the lantern on the left side in front of the Yasukuni Shrine.)

The Manchurian incident is concluded in May of that year.

1934

Triumphantly returns to the Yamagata Hara Regiment in May and in December completes his service and is discharged from the military.

1935

Joins the Tokyo Shibaura Electronics Company [Toshiba] at their Tsurumi factory.

1937

Works at the Toshiba Private Youth Academy as a drill instructor and teacher of kendo, jukendo, and sumo. Also holds down a joint position instructing at the Kawasaki Municipal Youth Academy. Joins the Third Close Protection Infantry Regiment for reserve officer training.

1939, the author as an instructor at the Youth Academy. The author is standing at the far left (taken in front of the Meiji Shrine).

1941

Called up in July and joins the Eighteenth Northern Yamagata Unit (formerly known as the Thirty-Second Yamagata Infantry Regiment), being immediately assigned to Manchuria's Heihe province (now Heilongjiang province in China), involved in shoring up defenses along the border with the Soviet Union.

1942

Appointed as a special swordsmanship instructor to the forces in Manchuria.

1943

In September, assigned to the Second Yamashita Army Group Southern Special Attack Unit as an instructor in practical battlefield martial arts and instructs those officers with a duty to carry military swords in the gunto no soho sword-handling methods and tameshigiri using their own blades. During this period is assigned to the southern advance on as many as three occasions but each time recieves orders to be swapped out with someone else due to his role as a special swordsmanship instructor.

The author in 1943 as a squad leader in Manchuria's Heihe province, shoring up defenses along the border with the Soviet Union.

1945

Under Nakamura's supervision the Yamagata Regiment achieves a record three victories in a row in the interunit kendo competitons held at the Imperial birthday festivities in February, and he is presented with a medal for these efforts before the military standard.

In April is reassigned to Fukuoka to prepare for the final battle for the homeland and travels around the various regions of the prefecture as a swordsmanship instructor, training civilian militia units in the "sure killing of a single enemy" ideology for bamboo spear patrols and sword handling. Sees out the War in Hakata and is demobilized.

1949

Opens the Tsurumi Shiseikan dojo and instructs the youth in kendo, including competition with bamboo shinai.

1951

In October holds an all-Yokohama kendo tournament at the shisei-kan with the mayor of Yokohama, Hiranuma Ryo sensei, as the chief official.

1952

In April starts up activities to restore the Hayashizaki Iai Shrine in Yamagata prefecture's Murayama city. Declares the first launch of the movement in the square in front of the Yamagata prefectural offices alongside Yamagata municipal councillor Yamada Saburo.

Participates in the All-Japan Shinai Fencing Tournament held in Nagoya in Aichi prefecture.

1953

In May is awarded the teaching rank of kyoshi in kendo.

1958

In April wins the individual category of the second All-Japan Jukendo Championships representing Kanagawa prefecture. Goes on to achieve third place in the individual event of the third championships and reach the semifinals in the team event at the fifth.

Photo taken in April 1958 to commemorate the author's victory in the individual event at the second All-Japan Jukendo Championships. From front right: second son Yasunori, wife Chieko, second daughter Tomoko. Rear row from right: eldest son Akihiko, eldest daughter Kyoko, author.

The author appearing on NHK's *That's Me* program in 1960, performing spear versus sword kata with his eldest daughter, Kyoko (a fourth dan in jukendo).

1961

Is awarded seventh dan in kendo. In June the restoration of the Hayashizaki Iai Shrine, one of Japan's sacred worship sites, is completed with a new reinforced shrine building of around one hundred square meters in area. The restoration efforts owe much to the cooperation of volunteers from the local area and iaido enthusiasts.

1962

Is awarded eighth dan in iaido.

1966

Is awarded the teaching rank of hanshi in iaido.

The author with the Yokosuka Youth Sciences Academy iaido club in 1970. To the center left [from the viewer's perspective] is his assistant instructor, the late Self Defence Force Sergeant Inoue Kaoru.

The stone plaque dedicated to the Hayashizaki Iai Shrine in October of 1972 (calligraphy by the late former Prime Minister Ikeda).

1972

In May is awarded the Seventh Order of the Sacred Treasure.

In October cooperates with Matsuo Kenpu sensei and has the calligraphy *kenshin* [heart of the sword] brushed by former Prime Minister Ikeda engraved on a stone tablet that is then dedicated to the Hayashizaki Iai Shrine.

1973

Is awarded the teaching rank of hanshi in jukendo.

Celebrates sixtieth birthday and, to commemorate, publishes the sister volumes of *Iaido* and *Iai kendo*. As part of the celebrations at the commemorative tournament to mark the publication dedicates a "divine vessel" to the Hayashizaki Iai Shrine. (This is shown on the Yamagata television station.)

Appearing on the NHK television program *Surprising New Japanese Records* in April 1973 (filmed at Soujiji temple).

1974

Is awarded ninth dan in iaido.

1975

The gunto no soho system created at the former Imperial Army Toyama Military Academy is renamed as Toyama ryu battojutsu. Nakamura opens a study group and prepares to unite the Toyama ryu into one body.

1976

Founds the All-Japan Toyama Ryu Battojutsu Promotional Federation [Zen Nihon Toyama Ryu Battojutsu Shinko Renmei] and becomes its chief instructor [So Shihan]. Mr Tokutomi Tasaburo takes on the position of chairman. Has interactions with Yamaguchi Yuuki sensei from Hokkaido and from Morinaga Kiyoshi sensei from Kansai.

1977

Holds the first All-Japan Toyama Ryu Tameshigiri Tournament at the Tsurumi Kaikan venue in Yokohama.

1978

Holds the second All-Japan Toyama Ryu Tameshigiri Tournament at the Taiyo Kaikan hall in Tokyo.

1979

Is awarded ninth dan in battojutsu.

Holds the third All-Japan Toyama Ryu Tameshigiri Tournament, again at the Tsurumi Kaikan venue in Yokohama, combining the event with a memorial for the late Ishida Kazuto sensei (head of the All-Japan Kendo Federation).

In April renames the All-Japan Toyama Ryu Battojutsu Promotional Federation (Zen Nihon Toyama Ryu Battojutsu Shinko Renmei) as the All-Japan Toyama Ryu Iaido Federation (Zen Nihon Toyama Ryu Iaido Renmei). Kouno Kenzo sensei accepts the position of chairman.

The author at his residence with All-Japan Toyama Ryu Iaido Federation Yamato City branch head, Mr. Shibamoto Akira (taken in 1979).

In front of Hirosaki Castle in Aomori prefecture on the occasion of the All-Tohoku Regional Jukendo Championships. From left to right: the author's comrade in swordsmanship, Mr. Tamauchi; the author; the author's wife, Chieko (taken in 1979).

The Silver Dish for achievements in the martial arts.

Certificate of award for achievements in the martial arts.

Certificate entrusting the author with the position of battojutsu shihan from the International Martial Arts Federation (from 1980).

In November the Shinbukan dojo facilities are completed at the Hayashizaki Iai Shrine thanks to the efforts of many from the All-Japan Toyama Ryu Iaido Federation. To commemorate the laying of the keystone, it is decided that a plaque be engraved with the motto *hyakuren jitoku* [long and constant practice leads to one's mastery] and dedicated to the shrine under the name of Kouno Kenzo sensei. This is currently being crafted and the unveiling ceremony is planned for May 1980.

In November is awarded the Silver Dish for achievements in the martial arts by former Prince Higashikuni Naruhiko, head of the International Martial Arts Federation, in recognition for his many long years of efforts in promoting and developing the martial arts.

The author receiving an award for achievements in the martial arts in November of 1979. At the front left from the viewer's perspective is former Prince Higashikuni Naruhiko, head of the International Martial Arts Federation.

1980

In January takes on the position of inaugural chief instructor for the battojutsu department of the International Martial Arts Federation.

In February the All-Japan Battojutsu Federation [Zen Nihon Battojutsu Renmei] is formed and Nakamura becomes its inaugural head.

1981

In November a monument is built in Nakamura's honour at the Daihonzan Sojiji temple in Tsurumi, Yokohama. The construction and dedication is organized by a devoted battodo practitioner.

1984

In November is awarded tenth dan in battodo from Prince Higashikuni Naruhiko.

1985

Performs a demonstration of battodo at the Sakura Festival in Seattle, Washington.

1986

In November publishes the book *Battodo* and the video *Visual Battodo.*

1988

Performs a demonstration of battodo in Los Angeles that is broadcast on American television.

1990

In May creates the official densho scrolls for the initiation of his forty-three highest-ranking disciples.

In November performs a demonstration at Taiwan Central Police Academy.

1991

Performs a demonstration of battodo in Berlin at the ceremony to mark the reunification of Germany.

1992

In April the first tameshigiri seminar is held for the students of Kinki University in Osaka. Nakamura celebrates his *sanju* (eightieth birthday).

1993

Publishes *Katsujinken Battodo (Battodo of the Life-Giving Sword).*

1997

In November performs a demonstration at the memorial ceremony to mark the 120 years since the Satsuma Rebellion (Seinan War) in Kagoshima prefecture.

1999

In April renames the International Iai Batto-Do Federation (Kokusai Iai Battodo Renmei) as the International Batto-Do Federation (Kokusai Battodo Renmei). Nakamura celebrates his *beiju* (eighty-eighth birthday).

2001

Now ninety years old, Nakamura publishes *Nihonto Seishin to Battodo (Battodo and the Spirit of the Japanese Sword)*.

MAY 15, 2003

Nakamura passes away at the age of ninety-two years old. His official funeral is held at the Sojiji temple in Yokohama, Kanagawa prefecture.

FOREWORD:
COMMEMORATING THE PUBLICATION OF *SPIRIT OF THE SWORD*

The original Japanese edition of this book was published by Kodansha in 1980 under the title *Nihonto tameshigiri no shinzui* (The essence of test cutting with the Japanese sword). My father, Nakamura Taisaburo, authored the work when he was sixty-eight years of age, and it can be seen as the culmination of the Nakamura ryu battodo system that he created from his long years of experience and training. I am truly glad that some thirty-three years on, it is getting an English-language version. By strange coincidence, 2012 marked the anniversary of exactly one hundred years since my father's birth. I am filled with happiness that the plan for the English edition was put into action and realized in this memorable year. I am sure that my father himself would also be pleased by this.

My father, Taisaburo, studied deeply into the shortcomings of both the classical schools of iai and modern kendo, and he created the *happo giri* method of sword handling based on his many long years of experience with the Toyama ryu battojutsu system of military swordsmanship and with practicing tameshigiri, also taking inspiration from the *eiji happo* that forms the basis of calligraphy.

This volume expounds in great detail on the experiences that led to the formation of these methods and their technical content.

In his quest on the path of true "live" swordsmanship, my father always emphasized the technical fundamentals, such as circular motion, subtle grip control, and cutting angle, and warned vehemently against base and misguided practices in which the purpose is simply cutting for cutting's sake. This was due to his belief that the true purpose and meaning of the sword lies in its being a *katsujinken*, a life-giving blade that enriches people. Cutting with a live blade places you in a state on the edge between life and death. It has tremendous value for polishing and forging mental concentration and its harmonious alignment with the physical body. Such an effect is inimitable by any other practice, and this volume details practical methods to achieve these goals.

This book also goes into great detail about the function and characteristics of Japanese swords, the specifications of swords that cut well, and even topics such as how to handle and maintain swords. There are also points of caution and a discussion of the correct mental attitude to take when test cutting, making this a great reference for all students of the sword arts.

I sincerely hope that this book will promote a correct understanding and aid in the spread of the Toyama ryu, Nakamura ryu battodo, and tameshigiri.

Finally I would like to express my thanks and gratitude to all the people who devoted themselves to the production and publication of this book. In particular, I would like to thank Mr. John Evans, head of the UK branch of the International Battodo Federation (IBF), who first proposed the publication and has driven the project forward with passion and enthusiasm; Mr. Yoshitaka Nomura, vice president of the Kakuseikai, who has lent his support in the valued role of coordinator; Mr. Gavin J. Poffley for his superb translations; photographer Mr. Coneyl Jay for reproducing and retouching the vast number of photographs; and Ms. Erin Wiegand and Ms. Susan Bumps from Blue Snake Books. Additionally, I would like to extend my gratitude to all those who have contributed donations to cover some of the production costs. The publication of this book would not have been possible without the help of these people, and I am overcome with sincere gratitude at their kindness. I wish heartfelt thanks to you all.

TOMOKO NAKAMURA
Head of the International Battodo Federation
Second-generation soke of Nakamura ryu battodo
Spring 2012

TRANSLATOR'S COMMENTS

First published in 1980, Nakamura's writing is a time capsule that lets the reader gaze upon the attitudes and events of Japan and, in particular, its martial arts world during the turbulent twentieth century. This book reads very much like an open letter to Japan's martial arts community, praising the good and pointing out what he thought needed changing in uncompromising terms.

The structure of Nakamura's writing is somewhat loose at times, making new points abruptly and adding important or relevant details as they come to him. This style wonderfully conveys his personality, and I can imagine that it is exactly how he spoke to his students face to face. I have strived to maintain that feeling rather than reorganizing the arguments to fit a more logical but much less expressive structure.

Nakamura's writing is, on the one hand, very frank and open; he gives his opinions without holding back. On the other hand, he tries to adhere to the constraints of formal Japanese writing and propriety. This dichotomy beautifully sums up the man himself as a direct, honest, and unpretentious individual who deeply respected the tradition and formality of his culture.

Nakamura assumes a huge amount of background knowledge on the part of the reader—I think it unlikely that he would have written with an international audience in mind. This might make certain topics somewhat inaccessible to those who have not lived in Japan or studied its history and culture in depth. I have thus chosen to translate the main body of the text as is, keeping the original flow and style, but I have also endeavored to provide background information and explanations of the more obscure topics and references in footnotes throughout the book. (All footnotes throughout the book are mine.) I am assuming that the reader of this book is interested in the Japanese sword arts or in Japanese culture in general and will not be turned off by having to deal with possibly unfamiliar concepts.

There are also a number of other, very Japanese idiosyncrasies in Nakamura's writing that may be a little jarring to the average Western reader. The somewhat fluid use of terminology is one; his practice of personally praising and thanking those individuals whom he respected is another. The terms for the martial arts in general or for sword arts in particular are somewhat interchangeable, so you will see *budo* and *bujutsu*, *kendo* and *kenjutsu* (and sometimes also *kobudo*), all referring to the same thing. When the author wishes to be more specific, he will talk about *shinai kendo* or "the classical ryuha of iai," for example.

Translating this book from the original Japanese into English was a fascinating endeavor and has been a great privilege for me. I would like to thank Ms. Tomoko Nakamura, the current soke of the Namakura ryu, for letting me translate this book; Mr. John Evans for organizing the whole endeavor; Mr. Chris Barron for recommending me to John when he was searching for a translator; Professor Stephen Chan, OBE, for his sagely advice and guidance; and my dear wife, Taeko, for all her love and support.

GAVIN J. POFFLEY
London, 2012

INTRODUCTION

The ultimate meaning of the path of the sword is not found in killing but in the polishing of one's own spirit. The ideology of modern kendo and iaido shows a reverence to respect and courtesy based on the spirit of the Japanese sword and has as its objective the methods of spiritual purification unique to the Japanese people. It has a great role to play in improving upon the mistaken societal trends of democracy since the War.

The Japanese sword may not be practically applicable in this age of civilization we live in, but it must not be forgotten that one of the three divine relics of the Imperial panoply passed down by our Yamato race is a sword, and swords have been valued since ancient times as the soul of the warrior. The Japanese sword is also an object of fantastic artistic beauty with no analogue anywhere around the world.

The essence of budo can be found where the Japanese sword is used to forge and discipline the body and spirit. In November of 1978, the film *Eien naru budo* [literally "the eternal martial arts," released in the West under the title *Budo: The Art of Killing*], which expresses the essence of the Japanese martial spirit, won two gold medals for best picture and best editing at the first Miami International Film Festival held in the state of Florida in the United States.

This film depicted scenes of deadly, focused blood-and-sweat training in the various martial art disciplines that come from the creed of bushido, contrasting the stillness and motion, life and death within them and approaching the true essence of bushido. This follows the theme put down in the *Hagakure* that "the path of the Warrior is to live constantly as if one is already dead." This film took around three years to make and included vistas of Japan's stunning natural beauty, showcasing our four seasons. It is a most joyous development that such a work should be chosen for the greatest honor from more than eighty films from all around the world, and I must show my deep appreciation and respect for the efforts of the crew who created such a wonderful picture.

I myself was also part of the cast of this film and demonstrated Toyama ryu and Nakamura ryu tameshigiri and kumitachi kata for it. Especially for the tameshigiri scenes, the filmmakers put in great diligence and effort to capture my movements in two-thousand-frames-per-second slow motion. This effort was well worth it, and the memorable footage that resulted accurately captured the correct circular path of the blade arc and cutting angle, vividly getting across the feeling of cutting with a Japanese sword.

The film ended with a scene of a duel pitting sword against sword that, while perhaps unfavorable to the prevailing tastes in this day and age, was amazing to watch.

In 1973 I commemorated my sixtieth year of life by publishing the sister volumes *Iaido* and *Iai kendo*. I wish to express my heartfelt gratitude toward all the support and approval I have received for these books from enthusiasts everywhere and the development within the sword arts that they have sparked. There are many fine kendo and iaido training manuals available but very few publications that are both bountiful in information on the Japanese sword itself and that holistically integrate the disciplines of kendo and iaido with the vital practice of tameshigiri, which gives immediate and important technical feedback. In addition to commemorating *Eien naru budo*'s historical success, it is thus that I decided to take up my pen again and write this book. Even though I feel some resistance in light of the prevailing attitude of the times, I have endeavored to breathe new life into the grand traditions of the Yamato people and promote the spirit of the Japanese sword.

This book brings together my experiences during the War as a special practical martial arts instructor for the Second Yamashita Army Group's Southern Special Attack Unit, making use of the *gunto no soho* military sword methods in instructing tameshigiri exercises. I also applied my further personal research and training in swordsmanship under the ethos of *hyakuren jitoku* [long and constant practice leads to one's mastery], as well as the results of my studies into the secrets of the densho from a multitude of iai schools. I created the happo giri used in my Nakamura ryu battojutsu system as a logical sword-handling exercise in response to the teachings of Shu-ha-ri and taking inspiration from the eiji happo that is the basis of calligraphy. There would be no greater joy for me than if readers would use this exercise in particular as a resource for their training.

This volume is based on my honest experiences, but alas I am not skilled in letters and I fear there are many areas of the text that are not up to scratch. I humbly request that you forgive these faults and welcome readers to point out anything that they may notice.

Furthermore, I am greatly indebted to the following people for their polite forewords to my book:[1]

Kouno Kenzo sensei: chairman of the Nihon Taiiku Kyokai [Japan Sports Association] and former speaker of the House of Councillors

Hatta Ichiro sensei: chairman of the Zen Nihon Jukendo Renmei [All-Japan Jukendo Federation] and former member of the House of Councillors

Kiyoura Sueo sensei: chairman of the Kokusai Budoin Renmei [International Martial Arts Federation] and former major general in the Japanese Imperial Army

Mr. Fushimi Ryu: chief executive officer of the Zen Nihon Toyama Ryu Iaido Renmei [All-Japan Toyama Ryu Iaido Federation) and CEO of the Kokusai Keibisha Company (Kokusai Security Services Co. Ltd.]

Mr. Hayashi Kunishiro: chairman of the Nihon Bugeki Kai [Japan Martial Film Association] and head of the Toyama Ryu Geinokai Shibu [Toyama Ryu Entertainment-Industry Branch]

---

1. Please see Appendix 1 to read these forewords.

I would also like to express my immense gratitude to the following officials of the Toyama ryu for their cooperation:

Former Chairman Mr. Tokutomi Tasaburo
Vice Office Manager Mr. Tanabe Tetsundo
Director Mr. Tanaka Tatsuo
Mr. Soga Yoshiharu

NAKAMURA TAISABURO
Zen Nihon Toyama Ryu Iaido Shihan Chairman of the Zen Nihon
    Battojutsu Renmei [All-Japan Battojutsu Federation]
Shodai soke [First-generation headmaster]
    of Nakamura ryu battojutsu
Spring 1980

CHAPTER 1

KOBUDO AND SHU-HA-RI

Gyaku kesagiri (reverse diagonal cut)

The Teachings of Shu-ha-ri

In this day and age all things evolve and advance at a tremendous pace and, as is shown most clearly by modern science, new discoveries are made rapidly and without pause, the march of progress knowing not of idleness.

Against this backdrop, it is most lamentable that the technique and *kata*[2] of modern iaido swordsmanship is too rigidly obsessed with the traditional *ryuha*[3] and little technical progress can be seen.

The martial spirit of our forefathers, as they risked life or death, was greater than most nowadays can imagine, and that spirit is indeed still alive today. However, most modern study of iai methods that should be based on their teachings of *Shu-ha-ri*[4] is not realizing its full potential.

---

2. 形 (literally "form") or 型 (literally "mold"); the prearranged training exercises of traditional Japanese arts.

3. 流派; the feudal, guild-like organizations dedicated to the practice and teaching of martial arts, often rendered into English as "school" or "style" but closer to "lineage." The word literally means "branch of a flow," referring to the flow of tradition and teachings down generations of practitioners.

4. 守破離; a term that sums up the traditional three-stage process of mastering any art, the three kanji characters that represent each stage literally mean "adherence" (*shu*; 守), "breaking" (*ha*; 破), and "separation" (*ri*; 離).

The "shu" stage of the Shu-ha-ri process, when related to the study of iai and kendo, is faithfully following a teacher's instructions, adhering to the unique teachings of one's style, and learning and practicing its kata and individual techniques unwaveringly and single mindedly to internalize the lessons.

The "ha" stage comes when the teachings, kata, and techniques that have been learned are fully internalized. The trainee naturally moves on to absorb the teachings of other style's teachers and adopts the good techniques from other sources. Through doing this, one breaks out of the techniques in the kata thus far strictly followed and develops one's own mental approach and physical skill.

The final stage of "ri" comes after further practice and training at the "ha" stage. Here the trainee is no longer caught up with adherence [shu] or consciously breaking away [ha] and moves from singular, fixed forms and set ryuha systems to his own innovations, creating something new and diligently training in it.

The spirit of this Shu-ha-ri process is not just limited to iai and kendo but also has great importance in how one lives one's life.

One issue that I stress repeatedly at iaido seminars and in martial arts magazines is the viability of sword methods that start from the *seiza*[5] position.

The bushi of the past would wear paired swords when out and about his business, and although he might keep the smaller *kodachi* (also known as a *wakizashi*) in his belt, when seated in seiza he would never have worn the longer katana in that position.

However, the mainstream practice of modern iaido has an abundance of long-sword methods starting from seiza.

In the years before the War, the *gunto no soho*[6] (Toyama ryu iaido) system of sword handling was formulated in the old Imperial Army Toyama Military Academy as seven purely standing techniques

---

5. 正座; Japanese formal seated posture.
6. 軍刀の操法; literally "military sword-handling methods."

based on the understanding that seiza is an unrealistic posture for sword use.

In the same vein, Takayama Masakichi sensei, kenjutsu shihan for the Japanese Imperial Navy, came to an enlightened understanding of the differences between kendo training with bamboo shinai and the handling of actual sharpened swords. He went on to acquire actual combat sword experience, founding his own ryuha under the name of Takayama ryu battojutsu, which he taught and promoted around the country. It was centered at the former Imperial Naval Academy.

Furthermore, at the old Dai Nippon Butokukai[7] a system of five standing sharp-sword-handling exercises was created under the designation of battojutsu, and these corresponded closely with iaido.

It is often said, "Kendo starts and finishes with iai."[8] But it is absolutely impossible to reconcile sword methods from the seiza position with kendo practice. This is a problem in my sincere intention to unite both of these disciplines, effectively applying the teachings of Shu-ha-ri and further fostering the spirit of the Japanese sword.

In my personal and idiosyncratic way, I have done much research and study into the koryu iaido that was created by the masters of the past. I have put my forty-plus years of experience with tameshigiri to good use in creating the happo giri exercise. This is a logical method to teach sword handling and draws inspiration from the *eiji happo*[9] that is used to teach the fundamentals of calligraphy.

---

7. 大日本武徳会; an official organization created in 1895 with government backing to coordinate the teaching and practice of martial arts in Japan. (It no longer exists as a government body.)

8. The original meaning of the word *iai* (居合) is posited to refer to sets of techniques in classical martial arts curricula that cover fighting from seated or kneeling positions. The word is still used in this way in addition to the more common meaning of sword-drawing techniques. Thus this saying can be interpreted along the lines of "kendo starts and finishes with seated practice" as well as that "the core of kendo is sword drawing."

9. 永字八法; literally "the eight methods in the character of 永 (ei)." A fundamental penmanship exercise that utilizes the fact that all eight of the basic strokes needed to write any Chinese character can be found in the character 永.

At present my students, colleagues, and I continue striving in our studies to synthesize the Toyama ryu and Nakamura ryu systems, integrating practical tameshigiri. I sincerely desire to improve and perfect the technical quality in swordsmanship by studying the scrolls of transmission left by our forbearers and applying the teachings of Shu-ha-ri.

Points of Concern Regarding the Classical Schools

Between the Muromachi period (1336–1573) and the early years of the Meiji era (1868–1912), there were more than three thousand schools [ryuha] of the various martial disciplines extant around the country, but after wearing swords was banned in mid-Meiji, this dwindled to around one hundred schools.

When watching demonstrations of the koryu[10] arts today, there are many times I have serious doubts about the validity of the sword methods in the kata on show.

Today we see the different ryuha being exhibited at regional events all over the nation, but the scrolls that transmitted the core secrets of the koryu[11] were originally something intensely personal in which an individual would record the kata they had formulated based on their own ideas and experiences. When the information in these scrolls came to be passed on to the next successor of the school, it was not uncommon for the inheritor to be sworn to uphold utmost secrecy and be expressly forbidden to reveal the transmitted secrets, even to trusted parents, brothers, or relatives. Often the teachings were not permitted to leave the school or were restricted to being passed down

---

10. 古流; a contraction of koryu budo/bujutsu (古流武道／武術) referring to "classical" or historical schools of martial arts in comparison with modern gendai budo (現代武道). The official dividing line used to delineate the two periods is 1868, which is the first year of the rule of Emperor Meiji and designated as the start of the modern era in Japanese national chronology.

11. 伝書 (densho) or 極意書 (gokuisho).

only within a single dojo or a single province. It is even said that there were those who were cut down on the spot for seeing the kata of a ryuha that were deemed to be strictly secret.

From 1872 when the requirement for the samurai class to wear swords in public was lifted, the practice of kenjutsu began to atrophy. Five years later in 1877, when the public wearing of swords was forbidden, ordinary citizens outside of the police or military were prevented from even practicing the sword arts. It is due to these events that a "lost era" came about in the transmission of the inner mysteries of swordsmanship.

About halfway through the Meiji era, the senior martial artists in the police department got together to create the *keishicho ryu*[12] style of swordsmanship, taking kata from various koryu schools and subjecting them to further study and research.

On December 20, 1912, the Dai Nippon Butokukai held an executive meeting. These discussions resulted in a council to oversee proposals for creating a set of nationally endorsed, official kendo kata known as the Dai Nippon Teikoku Kendo Kata (Kendo Kata of the Grand Imperial Japanese Empire). Twenty-five expert swordsmen were selected to sit on this council, including five masters currently holding hanshi rank and various teachers of kyoshi rank from around the country. From these twenty-five authorities, five were chosen to act as chief auditors and entrusted with creating the technical proposals themselves.

In June of 1913, the first chief auditors meeting was opened at the Butokukai headquarters, attended by the following five luminaries:

Negishi Shingoro: Shinto munen ryu (hanshi, Tokyo)
Tsuji Shinpei: Shingyoto ryu (kyoshi, Saga)
Monna Tadashi: Hokushin itto ryu (kyoshi, Butokukai headquarters)
Naito Takaharu: Hokushin itto ryu (kyoshi, Butokukai headquarters)
Takano Sasaburo: Ono itto ryu (kyoshi, Tokyo Shihan Gakko)

---

12. 警視庁流; literally "police department school/style."

These five expert kendoka came together and created today's Nihon kendo kata that have remained in their current form since then with only a few minor alterations.

Details of these events are covered by Shoji Munemitsu sensei (former chief executive of the Kendo Renmei) in his publication *Kendo gojunen*,[13] so I will not go further into them here.

The fundamental kendo instruction for tournaments that is carried out nationally today is based on these kendo kata. Kata is training and training is kata. These forms are the basis for all modern kendo instruction, teaching students to apply the lessons on courtesy, posture, attitude and bearing, *kamae* (mental and physical preparation), and striking theory in the techniques contained within them. However, the fact that modern training and instruction for kendo tournaments no longer includes the kata covering methods such as *hasso no kamae, waki gamae,* or the three kodachi forms demands serious consideration from instructors.

In 1978 and 1979 the first and second Zen Nihon Kobudo Enbu Taikai[14] events were held at the Nihon Budokan in grand style. These events were indeed successful, but deeper problems could be seen in the performances showcased there. This is eloquently summed up in a letter to the reader's discussions section of the May 1979 edition of *Kendo Nippon* entitled "Responsibilities of the koryu" and submitted by Mr. Tada of Katsuura of Chiba prefecture. This letter is highly critical of the performers at such events, and it goes without saying that I am in total agreement with Mr. Tada's sentiments. I would like to print an extract of his correspondence here:

> I think that it is a wonderful thing that Kobudo is still alive and breathing today after such a long history. However, I believe that there are more than a few of my fellow martial arts enthusiasts

---

13. 剣道五十年 *(Fifty Years of Kendo).*
14. 全日本古武道演武大会 (All-Japan Classical Martial Arts demonstration).

who, like myself, notice many points of concern in public performances of the various ryuha, their techniques, and the swordsmen of today. In these national-level events the performers have considerable determination and require a total mental commitment to exhibit the techniques of their style, but unfortunately, with the exception of a few ryuha, what I see is that the vast majority of practitioners have not trained enough, as is obvious from the bluntness and heaviness of their body control. One can also often see martial artists who, due to their extreme age, can no longer even stand, kneel, or move satisfactorily.

It is admittedly very admirable that these senior martial artists have continued their training for so long into their advanced years but one must wonder about this in the context of the essential pillar of martial arts that is *shin-gi-tai,* the perfect unification of one's mental, physical, and technical powers. It is, after all, only right and natural that martial performances are carried out by hale and skilled practitioners in their prime.

If this is not paid the due concern then there is a danger of our deep and painstakingly practiced and perfected bujutsu being shown at nothing more than an elementary level and the true essence of the martial arts being warped . . . I believe that if one only practices to preserve and pass on the kata then the true significance of these exercises will eventually become lost, reducing the practitioner's training to an empty formality removed from its original intent. It is said that we are now seeing a renaissance in the kobudo arts, but in the majority of cases what is being shown is still in the realms of the martial novice when looked at by the specialized eye of the *gendai budoka.*[15]

---

15. 現代武道家; practitioner of a Japanese martial discipline founded after 1868, such as judo, kendo, or aikido. These disciplines tend to specialize in one aspect of martial technique and thus have achieved greater technical advancement within that area than the more generalized koryu.

Of course, there are experts in the koryu bujutsu of the same proficiency level as the kyoshi and hanshi of the gendai budo but it is unfortunate that these people are rarely motivated to show their skills at these kinds of national display these days.

It is for these reasons that I despair at the kind of underdeveloped technical proficiency described above.

For kobudo to exhibit true meaning it must have potency enough that a gendai budoka would accept it as valuable, and if it is only found interesting by novices or those outside of the martial arts then it is merely an anachronistic curiosity. This potency will only come from dedicated practice and training. Kobudo needs to have a level of technical quality such that the majority of gendai budo can look at a koryu performance and participate on a deep level. After all, kobudo is very much the foundation and source of Japan's martial arts that attract attention from around the world . . .

As martial arts enthusiasts we must take care to put in enough training and practice for demonstrations at these events so that we do not attract this kind of criticism. Kobudo has been passed down through the tradition of transmitting its core secrets in the densho, but times have changed. Today it is exhibited in front of the public eye. Those who inherit and continue a ryuha have a responsibility to the spirits of their forefathers to diligently study the densho and put utmost effort into their training.

Abstract and Unclear Scrolls of Transmission

Today the various koryu schools interact with each other and hold public demonstrations, but in the past there were no competitions where the practitioners fought using protective armor. Most training was done bareheaded, performing kata using wooden swords. This was a type of training in which one's life was constantly put on the line, and a single mistake could be fatal. Considerations such as correct stance, posture, and attitude were a distant second priority to survival. Those who went through this would go on to formulate their personal techniques and write their own densho.

To give some idea of the kind of names given to kata of swordsmanship in the densho, we can see examples such as *yokogumo, tora issoku, iwanami, taki otoshi,* and *yamaoroshi;* and in the kodachi kata, *dai harikomi, surikomi, makikaeshi, hyakkan ashi,*[16] and so on, which all cover iai techniques. Looking over these names, we can see that they are all written with kanji, the meaning of which is largely cryptic and unclear.

In 1978 a densho from around two hundred years ago was discovered at the former house of Kaneko Sadao sensei, chief executive of the Gunma prefecture branch of the Toyama ryu, and I was graciously allowed to view it. All I could make out was that there were lists of names on the paper, but I could not read most of them, written as they were using the kinds of characters described above. All I got was that it was a scroll concerning the secrets of the sword. In short this document eschewed recording practical directions in sword handling and instead simply had lists of esoteric names, such as *myoken, hiki honkaku,* and *kogaimakura.*[17] In order to make any more of this I decided I had to consult an authority on such things.

---

16. 横雲 *yokogumo* (literally "horizontal cloud"); 虎一足 *tora no issoku* (literally "single tiger's foot");岩波 *iwanami* (literally "wave on rocks"); 滝落し *taki otoshi* (literally "waterfall drop"); 山嵐 *yamaoroshi* (literally "wind blowing from the mountains"); 大張込 *daiharikomi* (literally "grand ambush"); 摺込 *surikomi* (literally "grinding"); 巻返 *makigaeshi* (literally "wrapping reverse"); 百貫足 *hyakkan ashi* (literally "one hundred kan" [375 kg] foot). One explanation for the esoteric and confusing nature of these names is a requirement for secrecy so that the densho would be of little use if they fell into the hands of rivals who would not be familiar with the ryuha's shared codes and metaphors.

17. 妙剣 *myoken* (literally "wonderous sword"); 引本覚 *hiki honkaku* (literally "pulling Honkaku"); 笄枕 *kogai makura* (literally "hilt knife pillow").

Kumitachi Kata Involving the Collision of Blade on Blade

In some sets of *kumitachi*[18] kata, you can see forms in which one practitioner stops the sword of an opponent who is making a powerful cleaving cut using the center of his blade.

I recall a particular kobudo demonstration event in Osaka in 1978 where, during a kata performance, an exponent of a particular ryuha received the opponent's cut on his own blade in this manner, snapping his sword clean in two as the fragments flew across the field. It was very fortunate that nobody was injured. In other ryuha's kata, there are also situations in which one swordsman meets an opponent cutting with full-body power using a horizontal ichimonji uke block impacting at the dead center of their blade.

It is not important that things were taught in this way in the densho from the past, and we must always study to improve our sword-handling methods. At the very least we should reconsider the dubious merits of this practice in terms of preserving the sword itself and preventing danger in training. In 1949 at the former Shiseikan dojo, we carried out some experiments into the durability of swords. At this time the occupying forces would confiscate swords if they saw them, so we decided to buy eight cheap blades in the understanding that it would not matter if they got confiscated, since they probably would be anyway. With these swords we tested the effects on the blade of cutting through copper, forged iron, pig iron, and dried bamboo; and of striking to the back, the side, and the cutting edge of the blade while it was secured on a pedestal.

In the blade-on-blade experiment, sparks flew from the katana used to make the cut, and a deep crack was cut into the one receiving the blow, proving beyond doubt that a poor-quality sword would have snapped in two.

---

18. Formal paired training exercises.

From these experiments it is clear that blocking a cut on the edge of the blade in kumitachi practice is very dangerous, and receiving it at a dead horizontal angle could even threaten the practitioner's life. The sixth kata in the Nihon kendo kata also has the practitioners crossing swords, but in this case it features methods of parrying away and sliding down the opponent's sword using the side of the blade [*shinogi ji*], which does not hold the same such danger. However, this series of kata also features methods in which one receives on the cutting edge of the blade before spinning out in front of the opponent. The validity of this may need to be reconsidered.

Sometimes in kobudo displays you can see kata for the *bokuto* (wooden sword) in which blades will clash, but these methods belong in the fight scenes of period-action films. I would personally like people to treat wooden blades exactly as their sharp metal cousins and expect exemplary demonstrations using them that skillfully apply the koryu sword-handling methods.

The Absence from Training of the Instinctive Sword Technique of Right and Left Kesagiri

If I am to give my personal and honest opinions when considering the sword-handling methods in the koryu schools that exclusively practice iaido, then I must express my sadness that the natural and instinctive technique of correctly performed right and left diagonal cuts [*kesagiri*] is not incorporated into their training.

There are statistics available proving that the majority of casualties from sword wounds at the fiercest battle of the Satsuma rebellion at Taburazaka, as well as in the battles of the Ueno shogitai[19] and in the Russo-Japanese and Sino-Japanese Wars, were killed by the techniques

---

19. 彰義隊; an elite corps formed by the shogunate during the Bakumatsu period in Japan. The shogitai took a large part in the battles of the Boshin War, especially at the battle of Toba-Fushimi and the battle of Ueno, where they were nearly exterminated.

of right and left kesagiri and *tsuki* [thrust]. These are proof as to the value of kesagiri as a practical method.

Of course, modern kendo has its legal striking targets fixed as the face mask, the breastplate, the gauntlets, and thrusting at the throat guard, and so must be treated differently. But for the majority of iai schools that use sharp swords, even though correct vertical cutting [*shinchoku giri*] is widely practiced, left and right kesagiri is only occasionally incorporated or more commonly not covered at all. For example, in the eleven techniques of the Omori ryu not even a single one covers this method. This is indicative that the kata of this school are not based on experiences with tameshigiri and that it is a style concerned only with the formalities of kata.

I imagine that the reason there is no basic kata for kesagiri in most iaido comes from the bushi of the Edo period, who placed a great spiritual value on the sword as a symbol of a warrior's soul, and also the fact that a katana would be of great monetary value in and of itself. This led to warriors' preferring to train with bokuto and study the kata for those instead, rather than risk damaging a precious steel blade.

Furthermore, we sometimes see iaido sword-handling kata in which the practitioner makes a pushing cut with one hand on the back of the blade (known as the *mine*), such as the ukigumo, yamaoroshi, and iwanami kata from the Hasegawa Eishin ryu. However, this too is not a feasible technique from the perspective of real sword combat.

The November 1978 edition of *Kendo Nihon* featured the Hasegawa ryu and the Omori ryu as transmitted by Hayashi Rokudayu Morimasa,[20] ninth-generation inheritor of these iai systems. It was written that Hayashi was both a retainer and chef for the aristocratic Uchiyama family, and thus these were sword kata passed down by one who also wielded the kitchen knife. The teachings of this tradition show that whatever the situation, a pushing cut with a hand on the back of the sword's blade is an untenable technique. Whether preparing fish with

---

20. 林六太夫守政 (1661–1732.)

a knife or using a sword on a human opponent, this method will cut through flesh but not bone. The teachings of the koryu in relation to actual combat are clear that one must cut through both flesh and bone, and this can be seen in the densho.

There are also kata in which kesagiri is performed starting from the seiza position, raising the left knee, and then performing the cut from right to left. This too is an impractical and unnatural method. The fundamentals of kesagiri mean that when cutting to the right, you withdraw the left leg, and when cutting to the left, you withdraw the right. This is a safety precaution to prevent injury to oneself.

Many valuable lessons on the martial spirit are transmitted in the koryu budo, and we cannot fail to show respect toward these. But when one examines and studies the kata itself, there appear to be a number of problems. I firmly believe that looking to the old while learning the new will lead to progress and improvement in technique. This is also the path set out by Shu-ha-ri.

Stamping In with the Forward Leg Is an Incorrect Drawing Technique

There exists a trend in solo sword-drawing kata of making a large step into the draw with the right leg while vocalizing a loud noise in the manner common to shinai kendo. This could be seen among many iai exponents before the War and can still be observed today. Stepping in with vigor while drawing and vocalizing with force certainly gives an impression of the integration of body, sword, and spirit. It looks imposing, and I myself also practiced this kind of stamping entry when I started training in iaido. However, this action is a mistaken drawing method that can occur only in solo practice where one is cutting the air. In stamping forward with the right leg, the left is not rooted and floats slightly, making it impossible to cut solid objects with this method and rendering it inapplicable to tameshigiri. To cut through objects it is important that a swordsman have a stable posture in the hips and feet.

For shinai kendo the stamping entry is a suitable method for entering into the opponent's space and correctly delivering a powerful strike with proper coordination of body, sword, and spirit, but it takes away the balance. So when cutting with a sharpened blade, it is not a practice conducive to making effective pulling cuts.

It follows that we should reflect on the fact that raising the right leg to stamp in is meaningless from the point of view of actual sword handling and adjust our practices accordingly.

We must note however that for practical two-handed thrusting techniques a stamping entry is viable and useful for the proper coordination of body, sword, and spirit, so this does not apply across the board.

Overattachment to Style

The masters of the past thought out their personal combative methodologies based on their experiences in life-or-death struggles and mortal combat and recorded their teachings and secrets for posterity in the densho. These are now appreciated and revered as items of cultural heritage and, because duels with swords are no longer a reality in this age of civilization, the various schools of swordsmanship enact the teachings for spiritual enrichment and training. It is the sad situation today that the inheritors of the classical ryuha who continue these traditions now present only formalized kata in front of the public gaze at demonstration events around the country. The majority of schools have become unable to move with the times, and even ryuha that have been handed down since ancient times have naturally died out, leaving some that exist today only in the densho scrolls.

Up until the Meiji period the iai of the Hasegawa Eishin ryu was passed down as a closed tradition in the Tosa fiefdom, but in 1917 Nakayama Hakudo sensei began his training in this school, taking an oath not to interact with other schools and to reveal nothing to outsiders, be they family or otherwise. Even though he was stifled and obstructed by these rules, Nakayama sensei went on to formulate his own iai in line with the universal principles of the sword and opened the door to the development and spread of modern iaido across the country. The development of modern iaido could not have happened without Nakayama sensei.

What I have to say may be discourteous to those who have mastered the path of the sword, but when considering the modern situation from the point of view of the teachings of Shu-ha-ri I am certain in my belief that had there been effort to formulate and promote training in a system of standing iai (sword-drawing techniques from a standing position) from the start of the modern era, we would not have the disparate system that exists today. Instead, an iaido intimately aligned and unified with kendo would have spread both before and after the War. We must bear in mind the principle that the roots of kendo can be realized only in iai, a principle summed up as *Iai kendo ittai* [literally "kendo and iai as one"], and this is of particular relevance to sword methods from the seiza position.

That is to say that the mystery of why iaido did not spread or develop much before the War is because it was mainly practiced as techniques from seiza. I consider that had the iaido world managed to formulate a method consistent with the official kendo kata, then the art would have developed and branched out in unison with kendo from inception. The oneness of kendo and iaido is often alluded to in theory with philosophies such as *keni ittai* and *iai soku kendo*. As far as theory goes this is laudable, but it is the sad truth that in the current era the technical methodology of kendo and the kata of iaido are far from being unified.

Of the seven techniques that make up the current iteration of the Zen Nihon Kendo Renmei Seitei Iai kata set, there are three performed from seiza, one from *tate-hiza* (the raised-knee sitting posture), and three standing techniques. The reason that even these have not yet been logically reevaluated and improved is because they have been

Calligraphy by Nakayama Hakudo sensei, age eighty-eight, depicting the motto *Yama takaki ga yue ni tattokarazu*. ("A mountain is not mighty simply for being tall," meaning that something is not truly great just for looking the part; it must also have the inner substance to back it up.)

formulated without reference to actual tameshigiri experiences. In short they are a symptom of overattachment to styles and systems.

The fact that instruction in modern shinai kendo training for competitions strongly discourages stances such as hasso no kamae or waki gamae is also because of this kind of fierce yet misguided attachment.

Masters Ozonoe, Suzuki, and Tsujimura perform beneath the cherry blossoms.

CHAPTER 2

THE INTEGRATION OF IAIDO, KENDO, AND TAMESHIGIRI

Viewed from Abroad, Japanese Iaido Is Artistic Performance with the Katana, a Dance of the Sword

In 1973 I reached the sixtieth year of my life, and to commemorate this I published the sister volumes of *Iaido* and *Iai kendo*. Thanks to the support of many martial arts enthusiasts, these were critically received. After the publication I received numerous letters of correspondence from around the country but also from places like Hawaii, Taiwan, and Hong Kong. Among those letters there was one from a young

Decisive combative distance. Renowned swordsman Mr. Obata is on the left, the author on the right.

man in Hong Kong who had graduated from Japan's Keio University, which read as follows:

> I consider Japanese iaido to be an artistic performance with the katana, a dance of the sword. I was greatly impressed with your instructional manual for tameshigiri, which is logical and well written and has easily understood photographs analyzing the techniques. I am very much looking forward to the opportunity to go to Japan and meet you in person.

I have also received great support from Waseda University alumnus and kendo seventh-dan Huang Beihua sensei and several other individuals. In particular, special mention must go to Zheng Langyao sensei, who came to Japan in 1977 to participate in a three-day Toyama ryu, Nakamura ryu, and tameshigiri seminar at the Zen Nihon Toyama Ryu Iaido Renmei branch in Tochigi prefecture.

Furthermore, as of 1978 I am making preparations for a gendai budo friendship tour with the aid of Jian Xinzhe sensei, chairman of the Hong Kong and People's Republic of China Taiwan Province National Arts Association.

I keenly feel that we should reconsider certain widespread training practices and make iaido into a discipline that can be integrated with kendo. The same can be said of kobudo as well. Such integration would be most beneficial for promoting the spirit of the Japanese sword.

The Differences between Iaido, Kendo, and Tameshigiri

Kendo and iaido were originally one and the same art, with iai denoting all motions and techniques up until the sword is drawn, and everything after that being kendo. But in the modern day it is the usual situation that they are trained completely separately.

In my estimation, if we put aside school-age trainees, only around 20 percent of modern kendo practitioners practice kendo and iaido together.

Of course, even before the War there were few kendoka or other martial arts enthusiasts who would train both arts in unison. As I repeatedly point out, this is due to the fact that since the Meiji era iaido has largely been practiced as sword methods from seiza. This trend has opened up fundamental differences between kendo and iaido and has left no option but for them to be trained separately. This is, alas, an unavoidable sign of the times.

When I consider my many long years of study into the use of the sword and my experiences in its instruction, there are a few points I would like to make regarding the kata of kobudo, kendo, and iaido.

First, there is the fact that the sword methods in iaido, kendo, and kobudo kata are all predetermined solo exercises done without partners and striking thin air. This is especially true in the case of iaido, which is exclusively solo training in which one must imagine and visualize the opponent (enemy). Such training cannot teach the student important things like the correct combative distance [間合; *maai*] when making a cut.

Accordingly, there is little wonder that the discipline is described as "an artistic performance with the katana, a dance of the sword" in the letter from our friend in Hong Kong mentioned above. We must also think hard about iai being mainly practiced as techniques from seiza. Using a sword from seiza is not taught in kendo, and the width between the legs (approximately two steps) when drawing from seiza as seen in iai is an impossible method to apply in reality.

In arts like judo and karatedo, kata is practiced as kata, and then the trainees progress to exercises applying the movements with partners. However in the case of iaido, because it uses a sharpened blade, any application can be carried out only against a visualization of a foe in solo kata.

At the Hayashizaki Iai Shrine, one of Japan's Shinto prayer sites, there is a custom for iai practitioners to make offerings to the resident *kami* [spirits] that mark multiple tens of thousands of draws they have completed in training. One must respect the spiritual training achieved through such diligent and repeated drawing practice for tens of thousands of times. But as solo training without an opponent, this cannot possibly lead to improvements in the kind of technique that is forged by kendo training wearing armor and is thus a wasted endeavor.

Compared with this, the kata of kendo requires of the practitioner correct distancing, proper posture for striking, attitude, coordination of footwork with the sword, proud bearing, situational awareness, and technique, so practicing these paired forms and engaging in fiercely intense training with armor will lead to improvements in technical skill. I can thus thoroughly recommend the kendo kata on these points.

On the other hand, the iaido kata require hand positioning and control, correct blade trajectory, striking angle, and circular motion. Accordingly they are impossible for beginners to fully grasp but are suited to high-level yudansha with experience of tameshigiri. A good illustration of this can be seen at the Hayashizaki Iai Shrine in my home prefecture of Yamanashi.

It is the custom for martial artist pilgrims to the shrine to perform a *hono enbu*[21] on the mats before it, and if you look closely you will notice countless scratches and cuts made by sword tips in the surface of the tatami. If it were a wooden floor then this would not stand out as much, but because it is a matted surface it is immediately obvious that these are marks from sword tips and proves that the *tenouchi*[22] skills of the pilgrims are lacking.

---

21. 奉納演武; a demonstration of martial arts before a shrine done to venerate the kami that are said to dwell there.

22. 手の内; literally "within the hands," referring to gripping, hand positioning, and subtle manipulation of the sword handle.

This is all because they are using the sword from seiza and using a grip on the hilt that opens up the *tsukagashira* [pommel]. If they were performing from a standing position there would be no chance of cutting down into the mats. I believe that the majority of these hono enbu performances are by beginners, but it is still a point of sword handling that deserves special caution.

I participated in the martial arts display events organized by the Zen Nihon Iaido Renmei for the twenty years from that organization's inception until the twenty-first-generation soke succession problems split it into four smaller groups. Five years ago I did a performance of tameshigiri at such an event, but from the next time round there was a note on the program declaring that "tameshigiri will be strictly prohibited." I have not performed such a demonstration for them since. This prohibition is most likely for reasons of preserving the sword itself or fears of the danger that goes with the practice. (It must be noted, however, that caution is legitimately required when using valuable antique swords.)

However, demonstrations of tameshigiri should be allowed, as they are of great reference value for sword practitioners. From observing such a demonstration one can get vital points of reference for performing iaido kata solo, such as the unified use of the body, sword, and energy [ki ken tai ichi]; cutting trajectory [hasuji]; blade angle [kakudo]; correct circular cutting motion [enkeisen]; subtle handling of the sword grip [tenouchi]; how to stop the cut; how to flow out of a cut; and correct combative awareness [zanshin]. From observing the practitioners' form and the results of the cut, all these aspects are obvious at a glance, making tameshigiri training extremely valuable in improving technical skill.

The differences between kendo, iaido, and tameshigiri itself are made clear through such cutting demonstrations. They can prove whether the handling methods used in kendo and iaido are capable of actually cutting, and I believe that they are a vital key to improving one's skill in iaido if linked to the process of Shu-ha-ri.

Those Who Practice Only Iaido and Those Who Practice Iaido While Also Studying Kendo

In the November 1978 edition of *Kendo Nihon,* there was an article titled "The student reaches not the heights of the master's art" in which shihans Hayashi, Segami, Nakajima, and Danzaki, four of Nakayama Hakudo sensei's direct students, reminisce about him. Reading this it struck me that martial artists in particular are the model of outdated, feudalistic ways of thinking. The methods of instruction from the past put fostering a martial spirit as the first priority in training, with the acquisition of technical skill as a secondary or lesser concern. The old masters would not take trainees by the hand when instructing, and the student would have to find his own path to understanding after overcoming numerous hardships with barely a word of communication from his teacher. I have nothing but respect for those in the past who mastered the martial arts in this way, and I bow my head to them.

Compared to that, we now live in a time when it is even possible to eat ramen noodles at home by putting a little water to boil and waiting for two or three minutes. The Japanese martial arts are no exception and have also entered the instant age.

Of the students that I instruct in iaido, around 80 percent of new members to the organization have never held a Japanese sword before starting training. However after one or two years of training once or twice a week, the dedicated and passionate ones will reach the yudansha level, and after two to three years will enter the realms of fourth and fifth dan, at least in terms of technical skill alone. They also become proficient exponents of tameshigiri through the iaido.

This speed of improvement is due to there being no extraneous elements in my iaido system. Training is based on a natural walking posture and progresses in an orderly manner, starting with the five fundamental stances [*goho no kamae*] and moving through *chudan, gedan, jodan hasso,* and *waki kamae.*[23] After that the students master drawing *[batto]*, the initial cut *[kiritsuke]*, shaking off the blood *[chiburi]*, and re-sheathing *[noto]*. From then on the student will carry out cutting exercises with bamboo and straw targets at least two or three times a month in order to internalize the principles of tameshigiri, such as blade angle, cutting trajectory, circular motion, and how to stop and flow with the blade after cutting. (These bamboo and straw targets can be replaced with the upper layer from tatami mats, rolling up one to one-and-a-half sheets.)

Scroll penned by the author showing the Kendo gokun (five edicts of kendo). These are as follows:

1. 礼儀尊重 Reigi soncho (To value respect and propriety)
2. 心身鍛錬 Shinshin tanren (To forge the body and mind)
3. 根性養成 Konjo yousei (To cultivate willpower and determination)
4. 百錬自得 Hyakuren jitoku (To engage in long and constant practice in order to internalize one's art)
5. 誠意実践 Seii jissen (To practice honesty and righteous intent in everyday life)

Those young students who have trained hard for around five years improve technically at a terrific pace and have an even greater aptitude for learning than I had myself. In 1979 we held the third All-Japan Toyama Ryu Tameshigiri Competition and, of more than two hundred participants, not a single one failed to cut through their targets. Furthermore all who entered showed greatly improved technique.

Around 80 percent of the members of the Toyama ryu do not concurrently practice kendo, with 20 percent training in both kendo and iaido at once. Out of the former 80 percent, approximately 40 percent are also members of the Zen Nihon Jukendo Renmei,[24] and we expect great developments with the aid of that organization.

---

23. 中段 (middle level); 下段 (lower level); 上段 (high level); 八相 (vertical sword; literally "eight aspects," implying 360-degree awareness); and 脇 (rear sword; literally "flank or armpit") positions respectively.

24. 全日本銃剣道連盟; All-Japan Jukendo (bayonet fighting) Federation, commonly abbreviated to "Zenjuren."

Among the students who also train in kendo, there is obviously individual variation in levels of dedication and enthusiasm for training, but it has been observed that all of them undergo even more rapid technical progress. The skill of those young students who have done kendo is among the highest in the organization, and even the older practitioners who have years of kendo training learn quickly. Conversely, older members who have not done kendo do not improve very much. This is because those who do not have a fundamental grounding in kendo training will have problems with tenouchi and *tai sabaki*.[25] I can thus thoroughly recommend kendo to those who practice iaido. I would also like to recommend iaido to kendo practitioners.

Among the kendoka of the past there was a saying that "Practice iai and your kendo will not improve," and this is clearly because iaido was mainly seiza methods. There are certainly two or three times as many problems with technical improvement through seiza-based sword techniques when compared to standing sword techniques. But with a combination of purely standing technique–based iai and tameshigiri, there are no problems at all.

Considering the future of iaido, seiza-based techniques do have a small place, but we should revise and reform the modern iai method to focus entirely on standing techniques. I would like to recommend establishing both iaido and kendo kata and uniting them into one system that also makes use of tameshigiri.

The Fundamental Basis of Both Kendo and Iaido Is Cutting

According to the gokui densho from the past, the majority of sword practice was kata practice wearing no armor and mainly using shinai

---

25. 体捌き; literally "body management," referring to movement and positioning in relation to the opponent and attack, usually in terms of evasion.

and wooden swords. This included using some specialized wooden swords among the different ryuha. However, one cannot get the feeling of the proper cutting trajectory, subtle gripping control, and distancing if one does not try to cut through physical objects with a sharpened blade. Due to this lack of experience in cutting through actual targets, today's kobudo demonstrations often show sword-handling methods that are completely improbable, and they have attracted much criticism for this.

There are some slightly more enlightened kobudo schools, how-ever, like the Jigen ryu of the old Satsuma province, which is a promi-nent representative for practical martial arts. Under the indomitable motto of "attack but no defense," they carry out suburi[26] and kirikaeshi[27] training, striking objects such as logs and pillars with an aggressive attacking spirit. Accordingly Jigen ryu practitioners will soon learn the correct tenouchi. This is laudable and a big improvement on cutting only the air but, without experiencing tameshigiri, they will still not acquire correct cutting trajectory or circular motion.

The same can be said for modern shinai kendo. Putting aside the case of those who have integrated tameshigiri with real swords into their training, even kendo practitioners with decades of training behind them will not learn tenouchi. Merely striking to the men, do, and kote with a shinai is not a method of training applicable to a real, sharp-bladed sword.

The development and evolution of kendo is of course intimately linked to iai, and it is widely known that modern kendo's tsuki tech-nique, in particular, was created from practical battlefield thrusting techniques for Japanese swords with a shallow curvature in the blade.

---

26. 素振り; training involving repeated practice swings. Also used outside of martial arts in training for sports such as baseball.
27. 切り返し; training similar to suburi but involving alternating cuts to the left and right.

It is also true that a real sword weighs two to three times more than a shinai, and from that fact alone it is clear that proper tenouchi will not be acquired through training with shinai exclusively. The circular path of the blade trajectory required when making a pulling-type cut is also a technical aspect that is unique to sharpened swords. I would like to expound here on a particular tameshigiri seminar that I held in 1976 for Mori Hisatoku sensei's Kozenkan dojo in Minami Tamiya in the town of Tokushima, Shikoku.

Mori sensei is an experienced master of iaido, has a keen awareness of the nature of the art, and has also mastered tameshigiri. Around fifty kendo and iaido enthusiasts from the local area came to participate in the seminar. Most ordinary folk outside of the martial arts think that a yudansha in kendo or iaido will be able to cut through something using a sword, but when it comes to actual tameshigiri this proves not to be the case.

The kendo yudansha who participated in the seminar had no experience of getting the correct cutting trajectory and circular motion for kesagiri, and so unsurprisingly most of them failed to complete the cut. Iaido practitioners too had problems, as there are differences in blade trajectory and grip control at the moment of impact between cutting a real object and only practicing cutting the air. At the same time there is a difference in the power that one must put behind the blade as the cut descends.

There were those who managed to cut through their targets, but there were also those who put in too much power and could not stop the blade as it cut down into the floorboards.

Having said this, after building up experience of several cuts the kendo yudansha learned for themselves the correct trajectory, angle, and circular motion required, and several of them went on to successfully achieve the objectives of tameshigiri.

Mori sensei was prolific in his studies into tameshigiri and even converted part of his home into a dojo so he could train there. I must express my heartfelt admiration for him in these endeavors.

When training iaido using the Japanese sword one must always strive to integrate and unify the whole of one's spirit, and this is the highest expression of mental forging and self-discipline in the martial arts.

Even if one does not actually use it for cutting people down, iaido is still a martial art, and the original form was trained with cutting as its core principle. Thus we have no recourse but to describe kata that cannot be used for actual cutting as "art swordsmanship," as in the letter sent by that young man from Hong Kong. I would like for iaido and tameshigiri to be seen as two wheels on the same axle and wish for their practice to first and foremost address being able to cut.

Tameshigiri Gives Instant Feedback on One's Technique, Making Theory Unnecessary

In other kinds of sports training and conditioning that are concerned with individual physical education, priority is placed primarily on actually going out and doing the activity, with theory coming in a distant second place.

In tameshigiri the results of one's mental and physical integration, blade trajectory and circular motion, cutting angles, and grip manipulation are clear and immediately obvious. Accordingly, regardless of how great the theory a swordsman expounds or however perfectly he understands the logic of it on an intellectual level, the results of that technique will never be known until he tests it with tameshigiri. With tameshigiri the effects of a technique can be seen immediately and obviously in the trajectory of a single cut, leaving no need for theoretical analysis. This is extremely useful in assessing one's technique, even for kendoka with high dan ranks who may already have great skill in the techniques of sword kata. Tameshigiri is ultimately something to be done without concern for theory. Furthermore, one needs to master the two skills of how to stop and flow with the blade after making a cut through a target in order to prevent unnecessary danger of injury.

The nature and aspect of the cut made is influenced by a swordsman's subtle gripping manipulation [tenouchi]. Even small errors in the blade trajectory can lead to bending of the blade and, depending on the object that is being cut, even cause it to snap. This is especially true when performing consecutive cuts. To prevent such errors one must regularly and repeatedly practice the correct motions with a centered and unified spirit. I personally practice tameshigiri once or twice a week, but if I don't manage to practice for two to three months, then errors will creep into my gripping and blade trajectory. Above all, I dedicate myself to training combining the objectives of spiritual unification and the promotion of physical health under the motto of *hyakuren jitoku* [long and constant practice leads to one's mastery].

Even if one does no other training, make certain to constantly practice tameshigiri in order to internalize the correct cutting angle and avoid errors in trajectory. This is the most important technical point when it comes to sword handling, because if the cutting angle is wrong, then however superlative a blade you are using, the cut will not succeed. So I urge all sword practitioners to heed this advice.

Is Kendo a Sport?

There seems to be a split in which 40 percent of people think of modern kendo as a sport, with 60 percent considering it a martial art.

Kendo technique itself is suitable only for a contest in which participants put on sturdy protective armor and strike each other in the face-mask, breastplate, and gauntlets using a bamboo shinai that weighs less than half of what a katana does. Thus I see modern kendo as "sports and physical education," a sport that developed from martial arts. Even though kendo instructors may teach that shinai and real swords are to be treated the same, this will not sink in for a young trainee who has never held a real blade in his hands before, as to him it will be nothing more than pure theory and imagination. A duel with real swords risked the combatant's very lives and was decided in a single blow. It required one to accept the possibility of one's own death and master the ability to kill or spare the foe at will. That is the true face of martial arts.

Modern kendo is a healthy sport and method of physical education that starts and ends with courtesy and respect, and there is no longer a need to overemphasize the martial spirit in it. After all, thanks to sport kendo the youth of today are physically and mentally growing and developing while training in a worthwhile activity and participating in spiritual training befitting a Japanese person. Technical proficiency has also risen markedly since the prewar days.

However, unless we renew our awareness of the authentic way of the sword as a martial discipline found in both arts, then iaido will be reduced to swordsmanship as an artistic performance and kendo will be nothing more than a sport of striking each other with sticks.

Reconsidering Shinai Kendo Based on the Japanese Sword

The spread and development of youth kendo is happening at a surprising pace, and this is a great thing for the art. Postwar kendo has now primarily become a sport. The levels of skill and technical development have improved greatly over what they were before the War, especially in the approach to competition seen at the All-Japan Kendo Championships and various other tournaments held around the country. It is in no doubt that the postwar reform of the judging rules has led to great leaps in the level of technique demonstrated, and especially in the popularity of techniques like the single-handed strike from a high guard [jodan no kamae]. This technique has risen to levels not seen before the War and improved vastly in its execution. This can be nothing but a joyous development for the sport.

Before the War instructors would teach the theory that the shinai is to be treated as a real katana. And, during training and in competition, it was customary for kendoka to shout an apology for their impudence [usually *gomen, goburei,* or *shitsureishimasu*][28] to the opponent whenever they adopted the jodan no kamae posture. If one were to adopt this posture when squaring off with the instructor or a senior student during training, he would be marked out as being antagonistic and picked on most harshly.

The old-school instructors deemed that single-handed strikes were not practical with real blades, and so there were many who, when judging in competitions, would not count such blows to the facemask or gauntlets as winning techniques under any circumstances. This philosophy was especially prevalent in those competitions held within the old Imperial Armed Forces. Thus the idea that a shinai is to be treated as a real katana is responsible for the lack of attention paid to single-handed strikes from jodan no kamae, even today.

Compared to the prewar situation, jodan no kamae has become much more prevalent today. We now see competitors such as the police department's Tokyo representative Mr. Chiba Masashi and the Kochi prefecture representative Mr. Kawasoe Tetsuo using nothing but jodan no kamae as they fight magnificently in the All-Japan championships and achieve numerous victories. Thanks to this development the overall nature of competition bouts has become much more interesting to watch as well. It has even led to the official competition rules being changed, and since April last year (1979) thrusts to the chest have been permitted against an opponent adopting jodan no kamae.

These kinds of developments are simply moving with the times, and it is good that technical skill is being improved through them. But we can also see numerous details that appear to have been forgotten when looked at from the perspective of handling real swords.

This practice does not take place everywhere, but there are some dojos where young novice swordsmen, being instructed in kirikaeshi

---

28. 御免、御無礼、失礼します。Varying expressions of politeness in apologizing for one's impudence.

exercises without using armor, are taught to grip the hilt when using the right hand but switch to grip the center of the shinai when striking with the left. If they were using a real katana then this would be the equivalent of gripping the blade itself, and is a method of instruction in conflict with the principles of the spirit of the Japanese sword.

It is important not to forget that the fundamental spirit that kendo begins and ends with is courtesy, but at the same time I would like instructors in general to reconsider the state of the art and return to training with the attitude of considering the shinai as a real sword.

The Link between Tameshigiri and Sadaharu's Oh Home Runs

In 1978 baseball legend Sadaharu Oh achieved his eight-hundred-home-run season and set the greatest record in the entire baseball world. Although this achievement was undoubtedly the result of daily training to perfect his special batting technique—which involved putting his entire body weight into one leg—and his uncommon genius and effort, I am certain that it was also the result of his experience with tameshigiri using the Japanese sword.

Decades ago Oh went daily to the dojo of Haga Junichi sensei and received instruction in the methods of tameshigiri, training to cut targets with the correct trajectory using the area of the sword known as the *monouchi*.[29]

If a baseball bat strikes the ball at its tip or with the midsection of the shaft, then there is no way it will fly many hundreds of meters. A home run can be hit for certain only if impact is made with the area equivalent to the monouchi of a sword blade.

---

29. 物打; the area of the blade optimal for cutting, extending from two-thirds up the blade length to just before the curve into the point at the tip.

I too have had some contact with the baseball world and, several decades ago, I was invited to the home of Coach Mizuhara Shigeru to demonstrate tameshigiri for his players to study. Oh Sadaharu, however, is thought to have found inspiration from the principles of spiritual centering needed in tameshigiri all by himself and applied the lessons he had learned from Haga sensei to achieve the greatness he did.

Occasionally Oh can be seen on television commercials spiritedly performing the horizontal cut *mayokogiri* from a reverse grip known as *giccho* (with the left hand by the guard and the right on the lower part of the hilt). This feat clearly shows his proficiency; while left and right kesagiri are natural and instinctive cutting methods, mayoko-giri requires a trained skill to apply.

In tameshigiri the straw stands in for human flesh while the bamboo simulates bone, but the swordsman will succeed in cutting through neither if there is an error in the circular motion of the blade trajectory. When cutting kesagiri with this correct trajectory, the top part of the bamboo above the cut will fly off horizontally at an angle of ninety degrees. If it flies away at 140 degrees or forward at 40, this means that the angle of the blade trajectory was not consistent.

Exactly the same principle applies in baseball. If the bat does not strike the ball correctly on the monouchi area, it will result in a foul ball or the ball flying straight up or not gaining the necessary speed and distance. Home runs are achieved only through the unconscious intuition to hit correctly at ninety degrees.

What is important is to not contract the arms and to swing with an expansive movement along a circular path, exactly as when cutting with a sword.

Whatever the quality of the sword used and however accurate the grip control and distancing (being the correct distance away to strike with the monouchi), if there are errors in the circular motion of the blade trajectory then the cutting edge can chip or the whole blade can snap. The Japanese sword and the baseball bat are the same in that their technical purpose cannot be achieved if the mental side of the execution is not solidly integrated and the mind stops during the swing. This is taught as the principle of *shishin*.[30]

I have repeated this many times before now, but the reason I so enthusiastically recommend the integrated practice of kendo, iaido, and tameshigiri is that I firmly believe the true and correct teachings of budo are not found simply in cutting but in the mental attitude needed to cut. Relating to this ideal, Oh Sadaharu's eight-hundred-home-run record, brought about through the integration of finely honed baseball-batting technique and the mental and spiritual unification from tameshigiri, is a magnificent and joyous achievement for the sword arts and deserving of my deepest admiration.

Observations from Fujita Toko's *Kaiten Shishi*

Professor Okada Kazuo sensei of Kokugaku University has written an excellent treatise on Fujita Toko[31] sensei's visionary work *Kaiten shishi*,[32] entitled *Fujita Toko—Hitachi obi*, in which he highlights discussions of historical changes in the character of swordsmanship throughout the Edo period (1615–1865).

This work divides the swordsmanship of the Edo era into three distinct time periods:

First period (until the third-generation Tokugawa shogun Iemitsu): the era of practical swordsmanship for combat.

Second period (until the Kansei era beginning in 1789): the era of flowery and aesthetically oriented swordsmanship for show.

---

30. 止心; literally "fixated mind/heart." A mental state to guard against the mind's being overly fixated on one concern and losing awareness of other important factors.

31. 1806–1855. A renowned scholar and politician from Mito province who theorized about Japan's national destiny and was instrumental in the "revere the emperor and expel the barbarians" ideology that brought about the Meiji restoration.

32. 回天詩史 1870.

Third period (until the later years of the eleventh-generation Tokugawa shogun Ienari): the era of recreational swordsmanship for
competition.

To one with a passion for the martial arts, this work is a most useful
reference to the history of swordsmanship, the like of which cannot be
found elsewhere, and it has much to teach us. Okada sensei provides
a deep and insightful examination and commentary on Fujita sensei's
wonderfully erudite essay, and I wish to express my deep admiration
for him.

What comes to mind while reading this essay is how the majority
of kata found in the various ryuha of the classical koryu schools are
fixated entirely on the second category mentioned above (flowery and
aesthetically oriented swordsmanship), exhibiting as they do practices
such as receiving an opponent's cut with a perfectly horizontal block
and clashing cutting edge on cutting edge.

This kind of kata is no longer bujutsu and has entered the realms of
bugei.[33] For example, the absence of the practical and natural methods
of right and left kesagiri and the inclusion of techniques from seiza,
even the footwork contained in the kata of the various koryu, clearly
mark them as bugei and are not practices that it is possible to integrate
with kendo.

It is thus that I feel no technical improvement can come from the
solely "bugei-based" kata practice of modern iaido, as it is fixated on
the various koryu belonging to the second period described by Fujita.

We no longer live in an age in which the primary objective of the
martial arts is to cut people down, but budo differs from other sports

---

33. Both *bugei* (武芸) and *bujutsu* (武術), along with *budo* (武道), are commonly translated into English as "martial arts" and even in Japanese can be used interchangeably
in casual parlance but have slightly different nuances and imply different ultimate
objectives. *Bujutsu* implies the practical and technical aspect for direct combat application; *bugei* is the aesthetic and cultural practice; and *budo* the lifelong path of spiritual self-improvement. It is this difference that the author references here.

in that it aims to conquer concerns about mortality and is a pursuit to be trained and studied throughout one's entire life.

Based on his lifelong practice of the martial and literary arts, Fujita sensei achieved the realization of the Mito Kodokan and Kobusho[34] through the thorough exposition in his work *bunbu fuki*.[35] Fujita sensei died in an earthquake in the 1850s, but his spirit lives on through those who learn kobudo, kendo, and iaido today. That spirit is found in the path of perfecting the character and forging the person.

---

34. Noted schools of learning and martial training, respectively.
35. 文武不岐; the inseparability of martial and literary pursuits.

Inside the Hayashizaki Iai Shrine

CHAPTER 3

THE CORRECT MENTAL ATTITUDE TOWARD THE JAPANESE SWORD

Calligraphy penned by former Prime Minister Kishi, dedicated to Hayashizaki Daimyoshin (resident deity of the Hayashizaki Iai Shrine)

One of the Three Items of the Imperial Regalia Is a Japanese Sword

The three divine relics of the Imperial family, vessels of the kami, are the following:

1. The Yasakani no Magatama jewel, which represents the emperor himself
2. The Yata no Kagami mirror, which represents the people
3. The Ama no Murakumo no Tsurugi sword, which represents the nation

It is important to note that one of these holy relics is a sword and that this sword represents the nation of Japan. Sometimes swords are kept in the shrines around Japan as physical vessels for the kami that reside there. Yet other swords have been passed down as heirlooms from ancestor to descendant in the houses of the *daimyo*, the bushi, and even the regular people of the nation, revered not just as weapons but as spiritual artifacts as well.

Before the War Imperial Japanese soldiers carried a *gunto* [military sword] and revered it as their very soul. The airmen of the Special Attack Squadron[36] would invest their body and spirit in their swords.

36. The air squadron formed as a last desperate gambit in World War II that is widely known in the English-speaking world as the *Kamikaze*.

Hono enbu at the
Yasukuni Shrine
(April 1977)

As I think of them bravely flying out to battle, swords alongside them and burning brightly with the martial spirit to nobly and beautifully fall like the cherry blossom, I am filled with admiration and respect and wish them nothing but the peaceful rest that their heroic spirits deserve.

The determination of the warriors of the past never to bring embarrassment or dishonor to the sword they carried is an attitude that originated in the majesty and virtue of the Japanese sword. As the martial arts of the past were something that decided life or death, training in their mysteries was training to forge and enlighten one's very soul. A spirit forged and forged again teaches lessons without limit, enlightening one about form and formlessness, and there were a great many among the masters of old who were deeply invested in the path of perfecting the character.

It is through the Japanese sword that the eternal rooted and immoveable spirit of the Japanese race is cultivated, and we Japanese are beholden to renew the nobility of the three divine relics.

The Sword Exists Not to Cut (Verse of the "Japanese Sword")

To own a Japanese sword requires one to first have a sufficient knowledge of and correct mental attitude toward it.

The Japanese sword was created with the unmistakeable purpose of cutting people down, but it is also the soul of the warrior. That the Japanese warrior came to be someone who constantly polished and perfected his heart, mind, and spirit finds its origins in the methods of spiritual purification unique to the Japanese people. This is intimately related to how the bushi, who engaged in killing for their profession, put into practice the most moralistic and virtuous creed of bushido.

The method for creating a Japanese sword is something that is unique to our nation and has no analogue anywhere in the world.

The artistic value and practical functionality of the artifacts that it produces are superior to the weapons of other countries, making the Japanese sword an object that receives great attention in all nations.

The Japanese sword focuses together our righteous intent with the divinity of the kami, as expressed perfectly in Fujita Toko sensei's poem "Seiki no uta": "The sword hardens to hundred-forged steel, and in its sharpness shall cut through helms."[37] Holding the Japanese sword and kneeling in seiza, composed and serene at the moment of drawing the blade from its sheath, we feel the pride of the Yamato race.

The popularity of iaido today exceeds what it was before the War, and the activities of sword collectors and enthusiasts are also stepping up, showing that there is something of a quiet renaissance of the Japanese sword going on. This is both a right and proper development for Japanese people and, I believe, shows a reawakening of the spirit of the Japanese sword.

Viewed by a foreigner, the cutting power of the Japanese sword may indeed make it appear a frightening weapon, but to us Japanese it is an object of reverence to the point of being a vessel for the divine. There is not a single classical ryuha of Japanese martial arts that does not have rituals of courtesy and respect toward the kami and the sword before and after its sword practices. That the expression of respect toward the sword is performed in the same way as it is toward the deities may appear to be slightly strange at first glance, but when one remembers that the katana is a spiritual object and a divine vessel, it is only right and natural.

Saijo Yaso[38] expresses in one of his poems that "the sword exists not to cut." (The full passage is shown below.)

To expound on this vital point, the Japanese sword exists for the purpose of cutting, but it does not exist only to cut. In short, the Japanese sword exists to perfect the heart and mind of its wielder

---

37. 正気の歌; verse of the just and righteous spirit.
38. 1892–1970. A well-known poet and writer.

through spiritual training, and it is taught that the sword that gives and enhances life must not become the sword that takes it.[39]

It must be noted, however, that the methods of many iaido and kendo practitioners, which are far removed from practical experiences with actual swords and which cannot even cut through bamboo and straw targets, can produce neither a life-giving nor life-taking sword.

Furthermore, learning proficiency in cutting is just the first step. Only through heaping training upon training and practice upon practice, polishing one's skill, and conditioning one's mind until one achieves a mental attitude of unflinching determination no matter the odds will the life-taking sword become the life-giving sword and the proper attitude of reverence and respect toward the Japanese sword emerge.

Through the efforts of iaido and kendo practitioners, as well as all enthusiasts who share a passion for the sword, we should rekindle awareness of the Japanese sword as the heart of the Japanese race and the noble pride of the Yamato people.

The verse of the "Japanese sword"
BY SAIJO YASO

1.
Colour of the misty night sky,
Colour of the cherry-blossom crescent moon,
The Japanese sword is drawn,
Beauty of the crystalline forged edge.

2.
If one looks with one's heart
Ah, the line at the hundred-forged point of the blade!
Noble spirit of the Yamato people,
Dances in my heart.

---

39. These are known respectively as *katsujinken* (活人劍) and *satsujinken* (殺人劍).

3.

The sword exists not to cut,
A fine blade to polish the heart,
And the words of the sages of old,
May yet quietly ring out.

4.

The straight blade shall be Goro Masamune,
The colour and vibrancy of myriad flowers,
The curved from Bizen Osafune,
Its serene form like viewing the moon.

5.

Ah, the beautiful Japanese sword
The sword that is our pride,
The justice of bushido, clear and unclouded
Shall shine on bright unto eternity.

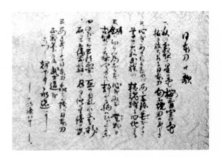

The verse of the "Japanese sword" by Saijo Yaso (Calligraphy by the wife of Aiki Shichirozaemon sensei of Takefu in Fukui prefecture)

The scroll shown in the photograph above was penned by the wife of Aiki Shichirouemon sensei, an iaido ninth dan who resides in the town of Takefu in Fukui prefecture, and it brings fresh significance to the poem.

The branch of the Aiki family that Shichiroemon sensei is the patriarch of is directly descended from Aiki Ichibe Nobufusa, renowned general of the Takeda clan forces at the battle of Kawanakajima, making him the twentieth-generation master of that august clan. The Aiki residence is designated as an important cultural treasure, and the longhouse gate and garden are maintained in the antique style. The view of this magnificent house is rated as the best in the Echizen[40] area.

---

40. Modern-day Fukui prefecture.

The Swordsmith's Battle with Iron and Fire

It is only natural that the respect and reverence we hold for the Japanese sword should first be directed toward the swordsmith who made it.

A Shinto shrine is placed in the forge where the Japanese sword is made, and the swordsmith will pray to the deity before investing his heart and soul in his work and battling iron and flame to forge a masterpiece.

A sword like this is both a weapon that protects the life of its owner and a work of art unrivaled in all the world, known for its characteristics of being light, unbendable, unbreakable, and having a wicked cutting power. More than any other art treasures these spiritual objects are the pride of the Japanese people.

The major swordsmiths of antiquity from the Nara period [710–794] were Tenkuni, Yasutsuna, and Sanjo Kokaji no Munechika. Moving into the Edo period [1603–1868] there were, among others, Kotetsu, Kunihiro, and Shinkai, with the end of that era being dominated by Kiyomaro, Yukihide, and Masahide. In the modern era [1868 onward] it is said that there are over four hundred smiths currently active around the country. Among the marvellous and artistically valuable blades forged by the smiths of today, there are many that exceed the swords of the Shinto[41] and Koto[42] periods, with some pieces that are so special they defy analysis by modern science. I bow my head and express great respect to the sterling efforts of these master craftsmen and wish for the continued success of their profession.

A Great Sword Is Realized through the Polisher's Art

The overall quality of a Japanese sword and whether it will be of a higher or lower grade owes much to the skills of the smith. However,

---

41. 新刀; "New-sword" period denoting blades forged between 1596 and 1760.
42. 古刀; "Old-sword" period denoting blades forged before 1596.

the final quality is truly realized only through the efforts of the polisher. Just as a jewel will not sparkle unless it is buffed to a shine, the art in the Japanese sword will not come through without the polisher's diligent craft, taking it from a dull blade to a masterwork. As iaido practitioners we do not require our blades polished to a particularly high sheen, but when it comes to the polishing of shrine presentation swords and art swords, an unimaginable level effort is essential to bring out the necessary quality. The burden on a sword polisher is heavy, and to live up to that expectation shows uncommon dedication. I must express my great admiration for their craft.

Regarding Sword Fittings (*Koshirae*)

The fittings used on swords both ancient and modern first emerged in the Heian period [794–1185] and have continued to be used to this day, although continuous changes have been made throughout their history. The different types of fittings are divided into a number of styles and categories depending on the type of sword they will be fitted to, such as *tachi koshirae, handachi koshirae, uchidachi koshirae, daito koshirae, wakizashi koshirae,* and *tanto koshirae.*[43] There exist many different sword fittings of both high and low grades and, just as clothes make the man, the fittings set off a Japanese sword and bring out its quality. Even a high-grade sword will not live up to its quality if the fittings are poor. Everyone will have their individual preferences, but it is only right and proper for a warrior that a practical sword intended for use must have practical fittings, from the scabbard to the hilt. After all, it is said that one must not forget war in times of peace.

The Edo period saw an era of peace across the nation when many warriors neglected their scholarship and turned to aesthetic pursuits. The changing times also had an effect on the sword, with fashions

---

43. Full-cavalry sword fittings, half-cavalry sword fittings, long-sword fittings, great-sword fittings, short-sword fittings, and dagger fittings.

leading to aesthetic concerns favored in blade and fittings design. One must, however, be aware of the differences between practical and artistic fittings.

Some sword guards and other fittings have various patterns engraved into them, and each of these will have a meaning and express cultural ideas. Such fittings are made to many different specifications, with some that are eminently practical and others that are for artistic display. The engraved patterns show things from our everyday lives and the natural world, and there are many that have great artistic value in their own right. However, these kinds of fittings are not needed on a practical warrior's blade.

The guard, hilt, and other metal fittings for a practical iaito should have practicality as their major concern. I personally find fittings of the Higo style (Hon Higo or Edo Higo fittings) to be excellent for actual sword-handling purposes and recommend them to my students and to the members of our organization.

Art Swords and Practical Swords

If you speak to swordsmiths in the modern era, most of them say the same thing—that they cannot sell a sword unless it is an ornate and flowery blade with a prominent and expansive, deeply applied hamon[44] pattern. As the majority of swords sold are for art purposes these days, it is admittedly only natural that flashy hamon patterns are favored.

On the other hand, those with experience of tameshigiri desire more practical swords and tend not to prefer the ones with elaborate and artful hamon. I shall look into this further later in the book. Swords from the Shinto and Koto periods are treated as antiques and have considerable value, so one cannot really use those for training. At the same time, one will not find any blades suited for practical use

---

44. 刃文; the pattern along the cutting edge of the blade created by the unique forging process.

among the dedicated art pieces seen at sword display meetings, which is, in my opinion, something of a sad state of affairs.

Among the swords of the Koto period one sees many with a short tang and a narrow blade width. Moving into the Shinto period there were many ornate art swords produced, due to the extended peace of the middle Edo era. As told by the words of the modern swordsmiths above, we are currently seeing a similar phenomenon today—in what is known as the new golden age of sword making in the Showa era [1926–1989].

The warriors of the past constantly wore two swords at their hip, and so the blades would have to be of a practical length and weight. However, as most swords today are forged for display purposes, they are made with a greater length, weight, and blade width, meaning there are few that are suited to use in iai practice. This is a situation that I find most unfortunate.

Points of Caution When Maintaining Swords of the Shinto and Koto Periods

Over twenty years ago a great and respected senior of mine, who had a high dan rank in kendo, showed me a pair of swords that he used for kata practice.

From the hamon and form of the blades, I could see that these were quality swords, but I was taken aback when I viewed the tangs.

One was a relatively recently forged blade, lacking a chrysanthemum crest, and it bore an inscription denoting that it was made by Inoue Shinkai. The other had the tang shortened and the name inscription filed away, but it was a Koto-period sword of the Tegai school and made by Tegai Kanenaga himself. Both blades would be worth a great deal today but had been used since before the War for sword-on-sword kendo kata practice and were in an irrecoverable state with several deep notches in their cutting edges.

The master was surprised at my appraisal and regretted his use of these swords for training, but this kind of use of antique swords for practical training happens all over the country. I would urge Japanese sword owners to employ sufficient caution when storing and maintaining their blades.

Practicing the kendo kata with live blades is, of course, very good for perfecting and enriching one's spirit, but in this day and age we have some excellent imitation swords [mogito] and for reasons of both sword preservation and moving with the times, practice with these is perfectly acceptable and sufficient.

For iaido too, there are masters who are proud that they use real swords of renown in their training. While this kind of blade is fitting for their status and authority, such famous swords will never be forged again, so I would strongly advise that to preserve these artifacts they refrain from putting them through the rigors of practical use.

Improvements to Swords Forged in the "New Genroku" Golden Age of the Showa Era

In March every year around five hundred newly forged swords are put on display at the Ueno Matsuzakaya department store. Some of these new swords are perfected to greater levels than even the swords of the past, and all have a generally fine form and are surely a shining example in the history of Japanese sword making. One can also observe the uncommon skill and efforts of the polishers in bringing these swords to life.

However, these swords are clearly created with display as the primary concern, with utmost importance placed on looking impressive; a situation that I feel is somewhat pitiable.

We do not live in an age where swords are used anymore, and so I suppose it is only right that swords are now made to look good. However, we must not forget that the Japanese sword is and always will be a weapon first and foremost. It should be understood that the ability to cut is its primary value with artistic value coming second.

Of course, the fact that it combines and excels in both practical and artistic qualities is part of the attraction of the Japanese sword. On top of this it is light, does not break or bend, and can cut. These four conditions are what make Japanese blades so revered around the world, and I believe we should focus on them when assessing and appraising a blade.

In the Edo period a samurai was required to wear twin swords, and the length of these was fixed by *bakufu*[45] edicts at 2 *shaku* and 3 *sun* (approximately 70 cm). Taller warriors could wear longer blades, but these were capped at around 2 shaku and 5 sun (approximately 75 cm), and there were restrictions on the weight as well.

In the Edo period, many of the longer blades produced in the earlier Muromachi era [1338–1573], even blades of some renown, had their tangs altered and the inscriptions filed away and were adjusted down to a more practical length and weight. It is lamentable that many blades became anonymous in this way.

Compared to this, the swords produced in the new Genroku golden age of the Showa era have a greater weight and more substantial dimensions, and usually a more deeply applied hamon.[46] As most are pieces forged with concerns only for display, they exhibit aesthetically pleasing measurements that are longer than would be practical in swordsmanship. If asked what percentage of these newly forged swords would be able to cut effectively, I would have to say that more than half of them could not be relied upon to go through a target.

---

45. Literally "curtain government/tent government," the military government headed by the shogun that effectively ruled Japan from the twelfth century to 1868. The name refers to the tents an army's officers would camp in when on campaign.

46. The "depth" of a hamon on a blade refers to how much of the blade it covers. The size and design are decided in the forging process by how and where a layer of clay is applied.

In the case of heavier swords, even though these may be fine for someone with a physique as imposing as that of a sumo wrestler, a regular user will not be able to muster the strength to swing them with enough speed, and thus the cutting power will be halved. As I keep saying, lightness combined with cutting power are the lifeblood of the Japanese sword. Swords with a high shinogi [the ridgeline along the back of the blade] are durable and thus suited to the rigors of combat, but the cutting ability of this design is not all that we could hope for and we must take this into account as well.

Blades with a deeply applied and flowery hamon, such as those made around the Edo-era Genroku[47] period have a tendency to be brittle and are thus easily chipped or snapped. The cutting edge itself is also very hard and thus the cutting ability is not excellent.

Through my research and experiences I have come to the conclusion that the ideal depth for a hamon is around a third to a quarter of the blade's overall width. A hamon applied during quenching to a depth of half the blade or more may still be strong but is not needed.

Swords quenched with the clay deeply applied to create large and flowery hamon, heavier swords, and those with longer measurements will look good but cannot be used practically. Accordingly, I feel we need to reverse and improve upon these trends in sword making in this so-called new Genroku golden age of the Showa era, for the benefit of future generations.

---

47. 1688–1704, a period known for a cultural renaissance of the creative arts and crafts.

CHAPTER 4

THE JAPANESE SWORD
AS A WEAPON

The author's calligraphy depicting the motto "hyakuren jitoku" [long and constant practice leads to one's mastery].

The Appeal of the Japanese Sword as a Weapon

The Japanese sword is an object of great art and craftsmanship, but it is unmistakeably a weapon first and foremost.

The reason that the warriors of the past staked their lives on the Japanese sword is because it is a weapon.

When the War was lost and the Potsdam Declaration accepted, all of Japan's weapons were discarded. However, efforts were made to emphasize that the Japanese sword is the historical heritage of the Yamato people, and, at the same time, an art treasure of the highest degree. The occupying forces were convinced and allowed the possession of Japanese swords to continue.

There are some in this age of developed civilization who view the Japanese sword as little but a brutal weapon of butchery, and I cannot help but be shocked at the lack of understanding and recognition that they should have as Japanese people. The Japanese sword is the soul of the brave and valiant warrior who valued it more than his life. It is the path of spiritual enrichment and enlightenment through the spirit of bushido.

The Japanese sword is made light, unbendable and unbreakable, and bestowed with cutting power through the skills of the swordsmith, painstakingly refined and further refined over many decades. These qualities are what give the sword its life-force and its appeal.

Furthermore, the attraction and appeal of the Japanese sword depends on the skill and craft of the polisher. No matter how fine the sword itself, if the polishing is poor it will not rise beyond the basest and dullest of blades. It becomes a true weapon only once skilfully polished to a captivating sheen. When gazing at the surface of such a blade, words are entirely insufficient to express the charm and draw of this masterpiece.

Study into Preexisting Blades

Of the sharp swords used for iaido practice, a large majority will have been forged and bought as a preexisting stock item and not tailored to the user. I would thus now like to look into the specifications of swords in general, and these pre-produced blades in particular, for the reference of all practitioners of the sword arts.

Japanese swords are categorized into four historical periods depending on when they were forged. These are *Koto* [literally "old swords forged before 1596"]; *Shinto* [literally "new swords forged between 1596 and 1760"]; *Shin Shinto* [literally "new swords forged between 1761 and 1876"]; and *Gendaito* [literally "modern-era swords forged from 1887 onward"].

Among modern-day iaido practitioners there are not many who own a sword that is well balanced for them personally, and I would estimate that around 70 percent are not using suitable blades.

I would thus like to consider this point in general, looking to my own experiences with tameshigiri.

There are few swords in existence that fit well with their user and are balanced in just the way they require to move naturally and harmoniously. Most are forged by swordsmiths using their own unique methods and to their own stock specifications. Modern-day iaido practitioners will try to adapt their technique to the idiosyncrasies of the blade in their training.

Using a badly balanced sword is a prime cause of the holes in technique that can be seen in many aspects of a swordsman's performance at demonstrations. One wonders how many of those training in iai bear in mind the following points when selecting a sword:

1. Blade length
2. Weight
3. Curvature
4. Overall appearance of the sword
5. Blade width
6. Nature of the hamon
7. Cutting ability
8. Flexibility of the blade
9. Positioning of the *menuki* ornaments
10. Positioning of the holes for the pegs that secure the hilt to the blade [*mekugi ana* and *hikae mekugi ana*]
11. The length of the tang
12. The practicality of the fittings

These points summarize the important specifications to pay attention to when selecting a sword for use in iaido training.

To preserve valuable historical swords, when selecting a sword for use in tameshigiri I will purposefully avoid blades of renown with engravings and instead will purchase a nameless blade with a few scratches on it.

Swords like this will often have various problems, such as being too long, too heavy, not having much of a curvature, or having a tang that is too short. In order to make these suitable for use it is important to carry out the following modifications to improve the balance:

1. For longer blades, move the hilt fitting grooves [*machi*] up the blade and resize it to more convenient dimensions.
2. For blades lacking in curvature, have them altered to curve more.
3. For blades with a short tang, have the base of the tang extended.
4. For blades that are too heavy, have a groove put in to lighten them.

Swordsmiths do not often have technical experience in the actual methods involved in using the swords they make and so will largely not understand the correct balance that is required. There are some smiths who create blades bearing in mind that the true essence of the sword is in being able to cut, but most smiths today look at the forging mainly in terms of creating artistic pieces. There are an especially large number of smiths who try to imitate the great works of the Koto and Shinto periods, and the swords they produce are judged by an appraisal panel from a museum, being passed or failed for a certain grade. That such smiths look to artistic merit as the primary concern when making new swords is an entirely understandable and unavoidable situation but still unfortunate.

In the Koto period, swords were sometimes forged by smiths who were illiterate, and these stalwarts would live for the making of the sword to the exclusion of all else—battling with fire and iron. The creation of a cutting edge was all-important, and the letters that would go on the tang were of little concern. As we can see today, these blades have come to be marked out and revered as swords of great importance or even national treasures. Compared to this what can we say about modern sword forging? Because swords are made primarily as art these days, it is often that we see the smith putting more attention into making the tang beautiful than the blade itself, trying to make the inscription as attractive and aesthetically pleasing as possible. There are even cases of modern swords being elevated to the status of blades of renown [meito] solely on the virtues of a pretty tang, designated as prefectural cultural treasures, and the smiths that forged such pieces being awarded the honored status of human national treasures.

Shinken, Iaito, and Mogito

As a rule all iaido enthusiasts are encouraged to practice using a *shinken* (an actual sharp sword). However, I feel we must rethink the practice of simply having all students use shinken without their first having any knowledge about the Japanese sword.

As mentioned previously there are cases, both before and after the War, of great and important kendo instructors using fine swords for kata practice and as a result damaging them beyond recovery.

In the first instance, if we consider the monetary value of swords, the economic struggle and hardship that some warriors went through to obtain a katana was far greater than most people imagine today.

It is also obvious when one looks at the sword fittings of those times that they did not practice iai in a cursory or desultory manner, like so many do today.

How the warrior viewed his sword before the Muromachi period can only be speculated upon, but from the Edo period onward he was raised and educated to see it as his very soul and treasure it more than his life itself. In this period high-grade swords with great intrinsic artistic value were almost never used for iai training. This was also true for both the sword fittings *[koshirae]* and ornaments of the time.

Before the War the former daimyo and the descendants of the old houses of the former warrior aristocracy *[shizoku]* were in possession of many tens or hundreds of swords. After the War many of these were put on the market and moved between various owners, but among such high-quality blades there are none that I would even think of using for iai. Instead these swords have passed into the hands of rich sword enthusiasts and are used exclusively for display purposes. This is a development of which I am glad, as the use of blades of renown from antiquity for rough iaido training does a great disservice to the traditions of the Japanese sword.

It is thus that I would encourage all practitioners of iaido to reconsider the use of imitation blades *[mogito]*. Today there are many fine and technically excellent mogito produced that are in no way inferior to real swords, a most joyous development for the spread of iaido.

In iaido training the concept of the unity of kendo and iaido as a single discipline *[ken i ittai]* is obvious and natural, and it is said of both arts that the practitioner should not get caught up with just the technical aspects and thereby forget the mental and spiritual side of practice. However, as the most important aspect, one must first put their art into practice with theoretical analysis a distant second priority. Regardless of whether he uses a shinken or a mogito, the student should take on board the spirit of bushido and practice single mindedly and relentlessly.

It is best for a novice student to practice the kata using only a mogito up to around the third-dan level and then gradually introduce the use of a shinken into training. There are instructors who emphasize the use of a shinken from the start of training, but this method is not conducive to good technical advancement. An individual's development in the spiritual side of the art and all that entails is ruled completely by their technical progression. It is thus more natural to start training with a mogito, as one's technique will improve faster through using such an implement.

However, for those practitioners looking toward performing tameshigiri, who do not have any kendo experience and who have come to training in the sword arts through the appeal of the Japanese sword itself, it is important that they learn proper gripping methods. Thus, from a technical point of view, I strongly recommend that they practice using the tanrenbo as described in chapter 6 of this book.

Some time ago I saw an article in the kendo press that criticized high-ranking practitioners who have won iai competitions held under the auspices of the All-Japan Kendo Federation for using mogito. Although the use of such imitation blades may present a problem from the point of view of cultivating the martial spirit, it is undeniable that there is a great difference in cost between shinken and mogito. And, depending on the individual economic situation of the practitioner, he may sometimes have no choice in what he can use. It certainly cannot be said that one should not practice iai unless he uses a shinken.

On the other hand, to consistently use nothing but a mogito can cause problems. This is in conflict with not only the ideals of the iaido spirit, but also the effectiveness of training, and it clearly limits technical development.

Taking pride in one's endeavors to foster the martial spirit and, in doing so, touching upon the spirit of the Japanese sword is without doubt a path to perfecting and enriching one's character.

Specifications of Swords Suited to Practical Use in Iaido and Tameshigiri Training

1. LENGTH

The standard length for sword blades as specified by the Tokugawa bakufu was 2 shaku and 3 sun (approximately 70 cm), with variations of between 2 shaku, and 2 shaku and 5 sun, depending on the height of the user. The standard length of the military swords [gunto] issued by the old Imperial Army and Navy was 2 shaku and 2 sun (approximately 67 cm).

The swords used in modern iaido practice are generally between 2 shaku and 3 sun, and 2 shaku and 5 sun (between 70 and 75 cm), with swords longer than this only used by special individuals. If one attempts tameshigiri using a sword longer than this, and the blade turns out to be slightly weak, it can snap clean off from the rebound of the strike, especially if the cut is made at an incorrect angle or trajectory.

When I had the honor of meeting the great master of iaido Nakayama Hakudo sensei, I inquired as to the appropriate length for a sword. He told me that a length of one's own height minus 3 shaku (around 90 cm) is a good length. In my case I am 5 shaku and 4 sun (approximately 164 cm) in height, and so this would mean that a blade of 2 shaku and 4 sun (approximately 73 cm) is optimal. However, this length is only optimal for solo iaido kata cutting the air and is slightly too long for tameshigiri. This fact is illustrated by a sword I was gifted with after the War by the archaeologist Ikeda Kenji sensei, who hails from Namamugi in Yokohama's Tsurumi

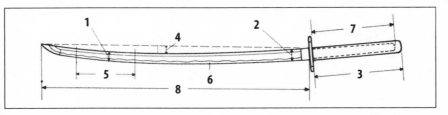

As the wielder stands up straight, the sword should be long enough that the tip just brushes the ground.

Standard dimensions for a sword suitable for use in iaido and tameshigiri

1. The blade should be about 8 bu (approximately 2.5cm) in width around the monouchi.

2. The blade should be about 1 sun (approximately 3cm) in width just above the guard.

3. The tang [nakago] should be about 7 sun (approximately 21cm) in length.

4. The blade should have a curvature [sori] of around 5 bu (approximately 1.5cm).

5. Monouchi

6. The depth of the hamon should be about 1/3 to 1/4 of the blade's width.

7. The hilt [tsuka] should be about 8 sun (approximately 24cm) in length.

8. The overall length of the blade should be between 2 shaku and 2 sun and 2 shaku, 3 sun, and 5 bu (approximately 67cm to 71cm).

ward. The blade was 2 shaku and 5 sun (around 74 cm) in length and forged by Kagaju Sadatoshi in the Bunmei era [1469–1487], making it a Koto-period sword. I used this sword for tameshigiri for around five years, but it would always bend when my grip control was even slightly at fault.

As a result I now use a blade of around 2 shaku and 3 sun (approximately 71 cm) for my own tameshigiri practice, and recommend to my students and the members of my organization that they use a sword of between 2 shaku and 2 sun (approximately 67 cm) and 2 shaku and 3 sun (approximately 71 cm).

2. WEIGHT

A standard katana that would be easy to use will weigh between 300 *monme* and 340 monme (between 1.1 kg and 1.3 kg) including the guard, hilt, and fittings. Swords heavier than this would be used only by those with sufficiently prodigious physical strength.

At demonstrations of iaido one will sometimes see performers who make the length of their blade shake spasmodically when stopping it after a cut or when carrying out chiburi. The cause of this is the use of swords that are too heavy, and it is a bad habit to get into. One must be wary of heavier swords.

3. CURVATURE

The ideal curvature for a sword of 2 shaku and 3 sun (approximately 70 cm) is around 5 bu (approximately 1.5 cm). Swords with a greater or lesser curvature than this are not good for practical use in swordsmanship training.

4. BLADE WIDTH

A blade that is around 1 sun (approximately 3 cm) at the base of the guard and tapers down to around 8 bu (approximately 2.4 cm) at the monouchi will have a good balance. Just as with the curvature, blade widths that vary too greatly from these measurements are not suitable for training.

5. DIMENSIONS OF THE TANG

The dimensions of the blade's tang control the overall balance of the sword and are an important factor to be aware of when selecting swords for use in training.

In general, swords of the Koto and Shinto periods have relatively short tangs of around 5 sun (approximately 15 cm), although there are exceptions. The standard length for sword hilts [tsuka] is 8 sun (approximately 24 cm), so if the tang is much shorter than this the blade may break at the tip of the tang when it cuts into a solid object.

If the hilt one is using is 8 sun in length, then a suitable tang should be 7 sun. When a longer tang fits well into the hilt then its weight will be retained there, and the blade will consequently become lighter, leading to a well-balanced weapon.

If the tang is too short and this is putting too much weight on the blade, then a good balance can still be achieved by inserting lead into the base of the hilt by the pommel.

6. DEPTH OF THE HAMON

Between a third and a quarter of the blade's overall width is a suitable depth for the hamon on a sword for practical use. In general, blades with flowery and deeply applied hamon have a tendency to be brittle and thus chip or snap easily.

7. POSITION OF THE MENUKI ORNAMENTS ON THE HILT

During the Muromachi period [1336–1573], most sword fittings were in the *handachi* [cavalry half-sword] style, in which the menuki ornaments were wrapped on the right-hand side of the hilt when the sword was at rest with the blade facing down. The military swords of the old Imperial Armed Forces also had their hilts wrapped based on this style, but in this case it meant that the ornaments would fit into the user's palm, making the grip more fluid and bringing out the user's technique.

The fittings of the Edo period, by contrast, were the opposite of this and had the menuki on the left-hand side.

Having the menuki too high up the hilt is also not good for handling. They were originally only ornaments to decorate the hilt and thus not necessary. Having said that, menuki can aid one's technique if wound into the hilt in the handachi koshirae style.

Ninety percent of the swords used by modern-day iaido enthusiasts have fittings in the style prevalent in the Edo period.

A large and flowery hamon

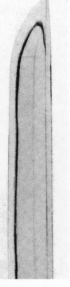

A blade with a straight hamon

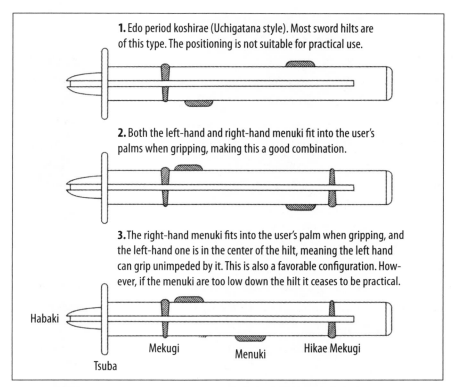

1. Edo period koshirae (Uchigatana style). Most sword hilts are of this type. The positioning is not suitable for practical use.

2. Both the left-hand and right-hand menuki fit into the user's palms when gripping, making this a good combination.

3. The right-hand menuki fits into the user's palm when gripping, and the left-hand one is in the center of the hilt, meaning the left hand can grip unimpeded by it. This is also a favorable configuration. However, if the menuki are too low down the hilt it ceases to be practical.

Habaki

Mekugi   Menuki   Hikae Mekugi

Tsuba

Positioning of menuki ornaments on swords of different periods, viewing the hilt from above with the back of the blade uppermost

8. PRESENCE OR ABSENCE OF A GROOVE [HI] IN THE BLADE

A sword with a groove running down the blade will make a sound when swung and thus many are not fond of them, especially high-ranking practitioners. On the other hand, there are those who like blades that make a sound.

In period films and plays the swooshing sound effects from a blade groove increase the dramatic effect and are generally appreciated by the audience. Additionally, to beginners, the sounds from a blade groove give them the impression that their technique is good. The same is also true of iaido demonstrations, in which the audience (although perhaps not experts) is generally more impressed by a performance where sounds are made.

There are tales that suggest it is impractical to use a sword that has a groove in some situations because it would make a noise even in the dark of night. It is also said that, in the past, the groove was known as the "blood runner," and acted as a channel so that the blood from a cut or thrust would flow away. Another tale would have it that, when thrust through an opponent's body, the blade would sometimes get stuck from the pressure; a blood groove would ease that pressure and aid blade withdrawal.

Additionally, even though it has no effect on a sword's cutting ability, the presence or absence of a groove will influence the sword's weight and is thus related to balance.

On top of this, when looked at from the point of view of the physical dynamics of a blade, one with a groove will be slightly weaker than one without. However, it will also have a greater flexibility. This can be clearly understood when one notes that exactly the same structure and principle is seen in the construction of a railway track.

Finally, the overall appearance of a sword with a groove is more elegant and appealing, and there are many who prefer this.

9. EFFECTS ON CUTTING ABILITY FROM THE HEIGHT OF THE BLADE'S RIDGELINE [SHINOGI]

The cutting power of a Japanese sword will vary based on the individual methods and idiosyncrasies of the smith who forged it, but what has most influence is the width of the blade and, related to this, the height of the ridgeline along it. Blades with a high ridgeline are good when cutting through harder targets, but against softer ones they fare poorly due to the absorption of energy. A high-ridged blade will lose about half of its cutting power when, for example, cutting the straw targets in *suemono giri*.[48]

---

48. An exercise involving the cutting of fixed targets.

Comparatively, blades with a shallow ridgeline generally have a better cutting ability, although this can vary with the blade's width. They are good at avoiding the energy absorption from softer straw targets and perform laudably when cutting these. However, if the user gets his grip handling wrong, such a blade can easily break. To give an example, the cutting ability of the blades made by Seki no Magoroku Kanemoto are said to be in the top class of the best and finest swords, the *saijo owazamono*. One of the characteristics of the swords that he made was a shallow blade-ridge, meaning that they would pass through targets with ease. By comparison, the cutting edge of a *dotanuki* or that of the Mito school blades from the Shin Shinto period were objectively superior to a Kanemoto. However, when it comes to the cutting of fixed targets in suemono giri and dai giri, the Kanemoto could slice through five bundles of straw, whereas the former blades would peak at only three. This is because blades with a high shinogi suffer considerably from the energy absorption caused by soft targets and proves that even if the blade edge itself is exactly the same, the height of the ridgeline has an effect on a sword's cutting power.

In short, this means that widening a blade and lowering the height of the shinogi will greatly improve its cutting ability.

On the other hand, when cutting bamboo, the blade's cutting ability will not be affected much by a higher ridgeline. A higher shinogi improves the flexibility of the blade, making it more suitable to cut bamboo. By contrast, a blade with a shallow ridgeline will not have such great flexibility and is not recommended for this type of cut. If the cutting angle and grip manipulation are incorrect, then the blade will often snap. This is best viewed along the same lines as using different blades to prepare different ingredients in the kitchen, such as using a cleaver to cut through harder ingredients and a vegetable knife to cut through vegetables.

Furthermore, the position of the shinogi line is an important factor. It is not desirable for it to be too central along the width of the blade and, when considered from the perspective of the blade's physical dynamics, being further toward the back of the blade [*mine*] will give a better cutting edge.koto

10. MONETARY VALUE

One will not find a sword on sale for less than 30,000 yen, however hard one looks. There are surely even people out there who use blades worth 50,000 to 100,000 yen.[49]

Under the economic conditions of today, buying such expensive swords is highly problematic. The number of iaido practitioners is constantly increasing and, given this proliferation, it is getting harder and harder to purchase swords. This is a problem that bears thinking about.

Differences in Cutting Ability of Swords from Different Regions

Many renowned masters of *suemono giri* emerged during the Edo period and up to the early years of Meiji. Of these, one man in particular, the renowned sword tester and executioner Yamada Asaemon, records details of contemporary swordsmiths in a four-rank hierarchy, noting twelve smiths ranked *saijo owazamono* [最上大業物], twenty-one ranked *owazamono* [大業物], fifty ranked *ryowazamono* [良業物], and numerous others ranked *wazamono* [業物].

It is widely accepted, as gospel, that the higher a smith's rank the more effective his swords would be. However, from my experience of performing tameshigiri with over two hundred different swords from the Koto, Shinto, Shin Shinto, and Gendaito periods, it can be said that as long as the smith has put his soul into the work and has been diligent in its forging, then there is not a great deal of difference in overall cutting ability between one blade and another. This is of course bearing in mind the caveat that the works of famed master

---

49. Prices current at time of original publishing in 1980.

smiths such as Kotetsu, Shinkai, Shigeyoshi, or Tadayoshi are price-less works of art, meaning that their cutting ability cannot be tested through tameshigiri to prove either way.

I would also like to make it clear that the same smith can produce ten different swords, and each one will not have exactly the same cut-ting ability—some will be better and others worse.

Furthermore, the overall strength and durability of a blade is mainly influenced by the way the hamon is applied during its cool-ing, but it is also greatly affected by the forging process itself. One sometimes sees mass-produced blades from the same smith that are of a lower quality and poorer finish than his bespoke pieces.

It is not as if I have personally tested the cutting ability of blades from every region of the nation. These are simply my observations and impressions based on the blades from regions I have experienced. I would very much like to write further on the merits of blades from different regions, but in doing so I would attract controversy both from those regions and from others I do not mention, so I shall refrain.

The Effects of Heat and Cold on Cutting Ability

There is a difference in the cutting ability of a sword depending on the season and temperature. These are not examples from inside Japan, but for the reference of all practitioners of the sword arts, I would like to expound further on the effects of season and temperature on cutting ability. These examples are based on my experiences of performing tameshigiri both in the over 35°C heat of China's Huanan region and in the bitter cold in the north of the nation of Manchuria (presently the northeast of China), which reaches between -30°C and -50°C degrees.

In July of 1942 I received the call to join the Imperial Army and was inducted into the Eighteenth Northern Unit (formerly the Thirty-Second Yamagata Infantry Regiment). The katana I owned at this time had the tang and name inscription filed down, but it was a fine-looking blade of the Koto period from approximately six hundred years ago. The blade measured 2 shaku and 3 sun in length and was slightly worn down from sharpening and polishing over its many years of service.

After joining up I was stationed in Beian in Manchuria's Heihe province (now Heilongjiang province in China), engaged in anti-Soviet strategic exercises. From November right through to early March of the next year the temperatures plummeted, recording a low of -48°C as Beian was hit by a particularly fierce cold spell.

One day during this severe icy season I found myself engaged in conversation with three officers regarding the cutting ability of a katana in cold environments. From various chatter about how a blade might freeze and snap, we made the decision to test it out for real, and soon preparations were underway for tameshigiri.

At this time rice sacks could not be obtained, so instead we rolled up rough *kamasu*[50] bags and soaked them in water in the base kitchens before carrying them back to the barracks buildings. Even during this short trip the mats froze over. Although these conditions were not perfect, I set the pace, demonstrating the fundamentals of tameshigiri with my Koto sword. On the third cut the blade buckled and bent, but even though the straw had frozen solid there was not a single chip along the cutting edge.

The first officer's sword was a gendaito, that of the second a shin shinto, and that of the third a shinto from the Kanbun era, making them all considerably younger than my own blade. All three of these swords received several chips along their edges, but fortunately none of them snapped.

My Koto-period blade had been worn down through years of polishing and sharpening, and its durability was slightly weakened, so on the third cut the blade buckled and bent around the monouchi. I managed to fix the bent blade by placing it on the cutting stand and striking

---

50. A rough bag made from low-quality straw or rushes.

the *mine* two to three times, but I was most surprised that it returned to its original curvature and did not get notched. About 70 percent of swords, both modern and ancient, will notch or snap when struck on the back of the blade like this when secured to a platform. My Koto blade had lost some of its core durability but was a mysterious and mystical weapon indeed, and even now I am deeply impressed by it.

A snapped katana blade

A bent katana blade

In summer of the next year I recalled our experiments with tameshigiri in a cold climate and, alongside two of the officers (the third officer had been reassigned to another unit), I set about preparing for testing our blades in hot conditions.

This time round, however, the shin shinto blades showed an excellent cutting ability that greatly contrasted with how they fared in the cold.

Under the heat my Koto was even less durable than it had been in the cold, and its cutting power was also poor. Thus, from my experiences, I have learned that when cutting in a cold environment the best sword to have is a Koto, whereas under conditions of great heat a shinto is better.

MACHINE-GUN CUTTER NAGANOBU

I once saw a newspaper article about an Imperial soldier cutting through an enemy machine gun with his military sword during the Russo-Japanese war. The sword in question was a Shin Shinto blade produced by Takahashi Naganobu, a disciple of the master smith Kato Tsunahide. This particular smith was hearing impaired, and from this he got the nickname "Naganobu the deaf." Nevertheless, the cutting power of his creations was exceptional. The Kato line produced many fine swords and smiths of the wazamono class, from Koyama

Munetsugu to Tsunatoshi, Koichi, and Munehiro. These blades are in the top ranks for cutting power among those forged in the Shin Shinto period, and I am very impressed by them. Once the Russo-Japanese war had ended "Naganobu the deaf" became known as "Machine-gun cutter Naganobu" and achieved great fame.

A kodachi short sword made by this smith is owned by Mr. Fushimi Ryu, the chief executive officer of the Zen Nihon Toyama ryu Iaido Renmei, and on occasion I have had the honor of viewing it. If this were a longer blade I would perhaps be unreasonable and ask him to relinquish it to me, but unfortunately it is just a kodachi!

Returning to this amazing "machine-gun-cutting sword," as far as I can envisage, it would be absolutely impossible for a sword, however sharp, to cut straight through a machine gun in one blow. This, I can state with certainty.

What I imagine happened was that when the soldier charged the enemy machine gun it had already fired many hundreds of rounds, heating up the barrel and chassis, and weakening the metal, the temperature making it possible for the sword to penetrate into it. We also cannot forget that this article was printed during a war, when newspapers will overembellish things for propaganda reasons, and the story became famous at that time.

Machine guns are made from tempered steel, which is a far cry from regular iron, and I state again in no uncertain terms that there is no way even the greatest of blades could cut through that.

Chipping the Blade When Cutting a Razor-Wire Fence

When I was still on active duty and sent out to the front during the Manchurian incident, at the battle of Beidaying in Jinzhou county (today known as Jinzhou county in Liaoning province, modern-day China), I was shown the military sword of a detachment commander who had used it to cut through razor-wire fences and thereby chipped the edge of the blade.

It is quite pitiful that the blade of a Japanese sword should be chipped cutting through something as flimsy as razor wire. The machine gun mentioned above would have been manufactured from tempered steel, but razor wire is only pig iron and should prove no problem if cut correctly. However, as always, the way the cut is made is important. If you cut straight down into the middle of a stretch of wire, where it is not as taut, then the wire will bounce and vibrate, and the sword will be rebounded, failing to cut and likely chipping the blade. In order to cut it successfully you must aim for the area by the mounting stakes, where the wire is fixed in place and there is not as much give. If this is done correctly then the wire can easily be cut through, although the blade may still chip slightly. Furthermore, the trick is not to cut the wire horizontally but at a diagonal angle (i.e., using kesagiri), and this will lead to success.

When making a cut, it is important to always get the correct cutting angle and trajectory, and to be aware that left and right diagonal cuts (left and right kesagiri) are both a natural and logical method. I would like for all sword practitioners to be aware that, when it comes to using live blades, vertical cutting is simply a method to train the fundamentals and is not suited to actual cutting.

Regarding Firearms and Bladed Weapons Registration

After the War, Japanese swords were put under a registration system by the occupying forces. I have no comments on how this affects guns and pistols, but I find it utterly lamentable that Japanese swords are treated in the same way as such base firearms.

Even though the Japanese sword is a weapon, it is the pride of the Yamato race. It is said that the bushi strives neither to cut nor to be cut by anyone, and the Japanese sword is his very soul. A heart that embraces the Japanese sword is intimately connected to our path of spiritual enrichment and perfection as Japanese people. After the swords were confiscated an appeal was made on the grounds that Japanese swords are world art treasures of the highest craftsmanship, and after much effort a registration system was secured. This system itself is indeed an issue, but the real problem is the restrictions placed on the number of swords that can be forged in the modern day.

These restrictions rule that modern swordsmiths cannot produce more than two Japanese swords per month. This is an unspeakably stupid ruling, and I strongly urge all associated parties to repeal it immediately.

I hear that there are over four hundred swordsmiths active today. The vast majority of swords they produce are for art purposes, being overly heavy, having wide blades and flowery hamon intended purely for display purposes. I would estimate that no more than 30 percent of these swords could be used as iaito. It must be said, however, that the sword smiths of today study deeply into the forging methods of antiquity and produce excellent blades that are in no way inferior to those of the Koto and Shinto periods. When iaido enthusiasts make an order for a shinken or iaito, they can expect a superlative blade made using these techniques. Such a blade will logically be of great use in perfecting one's technique in iaido practice.

Being light, unbendable, and unbreakable, as well as having great cutting power, are the life-forces of the Japanese sword, although in the current climate these ideals are slowly being lost. I would like for the swordsmiths themselves to take this current situation as an opportunity to reclaim and restore these essential characteristics to the objects of their craft.

As mentioned at the start of this volume, a Japanese sword has long been venerated as one of the three divine relics of the Imperial regalia. That sword can be said to be the very soul of the Japanese people. It is thus in the interest of fostering the spirit of the Japanese sword, and of preserving the swords of antiquity, that I wish to exhort the authorities to allow the sword makers of today to produce new blades, for sale at a suitable price, in the same manner as they could in the shinto and koto periods. I would also urge those same sword makers to produce practical shinken and iaito for the promotion and development of iaido.

I strongly call for organizations such as the Nihon Bijutsu Token Hozon Kyokai [Japan Art Sword Preservation Society] and the Token-kai [Sword Society] to come together and lobby for the support of politicians and the government, working with unified purpose toward the repeal of the restrictions that force swordsmiths to produce only two swords per month.

Words in Everyday Usage That Originate with the Japanese Sword

There are many words and phrases that we use in everyday conversation that have their origins with the Japanese sword. There may be some errors in how the Chinese characters are read, but I have listed some of these below, split into those that come from the names of parts of the Japanese sword and those that come from methods of sword handling.

WORDS AND PHRASES DERIVED FROM THE NAMES OF SWORD PARTS

Sword part: *Saya* 鞘.
English meaning: Scabbard.
Word/phrase: *Moto no saya ni osamaru* 元の鞘に納まる.
Literal meaning: "To return something to its original scabbard."
Usage: To return something to its original state or situation.

Sword part: *Tachi* 太刀.
English meaning: A cavalry sword [also a term for swords in general].
Word/phrase: *Tachiuchi dekinai* 太刀打ちできない.
Literal meaning: "Cannot clash swords with."
Usage: Cannot hold up against; is no rival for.

Sword part: *Hoto* 宝刀.
English meaning: A sword of great value; an heirloom sword.
Word/phrase: *Denka no hoto* 伝家の宝刀.
Literal meaning: "The family's valuable heirloom sword."
Usage: A final option; an ace up the sleeve; a secret weapon [metaphorically].

Sword part: *Ha* 刃.
English meaning: Cutting edge.
Word/phrase: *Ha ga tatanai* 刃がたたない.
Literal meaning: "The blade will not stand."
Usage: Cannot sort out; cannot deal with.

Sword part: *Tsuba* 鍔.
English meaning: Sword guard.
Word/phrase: *Tsuba zeriai* 鍔ぜり合い.
Literal meaning: "A desperate struggle pushing sword guards against each other."
Usage: A close contest; a well-balanced competition.

Sword part: *Seppa* 切羽.
English meaning: Thin metal washers on either side of tsuba to make a firm fit and cushion between the tsuba and both habaki and tsuba.
Word/phrase: *Seppa tsumaru* 切羽つまる.
Literal meaning: "The metal collar is stuck [in the scabbard]."
Usage: To come up against an obstacle; to be unable to progress or act satisfactorily; to be unable to act in the face of danger.

Sword part: *Shinogi* 鎬.
English meaning: The ridgeline on the blade.
Word/phrase: *Shinogi wo kezuru* 鎬を削る.
Literal meaning: "Wearing down each other's ridgelines."
Usage: A contest that is exactly equal; neck and neck.

Sword part: *Sori* 反り.

English meaning: Blade curvature.

Word/phrase: *Sori ga awanai* 反りが合わない.

Literal meaning: "The curvatures do not coincide."

Usage: Two people do not get along or feel differently about something.

Sword part: *Menuki* 目貫き.

English meaning: Ornaments wound into the hilt wrappings.

Word/phrase: *Menuki doori* 目抜き通り (The Chinese character used here is a variant on the standard one for menuki, but the root word is the same.)

Literal meaning: "A menuki ornament-like street."

Usage: A bustling main thoroughfare with many shops. The street will be a focal point of the town and draw the visitor's attention in the same way the menuki ornaments enrich a sword hilt and form a focal point.

Sword part: *Mekugi* 目釘.

English meaning: The peg that secures the tang in the hilt.

Word/phrase: *Mekugi ana* 目釘穴.

Usage: Used to describe something that fixes another object down or stops it from moving.

Sword part: *Mine* 棟.

English meaning: The back of the blade.

Word/phrase: *Mine* 峰.

Literal meaning: "The peak of a mountain."

Usage: The Chinese characters used to write them are different, but the words for a mountain peak and the back of a sword blade are homophones and their etymology is thought to be linked.

Sword part: *Koshirae* 拵え.
English meaning: Sword fittings.
Word/phrase: *Koshiraeru* 拵える.
Literal meaning: The verbal form of the noun "koshirae."
Usage: To manufacture or craft; also to prepare or season.

Sword part: *Kodachi* 小太刀.
English meaning: A short sword.
Word/phrase: *Kodachi* 小太刀.
Usage: A term for short swords in general.

Sword part: *Kantei* 鑑定.
English meaning: Appraisal.
Word/phrase: *Kantei* 鑑定.
Usage: General word for appraising something.

WORDS AND PHRASES THAT COME FROM METHODS OF SWORD HANDLING

Word/phrase: *Itto ryodan* 一刀両断.
Literal meaning: "A single decisive cut."
Usage: [Bringing something to] a decisive and clean conclusion.

Word/phrase: *Batto noto* 抜刀納刀.
Literal meaning: "Drawing and sheathing the blade."
Usage: Cannot act satisfactorily; cannot deal with.

Word/phrase: *Nukiuchi* 抜き打ち.
Literal meaning: "A cut from the draw."
Usage: A sudden and surprising occurrence.

Word/phrase: *Katate uchi* 片手打ち.
Literal meaning: "A single-handed cut."
Usage: One sided; biased.

Word/phrase: *Kubikiri* 首切り.

Literal meaning: "To behead; to cut the neck."

Usage: To fire someone. Decapitation is used metaphorically in Japanese to refer to losing one's job.

Word/phrase: *Hikigiri* 引き切り.

Literal meaning: "A pulling cut."

Usage: To cut something in a pulling motion with any bladed object.

Word/phrase: *Tsuki* 突き.

Literal meaning: "Thrust."

Usage: To thrust at or through something [in a general sense].

Word/phrase: *Futokoro gatana* 懐刀.

Literal meaning: "A concealed blade hidden inside one's jacket."

Usage: The lower part of the torso.

Word/phrase: *Yokogiri* 横切り.

Literal meaning: "Horizontal cut."

Usage: A horizontal line; the figure one. [The Chinese character for the number one is a simple horizontal line.]

CHAPTER 5

ESSENTIAL KNOWLEDGE CONCERNING THE JAPANESE SWORD

Knowledge of the Japanese Sword

It goes without saying that the warriors of old treated the Japanese sword with reverent care and consideration, as it was their very soul. They held their personal blades in great esteem, showing respect toward them, and through these blades they engaged in the perfection and enrichment of both mind and body, crafting and shaping their spiritual fortitude.

Even in this age of advancing progress and civilization that we live in today, the Japanese sword is still a vehicle for the nourishment of the spirit, as expressed in the saying that "a sword is one's heart and soul." The swordsman's wisdom, the philosophical teaching that one should strive to neither cut down an opponent nor be cut down oneself, is still very much alive and well.

Swordsman Tanabe Tetsundo

In iaido there is a saying, "*Saya no naka ni teki ari*" [literally "The enemy is within one's own scabbard"]. This relates to the ultimate expression of iaido, which is to face down the enemy without drawing one's sword and control the situation to achieve victory using only the dauntless and unyielding pride and willpower that one keeps within oneself. This level of mental strength, in which the practitioner's sword is in perfect harmony with all of his mental and physical energies, is the fruit of daily training and the forging of the self.

Swordsman Nakamura (right) and swordsman Haga (left) perform the Nippon kendo kata.

We are no longer living in an era when the Japanese sword is used in real combat, but it is still the pride of the Yamato people, steeped in history and tradition, and is valued highly around the world as a superlative work of art and craftsmanship.

The reemergence, development, and promotion of iaido, kendo, and the various other martial disciplines, which looked as if they were going to die out after the War ended, is a matter of great joy to me as an enthusiast of the martial arts. I am also surprised and delighted by the flourishing of study groups and other activities among today's younger generation of sword collectors and enthusiasts, feeling that traditions proper and befitting Japanese people are alive and well.

However, I find it most unfortunate and saddening that among the iaido and kendo enthusiasts of today there are those who have a poor knowledge of matters relating to the Japanese sword. As the kendo practiced today is almost entirely sports kendo, to some extent it is only to be expected that there is a lack of knowledge about actual swords. However, those who dedicate themselves to the path of the sword should rethink such an approach and should wish to deepen their knowledge of the Japanese sword.

The Example of Araki Mataemon's Blade Snapping

The tale of Araki Mataemon and the duel to the death at the Kagiya crossroads is one of Japan's three great tales of revenge, alongside that of the Soga brothers and the *Chushingura* [also known as *The Tale of the Forty-Seven Ronin*]. It also provides an example of how the sword can break. The sword that Araki Mataemon carried at that time was a shinto from the early Edo period, forged by the smith Izuminokami

Rai Kanemichi, and was 2 shaku, 7 sun, and 4 bu in length (approximately 84 cm).

When the servant Ichizo became desperate and came at Araki with a wooden sword, striking him with all his might, Araki swept the blow aside horizontally. In doing so, he snapped his blade at a point 1 shaku and 2 sun (approximately 36 cm) from the guard. Many decades ago I acquired a sword made by the same Izuminokami Rai Kanemichi, but it was clearly a showy piece forged to impress the layman, being wide of blade and having a large and ornate hamon extending over half that width. There are exceptions, but it is certain that hamon like this make the blade itself brittle and more likely to chip or break. Most newly forged swords are of this type and are suited more as display pieces for collectors than as useable weapons.

Swords with a hamon that extends over half the width of the blade are not suitable for practical use. Although an expansive and flowery hamon makes the blade itself more durable, it robs it of flexibility, meaning that on average it will snap more easily. A hamon of around a quarter of the blade's width will make the blade comparatively harder to bend or break and will also improve its cutting ability.

Furthermore, heavier swords tend to have a generally poorer cutting ability, although this does vary depending on the physical strength of the user. It is, after all, the very essence of the Japanese sword to be light, unbendable, unbreakable, and to have great cutting power.

It must be noted, however, that these characteristics of not breaking or bending and cutting well depend on the skills of the swordsmith who forged the blade. Furthermore, although Yamada Asaemon classified smiths and the swords they made into a hierarchy of four ranks (*saijo owazamono, owazamono, ryowazamono,* and *wazamono*) in his tameshigiri densho, different swords produced by the same smith will not always be the same. Depending on how the forging process went, there will be some that can cut well and others that cannot. There are also many other blades that are not ranked and categorized so highly but can, nonetheless, cut very well.

The Lieutenant Colonel Aizawa Incident

I would like to take up the example set during an incident involving the kendo master Lieutenant Colonel Aizawa Saburo, for what it can show us about the need to be aware of the differences between shinai kendo and handling a real blade. This will deepen our knowledge of the Japanese sword accordingly.

I will purposefully not touch upon the reasons for this incident here and stick instead to explaining the facts. On August 12, 1935, Lieutenant Colonel Aizawa cut down the head of the Military Affairs Bureau, Major General Nagata Tetsuzan. This became the spark that led to the February 26 incident[51] of the next year.

Lieutenant Colonel Aizawa was an instructor of kenjutsu and *juke-njutsu* at the former Imperial Army Toyama Military Academy and a master of those arts. The Toyama Academy was an elite institution that enrolled the most talented and generally superior commissioned and noncommissioned officers from the various units stationed within the motherland's borders, giving them special training and instruction in various disciplines and educating them in the martial spirit.

The Lieutenant Colonel had trained extensively in the ways of Zen Buddhism and had the bearing of a warrior of old, a soldier through and through. Unfortunately he did not have a great practical knowledge regarding real swords.

The army sword he carried was made in the Kanei period [1624–1644] by Musashi no Kami Fujiwara Kunitsugu, the second son of Kawachi no Kami Kunisuke.

Lieutenant Colonel Aizawa's first cut was aimed at Major General Nagata's left shoulder, but it failed to take him down cleanly and so Aizawa made a second strike that also failed to kill. As the Major General was writhing in pain, he turned away from Aizawa, who took

---

51. An attempted coup by around 1,400 troops from the Japanese Imperial Army that killed several high-ranking political figures and led to a brief occupation of central Tokyo.

his left hand away from the hilt of his sword and moved it to grip the center of the blade, taking up a left-handed diagonal facing stance [*hanmi*] and thrusting through the Major General's back and clean out his chest with the charging bayonet thrust motion of jukenjutsu. This final blow was the mortal one.

As he was gripping the center of the blade, with his fingers wrapped around the edge, the Lieutenant Colonel received serious cuts to the four fingers on his left hand that penetrated to the bone.

Regardless of whether he hesitated psychologically, that a master of shinai kendo such as the Lieutenant Colonel could fail to cut down the Major General, who was unarmed and wearing just a light summer uniform, in a single decisive blow was probably because the sword in question was a western-style sabre. Even so, this was clearly the result of his not internalizing the principles of actual sword handling and is most unfortunate.

Lieutenant Colonel Aizawa was sentenced to death, and from prison he expressed his regrets, saying "I find it most unfortunate and shameful that, as a swordsmanship instructor of the Toyama Academy, I could not kill in a single strike." He also commented, with regard to the sword itself, that from a technical point of view "a sword does not need a cutting edge from the center of the blade down to the guard."

One of the main differences between kendo and handling a real sword is that, while shinai kendo is simply a technique for striking, when using a real sword care must be taken that the cutting trajectory describes a circular arc. As iaido kata are training exercises that practice cutting only the air, practitioners should introduce tameshigiri into their training to learn the correct grip manipulation and cutting trajectory for using a live blade.

Furthermore, if a Japanese sword were to have a cutting edge only from the center of the blade to the tip, it would lose its value as art and become nothing more than a tool for murdering people. If looked at simply from the point of view of killing then, admittedly, a cutting edge from the center of the blade down to the guard is not necessary and carries with it a considerable increase in danger to the user. Over thirty years ago I, too, injured my left hand by fumbling my sword on its scabbard. However, once one has experienced the pain that results from making a mistake such as this, he will be extra cautious from then on and eager not to repeat it.

The Japanese sword has the appeal it does precisely because it has a cutting edge running all the way down it, and this is what makes it possible to use it as a vehicle for spiritual training.

The Martial Spirit of Yamaoka Tesshu's Muto Ryu

In owning a Japanese sword, one must hold safety and the avoidance of accidents as one's first priority and should under no circumstances handle the blade frivolously. One must show respect to the katana and value the proper decorum and formality regarding its handling, giving utmost devotion to one's own valued blade and adhering to the tenets of budo.

Yamaoka Tesshu sensei's realization of his martial philosophy, as expressed through his Muto ryu, is something truly great. His teachings state that "The principle of *muto* [literally "no sword"] is to bear no sword outside of one's own heart and mind. When facing down an enemy one should rely not on his blade but should strike with the heart." I have not studied the deeper mysteries of the unity of Zen and the sword myself, however, and so I do not fully understand the deeper significance of this philosophy.

Yamaoka sensei's philosophy looked far beyond the concept of the sword as a weapon, but at the same time the weapon he bore was a Fukuoka ichimonji—a sword of renown with scars on the blade from its practical use. He acted with a completely unflinching and centered spirit, and I have nothing but respect for this great master.

As a point of caution when performing tameshigiri, although straw targets may present few problems, when cutting bamboo targets there is a danger that the cut bamboo will be sent spinning away or that the mekugi in the sword's hilt will split in half while the cut is made and the blade will fly away. It is also possible that if the practitioner's grip on the hilt is not correct, the momentum of the blade can knock the whole sword out of his hands and send it flying. It is thus important to make sure that there is nobody standing in the path of the cut or the area extending beyond it. To maintain proper safety, when one cannot avoid spectators they should be kept a minimum of six meters away from the direction of the cut.

Breathing When Performing an Iai Draw

In some iai ryuha it is taught that when performing kata the practitioner should take two breaths and then, when he has finished inhaling, on the third breath make the draw. The purpose of iai techniques is to react instantly to how the opponent attacks and to draw into a strike in that fleeting moment of opportunity. As such I simply cannot understand the reason for waiting in front of one's foe to take two or three breaths before acting. In kendo kata and competition it is absolutely unthinkable for a swordsman to wait and take two or three breaths before striking. Such a practice deviates from kendo and thus should be improved upon from an instructional point of view.

It may be permissible at displays and such to make the draw after taking time to focus one's spirit, but this does not fit with the fundamental principles of iai and is clearly another of the mistaken teachings from the densho of the koryu. I am sure this is one of the reasons that Japan's iai arts are thought of as "artistic performance with the sword" and as "dances."

In the sport of weight lifting, competitors will take time to steady and focus their breathing before making the lift in one motion, but it is laughable to consider iai the same as weight lifting.

Around 1955 I had the opportunity to meet and converse with Kunii Michiyuki (Zenya) sensei, eighteenth-generation inheritor of the Kashima shinryu, at various martial arts demonstration and competition events. We watched many demonstrations of practical, combat-focused iai kata and kumitachi and discussed the finer points of swordsmanship. We came to the conclusion that iai has to come from a natural position, without adopting any kind of specific "ready" posture, the practitioner responding silently and instantaneously to whatever technique the enemy uses or however he attacks to secure victory. Specific methods of breathing have no relevance to this. Kunii sensei too finds the idea of iai practiced from seiza, taking time for two or three breaths before acting, as absurd.

The Toyama ryu and Nakamura ryu that I teach do not specify this method or that method of breathing, as such prescriptive instruction is unnecessary and counterproductive. All the kata are performed drawing from a natural stance, and tameshigiri especially is carried out based on these principles of natural movement. This has nothing to do with specific and contrived breathing patterns.

The teaching of practical sword methods using actual sharp swords may not be fitting for the times in which we live, but I have the greatest respect for the Kashima shinryu and the Jigen ryu as the premier schools of practical, combat-oriented iaido.

The Importance of *Netaba Awase* [Sharpening the Blade Edge]

When canny warriors of the past headed for the battlefield they placed great importance on knowledge of how to correctly sharpen and finely adjust the cutting edges of their swords [*netaba awase*].[52]

There are many today who do not have this knowledge and, although there are those who cut successfully with just a freshly polished and sharpened blade, the processes and importance of filing the cutting

---

52. 寝刃合わせ; refers to the practice of filing and sharpening a freshly polished blade to give it a slightly rougher finish and thus improve traction when cutting and protect the edge from damage.

edge are some of the most vital things to learn for tameshigiri. This has the same objective as when a butcher files his knives on an iron rod in order to cut through meat and fat effectively.

The aim of netaba awase is to protect the cutting edge against chipping while also improving its cutting ability, and it involves sharpening the point of the edge down to an angle of around thirty degrees using various grades of whetstone.

The most important point to remember, however, is that one should not simply file the blade regardless of the state it may be in but should file it carefully depending on what is needed. It would be outrageous to just brazenly and carelessly sharpen down the edge of a fine sword of renown, and this is likely to result in damage to the substance of the cutting edge itself or cause degradation to the surface of the blade. Sharpening the edge calls for great care and caution.

The whetstones that should be used are also important, and coarse stones [aratoishi] should be strictly avoided. It is recommended that one uses whetstones graded as "improving stones" [kaiseito], "Motoyama adjustment stones" [Motoyama awaseto], and "finishing stones" [shiageto]. When sharpening it is important to apply pressure evenly, so as not to scratch the surface of the metal, not to mistake the angle, and not to allow the cutting edge area to ride up from where it is secured.

Cross section of the blade:

between twenty and thirty degrees

The secret to netaba awase is to sharpen the cutting edge to an angle of twenty to thirty degrees

The Correct Mental Attitude When Cutting and the Importance of the Holding Pin (Mekugi/Hikae Mekugi)

When approaching a solid object and trying to cut it, if one hesitates and has doubts over whether he can cut through the target then, even if it can be done physically, the cut will fail.

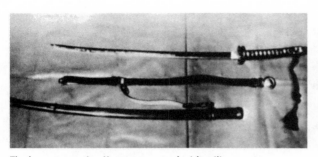

The later generation Kanemoto sword with military-type fittings used in the Mishima Yukio incident and still stained with blood

The determination and resolve that you will certainly cut through your target is most important. If the swordsman unifies and focuses his spirit; eliminates all uncertainty from the mind; and strikes with the willpower and vitality of sword, mind, and body in perfect coordination, perfected on the path of the ever-calm mind, and exhibiting the sublime quality of motion in stillness, then he will doubtless succeed in achieving his objective.

However, it goes without saying that a good mental attitude alone will not make the cut. Clearly the correct angle, blade trajectory, circular motion, and grip manipulation are vital, but a swordsman must also master how to stop and flow with the motion of the blade after the cut has been made. (These are covered in a later chapter.)

In addition to this, before the cut is even made, it is important to check whether the mekugi holding pin that keeps the blade fixed into the hilt is whole and undamaged.

In 1951, at a martial arts demonstration held inside the Meiji Jingu Shrine, I heard a story about an accident caused by failing to check the mekugi from the august Aoki sensei, eighteenth-generation inheritor of Miyamoto Musashi's martial teachings.

Aoki sensei was a shihan-level instructor of kendo in the empire's Taiwan province. At a martial arts tournament held at the Taiwan police headquarters during the War, he witnessed a certain respected practitioner of iaido fail to check his sword's mekugi before performing. During the display the peg snapped and the blade flew out into the audience and pierced the chest of one of the spectators. The spectator apparently later died from this injury.

Furthermore, although there is no way of knowing for sure, I believe that the sword used in the Mishima Yukio incident[53] that took place in 1970 at the Tokyo Ichigaya Ground Self-Defense Force base, the blade known widely as *seki no magoroku*, was actually my nameless blade with a *sanbonsugi* pattern hamon, forged by one of the later-generation Kanemoto smiths. I owned this sword eight years prior to the incident. I had bequeathed this blade to Mr. Funaita Hiroshi, CEO of the Taiseido bookshop by Shibuya station, to whom I taught kendo and iaido at the time. Mr. Funaita was a soldier who fought in the battle of Angaur in the Pacific War and miraculously managed to live through the heroic last stand of the Imperial Army there. When he published the memoir of his experiences during the War, *Screams of Heroic Spirits*,[54] Mishima sensei kindly provided an introduction. To show his gratitude Funaita presented him with the sword.

According to various stories, before the incident, it appears that Mishima sensei went to Saga prefecture and studied deeply into the Shinpuren uprising,[55] *seppuku*, and about the mekugi holding pins of

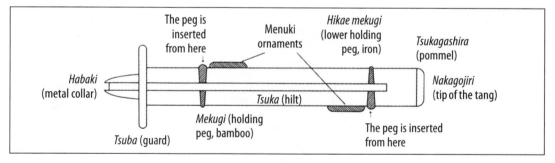

View of the hilt from above

---

53. The attempted coup by famed writer Mishima Yukio that culminated in his ritual suicide. Mishima was fascinated with the samurai code of bushido and was a practitioner of the sword arts.

54. 英霊の絶叫 (*Eirei no zekkyo*).

55. A rebellion by disenfranchised samurai against the new Meiji government that took place in Kumamoto prefecture in October 1876. The Shinpuren [divine wind federation] organization was staunchly against the modernizing and westernizing influences on the changing nation and desired to completely expel all foreign influence and turn the cultural clock back to feudal times.

swords. All swords used in iaido today have a single mekugi pin, and the vast majority of these pins are made from bamboo. With bamboo mekugi it is important to insert them into the cavity while facing the side with the bamboo's skin toward the pommel of the hilt.

As the members of my organization mainly practice tameshigiri alongside iaido kata, we aim for absolute safety and use two mekugi pins inserted into separate holes. One pin is made of bamboo, but the other is fashioned from iron and made to fit snugly into its mount so that the hilt will be firm and will not shift, allowing the practitioner to bring out their technique to the full.

Correct Gripping of the Hilt Is the Ultimate Secret for Iaido and Kendo

The Japanese sword,
Grip on the hilt should be pliable,
Not squeezing or loose,
Like squeezing a tea cloth.

With the handlebars of bicycles or motorbikes and the steering wheels of cars, a tight, stiff grip will rob the driver of any freedom of movement when driving and lead to traffic accidents. In the same way, gripping the hilt of a sword too tightly will stop users from applying their skill. Getting calluses on the palm of the hand is a mark of a novice swordsman.

I often hear people referred to as experts or veterans in kendo because they have calluses on their hands from gripping the shinai. I cannot help but laugh at this idea. A swordsman may have arms and wrists that have developed to be larger and sturdier than those of regular people, but if a practitioner has calluses on his hands then he is certainly not a master.

After Nakayama Hakudo sensei passed away, I heard one of my junior training colleagues, a man who graduated from the Busen academy[56] and was a high-level kendoka, tell of how he had heard that the area on the guard of Nakayama sensei's sword where his hand would rest was worn down and had a dip in it from the master's daily practice. He said that this showed how diligent and dedicated to training the master was. I could not help but turn away and smile painfully at this.

In 1951 Nakayama sensei honored me with a visit to my residence. We met three times after this, and he even penned a fine scroll of calligraphy for me. If a great iaido and tameshigiri master such as Nakayama were to grip the guard of his sword so strongly that it would cause a dent in it, there is no way that he would be able to bring out his technique. So it is clear that these stories are nothing but a fanciful fiction. The junior colleague who relayed this story dedicated his training to kendo alone, and so was impressed by the concept of Nakayama sensei training until he made an indentation in his sword guard. However, this proves that he had little knowledge of iaido.

When gripping the hilt, the most important hand is the left one, as this forms the base for manipulation. The grip should be made 70 percent with the left hand and only 30 percent with the right, and the thumbs on both hands should be pointed downward as shown in the photo below. The nature of how one should apply pressure to the hilt is exactly as explained in the poem at the start of this section, and correct grip manipulation is the deepest and most fundamental principle of swordsmanship.

Gripping not too tightly or too loosely and with the thumbs turned down

I will go into the correct *chakin shibori* [wringing the tea cloth] handling method later in this volume, in the chapter on how to stop and flow with the blade after making a cut.

---

56. Abbreviation of Budo Senmon Gakko (武道専門学校), a government-run national school for martial arts founded in 1911 as the Butoku Gakko (school of martial virtue). The school was closed during World War II.

I have not personally seen the sword guard that Nakayama sensei used, so I speak only from supposition here.

Paying Attention to the Tip of the Tang When Gripping the Hilt

One should check the length of his sword's tang and how far it inserts into the hilt before using it in practice. If the tang goes only a third to a half of the total length of the hilt (blades from the Koto period in particular tend to have short tangs), then take a grip that leaves the pommel open to prevent the blade from snapping at the hilt when practicing iaido solo kata cutting through the air. However, even though this grip will protect the sword when practicing kata, if one uses such a sword with a short tang for tameshigiri or suemonogiri and the wood of the hilt is too old and flimsy, then it will almost certainly snap, regardless of how one grips it.

This is not something to worry about if the tang is long enough though. If it is eight-tenths of the length of the hilt then there will be no need to worry about snapping, and the user can take a full grip on the pommel and express his technique to the fullest.

There are several gripping variations taught by the various classical ryuha. It is most lamentable that at iaido demonstrations and in kendo kata practice, one will see many practitioners of the sword arts who perform their techniques with a grip opening half a hand's width down to the pommel. One will never see anyone in kendo training or competitions with shinai performing a technique with a grip that exposes the pommel in this manner. It is only when it comes to kata using real swords that one sees such a grip and, although not all practitioners do it, unfortunately around half of them will make this error.

I would like to take this opportunity to caution all iaido enthusiasts who perform techniques opening up and exposing the base of the sword's pommel. This is an important technical point for reference.

The only reason to grip the hilt while exposing the pommel is to protect the blade from breaking if the tang is too short, but if this is not the case then a fuller grip, just strong enough not to damage the hilt, will allow the user to express his technique more fully. The unification of kendo and iaido should start with how the hilt is gripped.

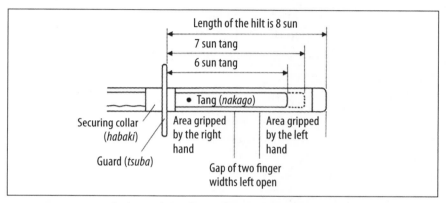

1. Safe positioning when gripping the hilt

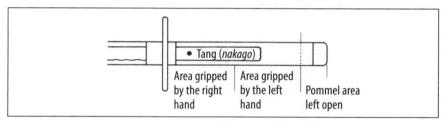

2. How to grip the hilt when the tang of the blade is too short (grip that opens up and exposes the pommel)

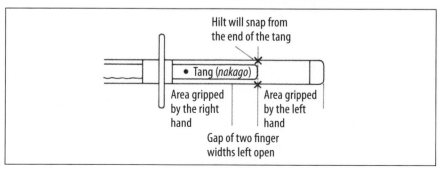

3. What can happen when the tang of the blade is too short and the usual correct grip (1) is used when striking a solid object

The *Tenouchi* (Gripping) Method of *Chakin Shibori* [Wringing the Tea Cloth]

The ratio of blade length and hilt length on a sword is not standardized across the different ryuha, but as a rule the hilt will be one-third the length of the blade. This means that a 2 shaku and 4 sun (approximately 73 cm) blade should have a hilt of 8 sun (approximately 24 cm).

I have touched upon the correct grip positioning before, and so I shall not repeat it here, but I must stress that the grip should be made with 70 percent of the strength in the left hand and 30 in the right, not holding the sword too stiffly or too loosely.

Through the correct gripping of the hilt [tenouchi], the practitioner ensures that the blade does not wobble when it cuts through a solid target. If the blade shakes when it makes impact with a hard object then the cutting edge will chip or the blade will bend.

Chakin shibori refers to the action at the moment of wringing out a wet cloth with the hands and is vital when stopping the blade after making a cut through a target. If the chakin shibori action is not pulled off correctly and the momentum behind the cut is not stopped, then the practitioner can cut down into his own foot, the tip of the blade can impact into the ground, and in extreme cases there are even examples of the sword flying clean out of the hands.

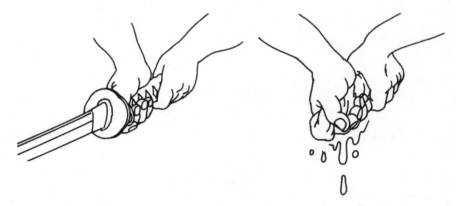

The grip in both hands is like wringing a teacloth (*chakin shibori*)

There is an enlightening example from my time during the War when I was in northern Manchuria (to the northeast of China), as a special practical martial arts swordsmanship instructor assigned to the Second Yamashita Army Group Southern Special Attack Unit, instructing a group of around fifty officers.

A young apprentice officer who had come out of university and had earned a third-dan ranking in kendo was cutting a simulated target with a descending diagonal cut from the upper right to the lower left (hidari kesagiri). He misjudged the distancing to the target and only grazed it with the tip of the blade, but there was too much momentum behind his swing and the military sword flew through the air, flying out of his hands and cutting into the young man's knee, finally coming to rest in the ground seven meters away (also see chapter 12).

His hand positioning on the hilt was also a factor, but this incident was largely because his grip manipulation [tenouchi] and chakin shibori action were not coordinated at the moment he made the cut.

Distancing [Maai], Cutting Trajectory [Hasuji], Blade Angle [Kakudo], and Circular Motion [Enkeisen]

In tameshigiri, regardless of how fine or renowned the blade one uses and however great its cutting power, if the distancing [maai], cutting trajectory [hasuji], blade angle [kakudo], and circular motion [enkeisen] are incorrect, then the cut will fail and, depending on the target, the cutting edge can chip or the blade bend out of shape.

Regarding maai, in shinai kendo students are taught to strike with the monouchi (the area from two-thirds up the body of the shinai to the tip), but as the blade of a katana has a cutting edge running all the way down it, those with no practical experience will try to cut with the middle part of it. This is a mistake right from the start, as if one cuts with the center of the blade then all the weight will fall at its tip, causing the cut to fail and possibly even causing the blade to bend at its central point.

The governing principle of cutting with a real sword is to impact with the area between the tip and the top third of the blade (known as the monouchi).

It goes without saying that the correct cutting trajectory, blade angle, and circular motion comes from tenouchi, but unless all of these factors are in coordination the cut will not achieve its objective.

There are various effective cutting trajectories, such as descending, rising, and horizontal cuts (see chapter 8: Nakamura ryu battojutsu happo giri), but in all cases it is important to cut in a perfectly straight line along the direction of the cutting edge.

Furthermore, even if the blade is swung in a straight line, unless the cut has the correct circular motion, it will not be a pulling cut and will fail to penetrate. This pulling cut motion differs from the "striking" motion employed in shinai kendo and is a major point of technical difference.

For example, when cutting tuna sashimi at a sushi restaurant or fishmonger, the professional cuts swiftly, cleanly, and efficiently, but an amateur will messily worry away at the edges and get the knife caught up in the fish meat, resulting in rough and frayed pieces.

The secret to cutting meat or fish like this is to make a pulling cut. In the same way, by making sure he does not mess up the circular motion and the associated blade angle, a student of the sword arts can learn and internalize the feeling of cutting correctly.

Good tameshigiri technique comes from synchronizing the above four factors and cutting with a strong will and an attitude of total coordination of the sword, the body, and all of one's physical and mental energy [kikentai ichi].

How to Stop the Blade from Shaking After Making a Cut

When viewing demonstrations of iaido solo kata, I often see the blade shaking back and forth when a practitioner stops after the cut or performs the blood-shaking maneuver [chiburi]. This happens in about 30 percent of cases and is obviously going to be an issue with beginners, but is often seen among older practitioners as well. It is a painful thing to watch from a technical point of view.

In short, the bamboo shinai used in kendo is very light and so can be stopped easily when doing kirikaeshi or suburi exercises. A real sword, however, weighs two or three times what a shinai does, and if the grip manipulation is not sufficient then the blade will shake when it is stopped after cutting. This is a point that needs attention from a technical perspective.

The causes of this shaking can be found in the practitioner putting unnecessary force or momentum into a cut while not properly synchronizing the chakin shibori gripping method with it, and, especially, in not extending the arms fully to make an expansive circular cut, keeping the elbows squeezed tight to the body. The student must always be critical of his performance and make sure to eliminate these mistakes.

Here too, experiencing tameshigiri will cultivate in the student an instinctive feeling for how much power and momentum to put into the cut, and will allow him to internalize the technique of coordinating his whole energy and being with the sword [kikentai ichi].

However, training with the tanrenbo (see chapter 6) will be more effective in teaching the correct tenouchi and chakin shibori gripping manipulations than simply practicing suburi with a real sword, and so I thoroughly recommend such training to all students.

How to Stop and Flow with the Blade After Making a Cut

I recall one particularly tragic anecdote regarding stopping the blade after a cut that I would like to share for the benefit of all practitioners of the sword arts.

This is a story that I heard from my comrade-in-arms, Sergeant Uchida Masakichi, who was sent out to fight in the Sino-Japanese War. Among the eleven kata practiced in the Omori ryu school of swordsmanship, not a single one covers the natural and instinctive diagonal cutting techniques of right or left kesagiri. The vertical cut shinchoku giri is the fundamental motion of this style, and it contains many kata covering the technique, allowing the student to master the correct cutting trajectory.

During the Sino-Japanese War, a certain platoon commander who had a third dan in kendo attempted to cut down a foe using this shinchoku giri vertical cut and misjudged the distance, only just cutting into the enemy's face with the tip of the blade. Because of the momentum behind the blade and the poor grip the commander was employing, the hilt slipped from his hands and the blade spun round to slice into his groin area, inflicting a serious injury. Both men writhing around with their respective injuries made quite a scene that Sergeant Uchida tells me he can still recall to this day. From my own experiences with the sword, this is a perfectly possible outcome.

Exactly this kind of outcome took place once while I was instructing tameshigiri, when the student failed to hit the straw target with the monouchi area of the blade and only scraped across its surface. Due to the momentum that had built up, the army-issue sword he was using came out of his hands and flew off, landing around seven meters away (see also the examples in chapter 13).

One occasionally sees performances at iaido demonstrations, competitions, and gradings in which the swordsman puts too much power into his cut and sends the tip of the blade cutting straight down into the floor. This is proof that he did not use proper chakin shibori when handling the hilt of his sword.

Even more than with solo kata practice, when performing tameshigiri it is very easy for the swordsman to get too caught up in the idea of cutting through the target and focus only on that, neglecting to stop the blade as mentioned above until it is too late. There are more than a few cases of performers cutting into their own feet or burying the blade into the ground, even though they may well have cut through the target.

The cardinal rule of stopping the blade safely and effectively after making the cut is to coordinate one's grip with the chakin shibori wringing motion and then bring the left hand holding the pommel of the sword to rest by one's navel, actually making contact with it.

The suemono giri exercise uses a vertical shinchoku giri cut, but it is the diagonal kesagiri that is the more natural and instinctive technique. When cutting with kesagiri, it is also possible to use the momentum of the descending blade [at the moment it cuts down diagonally from a high guard] to turn it on an axis and come up to a left or right hasso no kamae posture while maintaining proper situational awareness. This is the technique of "flowing" with the blade and, essentially, it involves letting the blade move away to the left or right of the body. To perform this stopping method in conjunction with tameshigiri requires quite a lot of training and practice.

The Technique to Cut through a Target and Leave It Standing in Place

In 1963 at the Fukui prefectural kobudo competition, I gave a demonstration of Toyama ryu tameshigiri. During the performance I made a horizontal sweeping cut from left to right, slicing through the straw target. However, once the cut was finished the target remained upright and the severed section did not fall to the ground. I have trained and practiced tameshigiri continuously, perfecting my technique for forty-two years—from 1938 to the present—but in all that time I have never managed to get a target to stay upright when performing a horizontal cut, either before or since that day. It was a special and awe-inspiring cut indeed.

It frequently happens that the target will remain upright after being cut with diagonal strikes such as kesagiri or johogiri/gyaku giri, but even I was overcome with surprise when it still stood after being pierced by a horizontal sweeping cut.

Basically, this phenomenon occurs when the circular cutting motion, the blade angle, and the trajectory are all in perfect alignment, and this causes a vacuum at the point of the cut (although it also depends, in part, on the way the water soaks into the straw being used as a target).

Furthermore, to get this effect one must cut the upper part of the target, above its central point. Cutting below the center will cause the weight of the target to act on itself, and the technique will not work. It will also fail if the base of the target is loose and can move around.

To get the target to remain standing after a cut is an advanced technique. The target will not stay up through trying to cut in a certain way or through simply willing it to remain vertical. The only way to achieve this is through perfectly synchronized tenouchi and the coordination of the whole of one's energy and being with the sword [kikentai ichi], avoiding all conscious thought and entering a state of complete egolessness while making the cut.

Shaking the Blood [Chiburi] and Re-sheathing [Noto]

There are many and varied chiburi blood-shaking motions seen throughout the classical koryu schools, but the concept of re-sheathing a bloodied blade after simply shaking it in the air once is a fallacy. Chiburi is simply a part of the formality of, and a ceremonial way to conclude, kata.

The scenes one often sees in period films and dramas in which a swordsman draws, cuts, and then returns the blade to the scabbard without the hand being seen is a silly party trick possible only with a *takemitsu*[57] imitation blade.

Re-sheathing the blade of the Japanese sword, soul of the warrior, by resting it on the left hand, salty with sweat, is also a somewhat dubious idea. From ancient times swordsmen have taken great care of their blades, making sure that even a breath does not touch the metal. A hand would have been completely unthinkable.

That aside, the common re-sheathing method of placing the *mine* [the back of the blade] onto the opening of the scabbard and drawing all the way down from the guard needs to be looked at further.

In my own organization students are taught to sheathe the blade by placing it on the scabbard one-third down the *mine* from the tip. As these motions are a modern form of art akin to a personal trial, a further level of research and study into the methods of re-sheathing is necessary. This goes without saying for sword techniques in general as well. (See also chapter 10: Nakamura Ryu Battojutsu [Kata], which includes the eight sheathing methods.)

Preventing the Suspending Cord [*Sageo*] from Getting Severed at the Bracket [*Kurigata*]

This will not matter at all if a sword is going to be used only for display purposes but, for an iaito that will be used in training, the suspending cord that is fed through the holding bracket on the scabbard will fray and sever after two or three years of use if a *hitodome*[58]

---

57. 竹光; an imitation sword traditionally fashioned by shaving down bamboo, although modern examples are more often made of wood. Originally carried by poor warriors who could not afford a real blade but still had to keep up appearances and fulfill the obligation to wear swords in public. Nowadays they are used as props in period pieces.

58. A metal fitting that goes around the inside of the kurigata.

is fitted. To be certain of preventing the cord from severing, an iaito should have fittings of the Higo koshirae type as mentioned earlier—a kurigata fashioned from animal horn and the hole through which the sageo cord passes rounded out with the corners removed.

The practice seen among some high-ranking instructors not to fit sageo at all is undesirable from the point of view of etiquette and expressing the correct respect toward the sword fittings and is a most idiotic idea. I would earnestly caution against it.

Toyama Ryu Iaido and Tameshigiri Instructional Course Implementation Plan

INTENTIONS OF THE TOYAMA RYU

Our federation's instructional plans involve the Toyama ryu iaido, also known as gunto no soho, a set of fundamental, practical kata to teach standing sword methods, created at the old Imperial Army Toyama Military Academy from actual combat experiences. From this year [1980] we are humbly receiving the support of the All-Japan Jukendo Federation, coming together as one with the Toyama ryu and preparing to spread and develop the art around the nation.

The Toyama ryu values and reveres the teachings of the classical koryu sword schools created by our ancestors and the martial spirit they displayed. By incorporating the paired Toyama ryu kumitachi kata into training, our federation members are putting these teachings into practice, as well as pursuing the unification of iaido, kendo, and tameshigiri (happo giri) into one discipline, striving for the glory and improvement of the art in accordance with the motto of "hyakuren jitoku" [long and constant practice leads to one's mastery].

INSTRUCTIONAL STAGE: 1

Main elements covered

Methods for conditioning using the tanrenbo and their effects.

Grip manipulation on the hilt [tenouchi] as the most fundamental
secret of swordsmanship.

Areas of study covered in instruction

1. Whole-body exercises for health promotion.
2. Learning the correct tenouchi and chakin shibori motions.
3. Learning about the hilts of real Japanese swords and shinai.
4. Whether students should make their own tanrenbo or purchase
   one.

Notes

1. Allows the practitioner to build physical fitness while cultivating pliability in the wrists.
2. Brings together kendo, iaido, and tameshigiri.

INSTRUCTIONAL STAGE: 2

Main elements covered

Knowledge of how to select a sword for iaido.

Areas of study covered in instruction

1. Sword length.
2. Curvature.
3. Length of the hilt.
4. Length of the tang.
5. Regarding the hamon.
6. Swords with high and low ridgelines [shinogi].
7. Selecting a sword guard [tsuba].
8. Presence or absence of a groove on the blade.
9. How to prevent damage to the sword tip.
10. The importance of mekugi securing pins [back-up mekugi].

11. How to insert the mekugi.
12. Blade weight and balance.
13. What to do when the weight falls at the blade tip [inserting lead into the hilt].
14. Safety with the scabbard opening [koiguchi].
15. The use of Higo-style sword fittings [Higo zukuri].
16. Swords that do not need registration.

Notes

1. Length should be between 2 shaku, 2 sun up to a maximum of 2 shaku, 4 sun [approximately 67 to 73 cm].
2. Weight should be between 200 monme up to a maximum of 220 monme [750 to 825 g].
3. Curvature should be between 5 and 7 bu [1.5 to 2.1 cm].
4. Blade width at the base of the blade should be around 1 sun [approximately 3 cm].
5. Blade width at the monouchi should be between 8 and 9 bu [approximately 2.5 to 2.8 cm].
6. Blades with deeply applied hamon are not suitable for practical use.

INSTRUCTIONAL STAGE: 3

Main elements covered

The logical instructional methods of the various ryuha.
Omori ryu iai (instruction in standing iai techniques).
Toyama ryu iaido (gunto no soho).
Nakamura ryu battojutsu.

Areas of study covered in instruction

1. Study into the application of the koryu's standing sword methods.
2. Gaining confidence from mastering the seven sword-handling kata created at the former Imperial Army Toyama Military Academy.

3. Study of the Nakamura ryu battojutsu (happo giri) logical sword-handling exercise, inspired in its formulation by the eiji happo that is the basis of calligraphy.

Notes

Natural posture and instinctive sword handling.

1. The eight stances [happo no kamae].
2. The eight cuts [happo giri].
3. The eight re-sheathing methods [hasshu no noto].

INSTRUCTIONAL STAGE: 4

Main elements covered

Toyama ryu kumitachi kata.

Areas of study covered in instruction

1. Entering and leaving combative distance should be based on the Nippon kendo kata, advancing three paces at the start and finishing by narrowing the width of the legs and then withdrawing five paces.
2. Learning accurate distancing.

Notes

1. Coordinating the whole of one's energy and being with the sword [kikentai ichi].
2. Opportunities for striking with thrusting or cutting attacks and the associated footwork.

INSTRUCTIONAL STAGE: 5

Main elements covered

Fostering the spirit of the Japanese sword.
General concepts of cutting ability in tameshigiri.

Areas of study covered in instruction

1. Changes in the characteristics of swords over the Koto, Shinto, Shin Shinto, and Gendaito periods.
2. The cutting abilities of heavier (including longer) and lighter swords.
3. Curvature, hamon, blade surface *[jihada],* and cutting ability over the different periods.

Notes

1. Differences in cutting ability depending on weather and temperature conditions.
2. Differences in cutting ability between blades from different regions.

INSTRUCTIONAL STAGE: 6

Main elements covered

Safety precautions for basic tameshigiri (danger prevention).
Information regarding *kiritsuka* [specialized handles for test cutting].

Areas of study covered in instruction

1. Back-up mekugi securing pins [hikae mekugi].
2. The length of the tang and its relationship to the balance of the blade.
3. The importance of netaba awase (fine sharpening).
4. Correct gripping when stopping, flowing with the blade after a cut, and maintaining situational awareness.

Notes

Referencing Nakamura's innovative self-assembly target-holding bracket, created from his tameshigiri experiences. Orders are being taken for these stands now. One stand costs around 3,000 yen.[59]

---

59. Pricing correct as of original publication in 1980.

INSTRUCTIONAL STAGE: 7

Main elements covered

The stages of tameshigiri

1. The materials used for tameshigiri:
   1a. Using the upper layer of tatami mats.
   1b. Securing around the targets with rubber.
2. Practical know-how for tameshigiri against solid targets.
3. Learning technique in logical order; gradually increasing the circumference of the targets used.
4. Left and right kesagiri (natural sword technique) as the primary method.
5. A fully developed mental strength.

Areas of study covered in instruction

1. Preparatory suburi exercises.
2. Cutting down from a high guard in a circular arc without contracting the arms.
3. The importance of correct cutting trajectory and blade angle.
4. Not mistaking one's distancing from the target (taking care to cut with the monouchi area at the top third of the blade).

Order of progression through steadily more difficult targets:

1. Thin bamboo.
2. Slightly thicker bamboo (cannot use the base).
3. Thick bamboo 3 to 5 cm (1 sun to 1 sun and 5 bu).
4. A single rolled upper layer from a used tatami mat to one and one-half layers, 12 to 15 cm (4 to 5 sun) thick straw targets.
5. When inserting bamboo inside a straw target use a piece with a width of 3 cm (1 sun) or less.

Notes

1. Students gain confidence from actually doing the training and experiencing tameshigiri for themselves.
2. Before performing tameshigiri, a distance of 6 to 8 m is created between the performer and observers.
3. When performing dai giri, make sure that woven straw mats are spread out beneath the stand.
4. Avoid cutting dried or desiccated bamboo.
5. The length of time to soak straw targets in water before use is between two and twenty-four hours.

(When sourcing the upper layers of tatami mats for cutting targets, it is ideal to use unneeded or discarded materials.)

INSTRUCTIONAL STAGE: 8

Main elements covered

How to repair a bent blade.
When the cutting edge is damaged.
Sword maintenance.

Areas of study covered in instruction

1. Never strike the blade with metal or wooden hammers.
2. How to resharpen the cutting edge when it has been damaged.
3. *Uchiko* powder is unnecessary.

Notes

Refer to "Tools used for sword repair": the chapter on how to maintain swords in *Iai kendo* by the same author.

Those who wish to study based on the syllabus above should not hesitate to contact the organization. If enthusiasts can gather a group of twenty or more practitioners in their region, regardless of ryuha or other organizational affiliations, then we can send out an instructor to hold study groups and seminars, contributing to the development of the sword arts, fostering the spirit of the Japanese sword, and encouraging interaction and relations between the various ryuha.

Any questions or enquiries regarding this syllabus are most welcome, and we shall endeavor to respond in writing.

Swordsman Tanida Kenichi
of Osaka

Swordsman Nishijima
of Tochigi

Swordswoman Hosaka Yukiko
of Koufu

Swordsman Fushimi Ryu, Chief
Executive Officer of the Toyama ryu
honbu dojo

Swordswoman Yoshida Keiko
of Tochigi

Swordsman Kaneko Sadao
of Gunma

CHAPTER 6

TRAINING WITH THE TANRENBO

The author instructs Mrs. Ougi Chikage in the use of the tanrenbo.

The Aims of the Tanrenbo

The most fundamental secret of both kendo and iaido is tenouchi: correct grip manipulation.

The core of tenouchi is in how one grips the hilt when cutting, and the most effective way to internalize the correct principles of gripping is through training with the tanrenbo.[60] Rather than making many hundreds of practice swings [suburi] with a shinai or a real sword, the same objective can be achieved with ten or twenty swings of a tanrenbo that weighs two or three times as much. This kind of training will also help to improve the student's physical fitness.

I thoroughly recommend tanrenbo training to all sword practitioners looking to integrate the disciplines of kendo and iaido, as the knack to performing many vital motions correctly is all in how the hilt is gripped and manipulated. Such motions include appropriate tenouchi while cutting, the chakin shibori stopping method, and properly stopping and flowing with the blade after making a cut.

It is important, however, that when attempting this kind of training the student uses a tanrenbo of a suitable weight. Too heavy an implement will have a detrimental effect on the user's posture and could cause muscle damage, so care must be taken when selecting the right size.

---

60. 鍛錬棒; *tanrenbo* literally means "forging stick," and the word is used metaphorically in this context to imply a wooden stave used to condition and forge the body and one's technique.

The Differences in Weight between Real Swords, Shinai, and Tanrenbo

The weight of a katana with full fittings is between 300 monme (approximately 1.1 kg) and 400 monme (approximately 1.5 kg).

The weight of a bamboo shinai is between 100 monme (approximately 375 g) and 150 monme (approximately 562 g).

The weight of a tanrenbo suitable for kendo practitioners is around 300 monme (approximately 1.1 kg), with one suitable for iaido practitioners around 600 monme (approximately 2.2 kg).

Making a Tanrenbo

Most tanrenbo available commercially have long handles, and the overall length is generally too long for practical training, so one should modify them in the following manner before use:

1. The handle should be adjusted to a length of around 8 sun (approximately 24 cm). If the handle is too long, then the implement will not be suitable and bad habits will creep into the user's tenouchi when performing suburi and kirikaeshi exercises.
2. The overall length of the tanrenbo should be adjusted to a suitable length of around 3 shaku and 8 sun (approximately 1 m and 6 cm). If a tanrenbo is too long, the weight will fall closer to the tip and make it harder to learn proper tenouchi.
3. As long as it is made from a heavy wood, any material is fine for a tanrenbo. The shape can be circular, hexagonal, or octagonal, but square tanrenbo are not recommended, as if the user accidentally strikes himself with the edge while swinging it there is an increased danger of injury.

One cannot internalize the principles of correct hilt gripping through practice with katana or shinai alone. Furthermore, swinging the tanrenbo enables the student to learn the correct chakin shibori method of stopping the blade.

Two tanrenbo

The larger hexagonal tanrenbo in the photograph to the right (left-hand side of photo) was created by Battalion Commander Shindo Iwao while his unit was stationed in Shenwutun in Manchuria's Heihe province (now Heilongjiang province in China) in 1943 and weighs three times what a sword would. At this time I requested that two or three such implements be prepared for each of the companies and used them for instructing the officers who carried military swords while also thoroughly encouraging their use for personal training. These tanrenbo were always kept ready in the battalion commander's offices, but before long Commander Shindo was transferred to the Hamamatsu Aeronautical Academy and left them in my care as a souvenir. In March of 1945, when my unit was reassigned to Kitakyushu for the final battle to defend the mainland, I brought these tanrenbo back with me. And in October when I was finally demobilized, I took them home and stored them in my house. These training implements bring back many memories of my times training the Southern Special Attack Unit in Manchuria.

The tanrenbo on the right weighs twice what a regular sword would and is beneficial for improving physical fitness if used daily.

How to Grip the Tanrenbo

Single-handed grip as viewed from above. Note that the thumb is facing down.

Single-handed grip as viewed from the side

Double-handed grip as viewed from the left. The left hand fully grips the pommel.

Double-handed grip as viewed from the right. The distance between the two hands is around two finger widths.

Double-Handed Left and Right *Kirikaeshi* [Repeated Cutting Exercise]

The most basic and fundamental training exercise is kirikaeshi as shown here, but performing this exercise with a shinai alone will not allow the student to internalize the principles of correct tenouchi. Additionally, a shinai will not have much of an effect in conditioning the body or provide sufficient exercise, so it will still be necessary to swing the tanrenbo before practice begins.

This exercise begins from chudan no kamae.

Single-Handed Left and Right Kirikaeshi

This single-handed kirikaeshi exercise is a very important one for both kendo and iaido practitioners to develop flexibility in the wrists. It is, however, not widely practiced. I recommend swinging the tanrenbo singlehanded, as it has a greater effect on technical improvement than two-handed exercises do. The photographs on this page show left and right directional one-handed kirikaeshi using the right hand.

Correct Method for *Shinchoku Suburi* (Vertical Practice Swings)

In both iaido and kendo *shinchokugiri* [the straight vertical cut down] is the most basic and fundamental of the core motions but is not a logical or practical technique on its own. It is, however, useful in cultivating flexibility in the body and strengthening the waist, hips, and abdominal region. It is also a good basic method of exercising the whole body.

This exercise is performed by widening one's stance to open up the legs, cutting down from a high overhead guard posture [*dai jodan*], and stopping the tanrenbo in place.

Repetitive Practice of Left and Right Kesagiri Motions (Natural Sword-Handling Method)

Kesagiri, as shown here, is the most fundamental method for kendo and iaido kata, but it is not commonly systemized into the forms of many styles. Regardless of whether one trains in kendo or iaido, when cutting with a real sword it will be kesagiri that is the most natural and instinctive cutting method to use.

I have previously mentioned a number of examples from actual combat and must emphasize that when it comes to sword handling, left and right kesagiri are without a doubt the most natural methods.

When performing the exercise make sure to pull back the left foot when striking from right to left and the right foot when striking from left to right.

Repetitive Practice of Left and Right Mayokogiri Motions (Yoko Ichimonji Giri)

Horizontal cutting [*mayokogiri/ichimonji giri*] is the most difficult of all sword techniques to perform. It is very easy to bend or break the blade when impacting on a solid target with this method, so it is not recommended.

This is not such a problem when trying to cut a softer target, however.

If the swordsman brings his arms in toward his torso when making a horizontal cut, the reverberation of the blow means he will not successfully cut through the target. It is thus important to make sure that the arms are extended fully when cutting and that the blade describes a circular cutting arc.

Holding the stick aloft and twisting to the left and right

Holding the stick aloft and bending sideways to the left and right

Holding the stick aloft and bending forward and backward

Holding the Stick Out to the Front and Resting on It to Stretch the Left and Right Legs (Achilles Tendons)

This exercise is to help prevent severing the Achilles tendon. It is quite common to see kendo yudansha severing their Achilles tendons during training and competition, so I would advise them to perform daily exercises designed to strengthen and loosen these tendons in order to prevent injury. These exercises consist of standing with the toes on a piece of wood or the raised area of a door threshold and moving the legs up and down several times. One should also stand with the body supported to the front by the tanrenbo and stretch the heels out alternately as shown.

Holding the stick behind the body and twisting to the left and right

Pulling the stick into the chest and bending both knees before thrusting it in the air again

Photograph analyzing the basic left kesagiri cut

CHAPTER 7

THE FUNDAMENTALS AND APPLICATION OF TAMESHIGIRI

How to Make Materials (Targets) for Use in Tameshigiri

1. The thickness of the bunched straw should be between 4 and 5 sun (12 to 15 cm) in diameter.
2. The bundle of straw should be around 2 shaku and 5 sun (75 cm) in length.
3. The straw should be tied off in five places, not too loose and not too tight.
4. The straw should be soaked in water for between three hours and a full day and night.

In the film *Eien naru budo [Budo: The Art of Killing]*, it is explained that the straw should be soaked for three days and three nights, but this is incorrect. It is especially important when making straw targets to ensure that no sand gets into the bundle between the straw. If any does get in, the blade can get scratched and the cutting edge will chip.

Furthermore, if a piece of green bamboo around a single sun (approximately 3 cm) in width is placed at the center of the straw bundle, this will simulate the same resistance as when cutting through human bone.

Straw can be hard to get hold of, does not come in a standard thickness, and is thus not a fair target to use for tameshigiri competitions. By comparison, the upper layer of a tatami mat is usually of uniform dimensions, and so it has been ruled that these are to be used in national competitions instead. If you can get a tatami shop to give you their old mat uppers that have been exchanged for new ones, then these can be even better for cutting than straw.

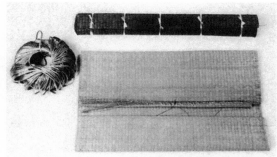

Rolling the mat into one single layer will make the target rather hard, so it is a good idea to fold it into two or three before rolling.

Fold in the edges and roll up the mat.

Once rolled, tie the mat off at four or five intervals. The length of time for which it should be immersed in water will vary between three hours and a whole day and night depending on the straw.

How to Grip the Hilt [Tsuka]

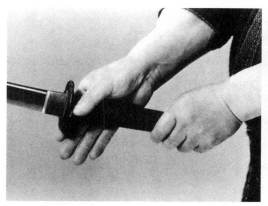

Right hand viewed from the left

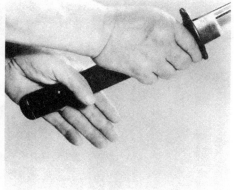

Left hand viewed from the right

The double-handed grip viewed from above

The double-handed grip held at midlevel height [chudan]

Equipment Used in Tameshigiri

KIT ASSEMBLY-TYPE STAND (TO HOLD UP THE BAMBOO TARGETS)

The four legs are around 1 shaku and 4 sun (around 36 cm) in length, and the central tube to which the target is affixed is around 1 shaku (around 30 cm) in height. The iron frame is cylindrical, so it does not get knocked down with any reverberations from the cut and can be made even more convenient if this section is designed to be removed and screwed in with a bolt.

UMBRELLA-TYPE HANGING TARGET STAND (SUSPENDS FOUR TARGETS)

The stand is around 5 shaku and 5 sun in height (around 1 m and 67 cm). If the central column is made from two sections so as to be extendible, not only will it be more convenient to transport and assemble but also it will be able to rotate to present the different targets.

Cutting Thin Bamboo Tubes—A Fundamental Education in Tameshigiri

This tameshigiri exercise involves cutting through a single thin piece of bamboo and allows the student to learn the fundamentals of distancing, blade angle, and circular cutting motion.

If the student starts out trying to cut through thicker pieces of bamboo, there is a danger of bending or chipping the blade or of getting too fixated on the cutting itself. It is common to see novices attempting to cut a substantial bamboo target, putting too much power behind the cut, and taking the blade into the floor or the ground, even if the cut is successfully made. If the student's grip on the sword hilt is incorrect then any number of mishaps could occur, such as the blade itself flying away or cutting down into their own foot. These kinds of mistakes and the injuries they can cause are described further in chapter 13.

Initially practicing with thin bamboo pieces places less pressure on the sword if it is mishandled and allows the student to get a fundamental education in tameshigiri without unnecessary risk. I thoroughly recommend that beginners start with this exercise.

It must be stressed, however, that students should not get complacent and cut in any old way just because the target is thin and comparatively easy. They must cut with a focused mind and take the same mental attitude as when cutting a thicker bamboo target.

Cutting Diagonally from a High-Guard Position [Dai Jodan] to the Lower Left
(Hidari Naname Kaho Giri/Left Kesagiri When Facing the Target) (Figs. 1, 2, 3, and 4).

One must pay particular attention to the direction that the severed tip of the bamboo flies away from the cut.

1. If the tip of the bamboo flies away horizontally (ninety degrees) then the angle taken toward the target is good.
2. If the tip of the bamboo flies away at 50 degrees or 130 degrees, then the angle taken toward the target is not suitable (poor), and the cut would not have succeeded if it were being made against a thicker piece of bamboo.

Cutting Diagonally from a High-Guard Position [Dai Jodan] to the Lower Right
(Migi Naname Kaho Giri/Right Kesagiri When Facing the Target) (Figs. 5, 6, and 7).

The students' stance and posture when cutting are important from a technical point of view. They must cut straight down in one motion as soon as the blade is lifted from a midlevel [chudan] to high-line [dai jodan] guard.

It is also important that the student does not pull his hips back when cutting (a practice known as *heppiri goshi*).

Regarding Right and Left Kesagiri

Kesagiri is the most fundamental of the core techniques of swordsmanship, and I will touch further on the mechanics of it later.

Kesagiri must aim to cut the target at an angle of between thirty and forty degrees. Twenty or fifty degrees will be incorrect, and one must always aim to keep the angle between thirty and forty as an inviolable rule.

The technique must be brought down from the correct dai jodan position while adjusting the blade angle and not initiated from left or right hasso no kamae. This rule should be paid due attention and committed to memory.

When making the cut one must initially move slightly forward and then shift one's whole body back to create a pulling cut.

When cutting, the following are of particular importance:

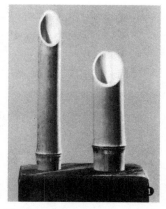

The cut bamboo viewed from the front

1. Not to pull just the hips back while leaving the upper and lower body forward (heppiri goshi).
2. To bring the pommel of the sword to rest in the center of the stomach (around the navel) at the end of the cut.
3. Stopping the blade after the cut has been made should be done using the chakin shibori [wringing the tea cloth] method, but it is also possible to flow with the impetus of the cut, using the circular motion to return to hasso no kamae.

THE ANGLE AND CUTTING TRAJECTORY FOR RIGHT AND LEFT KESAGIRI

When practicing tameshigiri, if the cutting angle and trajectory are incorrect then regardless of the quality of the sword used there is a chance of the blade's chipping or bending. Cutting at between thirty and forty degrees is the fundamental principle of kesagiri.

Side view of the cutting trajectory and angle

The bamboo to the right (the thicker piece) has been cut at forty degrees.

The bamboo to the left (the thinner piece) has been cut at thirty degrees.

Left Kesagiri

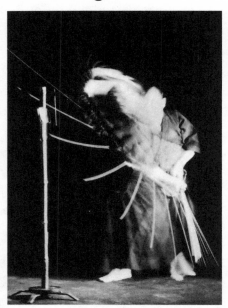

Cut down diagonally from the upper right to the lower left. Left kesagiri is intended to cut into the opponent's left-hand shoulder.

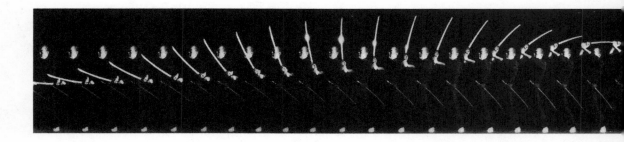

Right Kesagiri

Left: Cut down diagonally from the upper left to the lower right. Right kesagiri is intended to cut into the opponent's right-hand shoulder.

Right: Mr. Soga displays the *tsubame gaeshi* technique (literally "swallow reverse," a right kesagiri moving straight into a sweeping horizontal cut).

Left and Right Naname Joho Giri (Gyaku Giri)

When most students first attempt tameshigiri with the rising diagonal cuts [left and right naname joho giri], they will get the angle wrong and fail to cut through the target.

This is largely because these reverse-cutting angles are somewhat unnatural and problematic, and it is important when performing them to lower the hips and take the attitude of directing the cutting angle straight up toward the ceiling.

Left naname joho giri

Right naname joho giri

When the students have become more used to this technique, they will start to experience the correct squeezing feeling when gripping the hilt.

One must, however, exercise considerable caution when attempting this technique on a substantial target.

Left and Right Mayokogiri (Yoko Ichimonji Giri)

One must exercise caution when using these horizontal cutting techniques to cut hard targets such as bamboo. This is because if the trajectory of the cutting edge is incorrect then the blade can chip or bend.

When performing the technique, one must pay attention to the technical points of opening the legs by a single step to lower the hips, getting the correct cutting trajectory, extending the arms sufficiently, avoiding incorrect distancing, and getting the right circular cutting motion.

Left mayokogiri

Right mayokogiri

Cutting through Three Rolled Upper Layers of Tatami with Left Kesagiri

Whether you can cut through three, four, or five mats layered on top of each other is greatly affected by the cutting ability of the sword itself, but even more important than that is getting the correct distancing, angle, and circular motion on the cut.

It is also important not to loosen the grip [tenouchi] while cutting and to apply the correct wringing motion [chakin shibori] so you can properly stop the sword after the cut has been completed.

Because this cut requires a certain level of power to be effective, it is easy for the practitioner to get too focused on putting in that power and, through inaccurate gripping of the hilt, not stop the blade correctly.

This kind of multiple-layered target cutting presents many problems, and so I do not recommend it.

Renowned swordsman Tanabe Tetsundo cuts through four rolled tatami upper layers with right kesagiri.

Single-Handed Left Kesagiri
POINTS OF CAUTION WHEN CUTTING SINGLE HANDEDLY

It is said that the purpose of Miyamoto Musashi's two-sword style [二刀流; *nitoryu* / 二天一流; *nitenichi ryu*] was so that he could fight effectively with only the left hand if the right was injured in combat and with only the right if the left was rendered unusable.

It would be unthinkable to fight using a sharp sword in each hand in a real duel, and it is recorded that Musashi himself fought over sixty such duels to the death, but in none of them did he use two swords.

Similarly, the principle behind the initial one-handed drawing cut [*shohatto/nukitsuke*] in iaido is not to finish the enemy but to set up for the second, killing strike.

During the War I experienced having to learn to cut one handed, using only my left hand, after the right was accidentally injured during bayonet kata practice. That I managed to do this successfully was entirely because I had mastered the secrets of one-handed gripping through training with the tanrenbo.

It is impossible to gain an understanding of the correct gripping [tenouchi] through theory alone. The optimal way to learn this is through perfecting it with the tanrenbo, experiencing the feeling of gripping the hilt as you swing it down one handed.

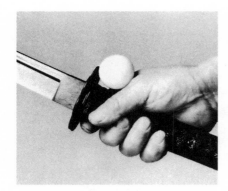

HOW TO GRIP THE HILT WHEN CUTTING ONE HANDED

(The same applies when using both the left and right hand.)

1. The thumb faces straight down.
2. It is best to grip the hilt at the point where an egg can be balanced between the thumb, forefinger, and the sword guard. (In the photograph a ping-pong ball has been used.)
3. Grip while maintaining a pressure that is neither too tight nor too loose (not squeezing or loosening the grip).

Single-Handed Right Kesagiri

Cut down from a high single-handed grip on the left side [katate hidari jodan] to the lower right. The left hand is placed on the left hip bone over the scabbard and the right side of the body is pulled back slightly as the cut is made.

Cutting Placed Targets [Suemono Giri/ Dai Giri]; Basic Method of the Zen Nihon Battojutsu Renmei (All-Japan Battojutsu Federation)

The practitioner widens his stance by around one step, and then brings the sword down from the high-level guard position [jodan] in one smooth motion, coordinating the movements of sword, body, and all his mental and physical energy. The grip on the sword hilt uses the "wringing the tea cloth" [chakin shibori] methodology, taking care not to retract the arms in and to drop the hips into the cut. The trajectory of the blade should draw a large circular arc.

Cutting a pile of four bundled straw targets

IMPORTANT POINTS WHEN PERFORMING SUEMONO GIRI

Suemono giri (the cutting of targets arrayed horizontally on a stand) is the most important of the tameshigiri exercises. It is an optimal method for testing the cutting ability of a sword and has been used since antiquity under the name of *dai giri* [literally "stand cutting"]. This method requires considerable power to be put into the cut and can thus lead to the blade's bending or snapping, or the hilt's breaking or becoming loose, worn out, and useless. It is for this reason that renowned sword tester and executioner Yamada Asaemon and other sword-testing professionals mainly used a specially reinforced hilt known as a *kiritsuka* [literally "cutting hilt"] when performing this exercise.

One must pay particular attention to the following points when practicing suemono giri:

1. To put sufficient focus and mental energy *[kiryoku]* into the technique (focusing ki into the lower abdomen).
2. To assume a correct posture and still the breath.

3. To grip the hilt correctly [tenouchi].

4. To widen one's stance by around one step and drop the hips.

5. To refrain from pulling back the hips while cutting or after the cut is complete.

6. The correct distancing for the cut is such that impact is made slightly below the monouchi, closer to the tsuba than usual. (The monouchi is the area from the base of the blade tip to one-third down the blade. It is a general principle that cuts should be made at a point exactly one-third down the blade.)

7. To refrain from bunching up or pulling in the arms, which must be fully extended into the cut. The shoulders should be relaxed.

8. To focus one's spirit on the cut and approach it with the mental attitude of cutting right down to the stand. It is no good to falter and wonder whether one can make the cut. One must be certain that he can cut through the target. This attitude and unshakeable belief that "I will cut this!" is vital. Belief is power, and one must have the necessary ardor and enthusiasm with an unwavering and dauntless spirit.

There are three ways to perform suemono giri:

1. Cutting the target exactly horizontally [blade at ninety degrees to the target]

2. Cutting the target at a diagonal from the right

3. Cutting the target at a diagonal from the left

The author displays suemono giri at a martial arts competition held at the Yokosuka Maritime Self-Defense Force Second Science and Technology Academy (1970).

Methods two and three above will give a cutting power twice that of the horizontal cut, but the basic method for performing all three is the same, with only the position of the body in relation to the target changing.

Suemono giri

Cutting at a diagonal angle

When viewed from the side

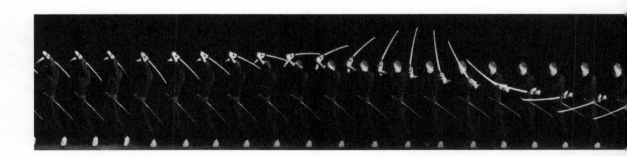

Left Kesagiri into Right Gyaku Giri; Basic Method of the Zen Nihon Battojutsu Renmei

Cut down from a high guard [dai jodan] to the diagonal lower left (left kesagiri), and then turn the sword back to cut up diagonally from the lower left to the upper right (right gyaku giri).

Right Gyaku Giri into Left Kesagiri; Basic Method of the Zen Nihon Battojutsu Renmei

Cut up diagonally from the lower left to the upper right (right gyaku giri), and then turn the sword back to cut down to the diagonal lower left (left kesagiri).

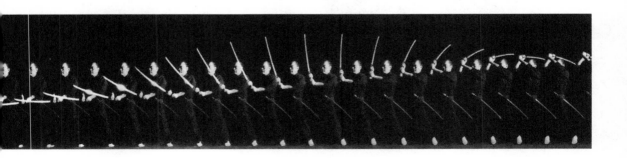

A seminar on Toyama ryu iaido and tameshigiri held at the Yanase dojo in Nara

CHAPTER 8

TOYAMA RYU IAIDO (FORMERLY GUNTO NO SOHO)

In praise of Toyama ryu iaido
BY MR. SATO SHIMEO

Severity of winter, flowers fall, the thousand-year dream.
Purity of our ancestors' wisdom gathered together,
Noble and radiant, the Toyama ryu.
Aware not, its renown, spread to the eight directions.
Ah Shikishima, the glory of old Japan shall waver not!
For as long as the heavens, the earth and our lineage of the
　　sword still exist.
To manifest righteousness and cut through evil, that is its
　　essence.
What tale does the blade at my hip tell?
The deep and infinite spirit of Yamato.
Forge the self one hundredfold and reap the benefits,
Passed on to the future generations.

About the Toyama Ryu Iaido

The Toyama ryu iaido is a scientific and logical sword-handling method created before the War at the former Imperial Army Toyama Military Academy. It is based on actual experiences of combat with the sword between the Manchurian incident[61] and the Sino-Japanese War,[62] including techniques from the various classical schools reformulated into a syllabus of standing iai techniques that are simple to comprehend and learn.

One feature of the Toyama ryu is that it consists entirely of standing techniques, meaning that as long as you have a belt to fasten the sword to your waist, it can be practiced simply and easily anywhere. You do not have to restrict practice to a dojo or sports hall and can train indoors or out. The kata can be practiced in sportswear or a shirt and trousers and while wearing regular shoes, sports shoes, or even slippers.

However, as martial arts must begin and end with courtesy and respect, one must train bearing this in mind and must not forget to perform the *torei* salutation to show reverence to the blade before and after practice.

OUTLINE OF THE FORMER IMPERIAL ARMY TOYAMA MILITARY ACADEMY

Although those who served in the armed forces before the War will doubtless be familiar with the Imperial Army Toyama Military Academy, there will be many from the postwar generations who will have little or no idea when they hear the name, so I shall give a simple outline of the institution here.

---

61. An incident in 1931 in which the Japanese Army detonated a section of Japanese-owned railway in southern Manchuria and used it as a pretext to invade and annex Manchuria as a puppet state.

62. This is referring to the second Sino-Japanese War from 1937–1945 rather than the earlier war in 1895.

The Toyama academy was originally founded in 1874 as a military dormitory. The purpose of the institution was to take commissioned and noncommissioned officers from various army units all over the nation, who excelled both academically and physically, and train them in marksmanship, physical fitness, swordsmanship, and all aspects of offensive and defensive warfare in order to create future instructors for the rank-and-file soldiers.

The academy was headed by such luminaries as Lieutenant General Kashii, the chief administrator of martial law after the February 26 incident, and Lieutenant General Ushijima, who later committed suicide during the Pacific War at the battle for Okinawa. It produced many fine officers whose lives were an embodiment of the soldier's martial spirit, such as Army Minister General Anan, who took responsibility for the end of the War and ended his own life in honorable suicide in the manner of the warriors of old.

Toyama Ryu and the All-Japan Jukendo Federation [Zen Nihon Jukendo Renmei]

The lost generation of martial arts after the War was first brought to an end by the foundation of the All-Japan Kendo Federation [Zen Nihon Kendo Renmei] in 1953 and then the All-Japan Jukendo Federation [Zen Nihon Jukendo Renmei] two years later. The first-generation head of the All-Japan Jukendo Federation was former Army General Imamura Hitoshi. The current head of the federation is former member of the House of Councillors, Hatta Ichiro sensei.

Today the "way of the bayonet" has been reborn as a competitive sport, practiced by former soldiers; regular citizens; members of the land, air, and naval self-defense forces; and by the nation's youth in general and at university clubs. The federation has expanded greatly and today has more than three-hundred-fifty-thousand members.

In 1970 the federation was accepted for corporate status and joined the Japan Sports Association, with jukendo featuring as an event at the 1980 National Sports Meet in Tochigi prefecture.

The All-Japan Jukendo Federation was founded with the principal of the former Imperial Army Toyama Military Academy, Uzawa Naonobu (lieutenant general), playing a central role.

Every year the All-Japan Jukendo Federation holds its national tournament at the Yasukuni Shrine's Grand Spring Festival as a hono enbu, to console the heroic spirits of those who fell during the War. The Toyama ryu also pays its sincere respects to these noble souls at the spring festival with its own votive performance at the *nodo* hall in front of the shrine.

The Toyama ryu Iaido Renmei has in its central ideology a dedication to consoling the heroic souls enshrined at Yasukuni, and I firmly believe it is a mark of pride in the old military ethos that the spirit of the old Toyama school continues to live on.

POINTS OF CAUTION WHEN PERFORMING THE KATA

1. The practitioner should calm his breathing when performing the kata and focus his energy in the lower abdomen in particular.

2. The practitioner should make sure that all actions in the kata are fully understood and execute them with the correct tension and relaxation.

3. When handling his sword, the practitioner should pay special attention to the angle of the cutting edge and how he applies power through the elbows, making efforts so that cutting and thrusting motions are large and expansive. The student must first learn and internalize correct and accurate handling movements rather than simply trying for faster technique.

4. As a principle, when making cutting or thrusting motions, the practitioner should project his voice, shouting "Ei!" or "Ya!" However, if techniques are performed with suitable mental and physical energy, then not vocalizing is also acceptable.

5. In order to prevent danger to himself and to preserve his valuable Japanese sword, the practitioner should pay due care and attention to his surroundings in all directions, including above and below, and should make sure he does not inflict injury on nearby people or other creatures or damage his blade.

Formalities

Begin practice by bowing and expressing respect to the kami, one's ancestors, and those who have gone before in developing the art. Then bow to the "upper seat" [joseki], which is where a presiding authority figure would sit, and finally to the sword itself. Once the necessary formalities have been observed, slide the sword into the sword belt.

Bowing to the kami [shinzen no rei]

Bowing to the joseki [joseki ni rei]

Bowing to the sword *[torei]*

Fixing the sword into the belt *[taito]*

First Technique: Enemy to the Front
[Ippon Me: Mae No Teki]

A single-handed rising diagonal cut to the upper right going into a descending diagonal cut to the lower left [katate migi naname kiriage, hidari kesagiri]

SIGNIFICANCE OF THE KATA

As the enemy approaches with his hand on the hilt of his sword and tries to draw, the swordsman's initial movement is a single-handed diagonal cut from the lower left to the upper right into the opponent's front elbow and his body.

The next motion is to cut down with a left diagonal cut [kesagiri] and then return to the midlevel ready posture [chudan no kamae] while maintaining correct situational awareness [zanshin]. From here perform the blood-shaking maneuver [chiburi], re-sheathe the blade [noto], and finally assume a rooted and unwavering posture [fudo no shisei] and return to the original position.

ORDER

While moving the right foot one step forward, unlock the blade from the mouth of the scabbard with the left hand. The right hand grips at the base of the sword guard, and the right leg advances forward one step while performing a single-handed diagonal cut from the draw, going from the practitioner's lower left to his upper right [figs. 1, 2, 3, 4, and 5].

Turn the sword back round to the left, into a high-guard stance [jodan no kamae], taking the sword with both hands. Then cut down diagonally to the lower left [figs. 6, 7, 8, 9, and 10].

Take up the midlevel ready position [chudan no kamae] while maintaining correct situational awareness [figs. 11 and 12].

Perform the blood-shaking maneuver [chiburi] and then pull in the left foot while re-sheathing the blade [figs. 13, 14, 15, and 16].

Assume a rooted and unwavering posture [fudo no shisei] and return to the original position [fig. 17].

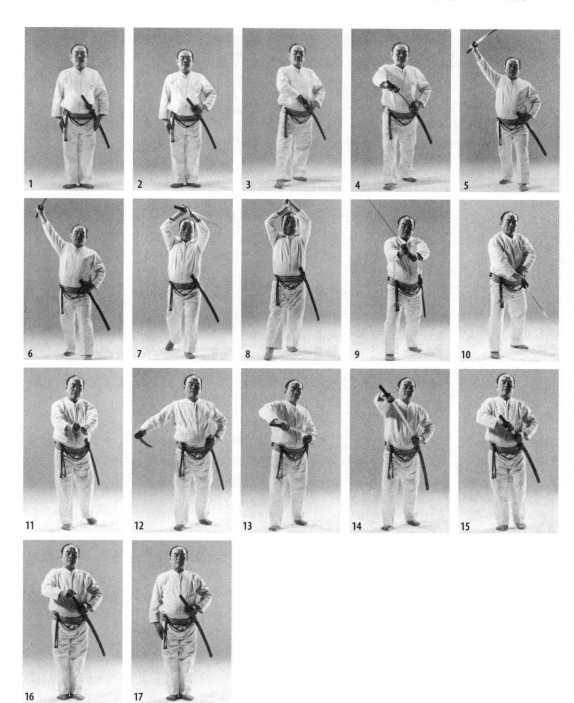

Second Technique: Enemy to the Right [Nihon Me: Migi No Teki]

A right, single-handed horizontal cut going into a right descending diagonal cut [katate hidari yoko giri, migi kesagiri]

SIGNIFICANCE OF THE KATA

Against an enemy approaching from the right in ambush, first cut to the side with a sweeping, single-handed blow, and then follow up into the enemy with a right descending diagonal cut. All motions after this are identical to those of technique one.

ORDER

Move first the right and then the left foot diagonally forward and to the right, and simultaneously turn the body toward the right. Step out with the right leg, and draw the sword into a single-handed horizontal cut to the right [figs. 1, 2, and 3].

Step the left leg forward, and assume a left-side-forward high-guard position [hidari jodan no kamae]. Cut down with a right descending diagonal cut [figs. 4, 5, 6, 7, and 8].

Step forward one pace with the right leg, and take up the mid-level ready position [chudan no kamae] while maintaining correct situational awareness [figs. 9 and 10].

Perform the blood-shaking maneuver [chiburi] [fig. 11].

Pull in the left foot while re-sheathing the blade [figs. 12, 13, 14, and 15].

Finish as for technique one [fig. 16].

Third Technique: Enemy to the Left [Sanbon Me: Hidari No Teki]

A single-handed thrust going into a left descending diagonal cut [katate zuki, hidari kesagiri]

SIGNIFICANCE OF THE KATA

Against an enemy approaching from the left in ambush, first stab into his chest area with a single-handed horizontal thrust [hira tsuki] and then, as he draws his sword and cuts down, receive and deflect the attack. Then counter with a left descending cut using a two-handed grip. All motions after this are identical to those of technique one.

ORDER

Extend the right foot [figs. 1 and 2].

Simultaneously step forward with the left foot [figs. 3 and 4].

Turn the edge of the blade diagonally left in the direction of the scabbard and draw [figs. 5 and 6].

As soon as the blade leaves the scabbard, proceed to stab with a right, single-handed horizontal strike [fig. 7].

Withdraw the strike and place the right hand on the right side of the hip [fig. 8].

While pulling back the left leg, turn the cutting edge of the blade to face forward, and extend the right elbow above the head to parry and deflect away the enemy's blow [figs. 9 and 10].

Move the left hand to take the hilt of the sword, making a double-handed grip, and then curve down into a left descending diagonal cut [figs. 11 and 12].

Take up the midlevel ready position [chudan no kamae] while maintaining correct situational awareness [fig. 15].

Perform the blood-shaking maneuver [chiburi] [fig. 16].

Pull in the left foot while re-sheathing the blade [figs. 17, 18, and 19].

Finish as for technique one [fig. 20].

Fourth Technique: Enemy Behind
[Yonhon Me: Ushiro No Teki]

A right, single-handed descending diagonal cut going into a left descending diagonal cut [katate migi kesagiri, hidari kesagiri]

SIGNIFICANCE OF THE KATA

Against an enemy approaching from the rear in ambush, turn 180 degrees and cut with a right, single-handed descending diagonal cut from the draw. Follow up with a left descending diagonal cut. All motions after this are identical to those of technique one.

ORDER

Look around to face the approaching opponent, extend the right leg forward, and at the same time turn the body 180 degrees to the right [figs. 1, 2, and 3)]

While withdrawing the right leg back, cut down from above the head with a right single-handed descending diagonal cut, finishing to the diagonal lower right [figs. 4, 5, and 6].

Take a two-handed grip on the hilt and move the sword to a high-guard [jodan no kamae] position; then step back with the left leg while cutting into a left descending diagonal cut [figs. 7, 8, 9, 10, and 11].

Take up the midlevel ready position [chudan no kamae] while maintaining correct situational awareness [fig. 12].

Perform the blood-shaking maneuver [chiburi] [fig. 13].

Pull in the left foot while re-sheathing the blade [figs. 14, 15, 16, and 17].

Finish as for technique one [fig. 18].

Fifth Technique: Multiple Enemies in the Forward Arc [Gohon Me: Zenmen No Teki]

A charging attack using three descending diagonal cuts, alternating between left and right [kesagiri]

SIGNIFICANCE OF THE KATA

Against multiple enemies attacking from the forward arc, charge forward raising the sword into a single-handed high guard above the head, and then cut down with both hands in a left descending diagonal cut. Use the momentum of the blade to return to a high guard, and then cut straight down into a right descending diagonal cut. Repeat the same motion into a second left descending diagonal cut. All motions after this are identical to those of technique one.

ORDER

Begin the kata in a rooted and unwavering posture [fudo no shisei], and move the right leg forward while drawing the sword and taking it up to a single-handed high guard [figs. 1, 2, and 3].

Move the other hand so both are gripping the hilt above the head, and then cut down into a left descending diagonal cut [figs. 4, 5, and 6].

Step the left leg forward, using the momentum of the previous cut [figs. 7 and 8] to extend both elbows out from the left, bringing the sword round and up above the head again. Then cut down into a right descending diagonal cut [figs. 9, 10, and 11].

From here step the right leg forward and, at the same time, use the momentum of the previous cut to extend both elbows out from the right, bringing the sword round and up above the head again. Then cut down into a left descending diagonal cut [figs. 12, 13, 14, and 15].

Take up the midlevel ready position [chudan no kamae] while maintaining correct situational awareness [fig. 16].

Perform the blood-shaking maneuver [chiburi] [fig. 17].

Re-sheathe the blade [figs. 18, 19, and 20].

Finish as for technique one [fig. 21].

1

Sixth Technique: Enemy in Front and Behind [Roppon Me: Ushiro To Mae No Teki]

A parry, followed up with a left descending diagonal cut that turns into a vertical descending cut [ukenagashi, hidari kesagiri, shinchoku giri]

SIGNIFICANCE OF THE KATA

One opponent is approaching from in front while another tries to strike an unexpected blow from ambush directly behind. Turn the body 180 degrees to the left, and deflect the second enemy's cut with a parry, following up into a left descending diagonal cut. Then turn back toward the first foe and deliver a vertical descending cut. All motions after this are identical to those of technique one.

ORDER

Step forward with the right foot, then with the left foot. Then step forward with the right again while simultaneously drawing the sword and turning the body 180 degrees to the left. Extend the right elbow up into a parry [figs. 1, 2, 3, 4, and 5].

At the same time move the left hand up to grip the hilt and come down into a left descending diagonal cut [figs. 6, 7, and 8].

Keeping the legs in the same position, raise the sword up to a high-guard position, gripping with both hands, and then turn on the spot 180 degrees to the left. Facing forward in the original direction, cut down with a vertical descending cut [figs. 9, 10, 11, 12, and 13].

Step forward with the right leg and take up the midlevel ready position [chudan no kamae] while maintaining correct situational awareness [fig. 14].

Perform the blood-shaking maneuver [chiburi] [fig. 15].

Re-sheathe the blade [figs. 16, 17, and 18].

Finish as for technique one [fig. 19].

Seventh Technique: Enemy to the Left, Right, and in Front [Nanahon Me: Hidari, Migi, Shomen No Teki]

A right, single-handed descending diagonal cut going into a left descending diagonal cut, then into a double-handed thrust

SIGNIFICANCE OF THE KATA

Against opponents approaching from the left and right, first cut down the one to the right with a single-handed descending diagonal cut using the right hand and continue to take out the one on the left with a left descending diagonal cut using both hands. From here step forward to attack an enemy directly in front with a two-handed thrust, withdraw a step, pull out the blade, and then raise it into a left-side forward high-guard position.

ORDER

Step forward with the right foot and then again with the left while simultaneously drawing the sword. Pull the right leg back and make a right, single-handed descending diagonal cut [figs. 1, 2, 3, and 4].

From here step the right leg forward, and at the same time use the momentum of the previous cut to bring the sword round out from the right and up above the head again. Then cut down into a left descending diagonal cut [figs. 5, 6, 7, and 8].

Take up a midlevel ready position [chudan no kamae], and make a double-handed thrusting attack forward [figs. 9 and 10].

Withdraw starting with the left leg, and pull out the blade before returning to the midlevel ready position [fig. 11].

Take up a left-side forward high-guard position and display the correct situational awareness [figs. 12 and 13].

Take up a midlevel ready position again [fig. 14].

Perform the blood-shaking maneuver [chiburi] [fig. 15].

Re-sheathe the blade [figs. 16, 17, and 18].

Finish as for technique one [fig. 19].

Eighth Technique: Cutting a Placed Target [Happon Me: Suemono Giri]

A single decisive cut [itto ryodan]

SIGNIFICANCE OF THE KATA

This kata teaches the basic motion for testing the cutting ability of a sword—the practice of cutting through a target on a stand [dai giri].

Widen the stance by stepping the right foot out to the side while serenely drawing the sword. Raise it above the head into a two-handed high-guard position with sufficient focus and energy. Then cut down with complete coordination of sword, body, and all one's mental and physical energy.

Demonstrate the blood-shaking maneuver before re-sheathing the blade. Simultaneously move the right foot back to the left, and finish in a rooted and unwavering posture [fudo no shisei].

ORDER

Step the right foot out to the side to open up the stance while drawing the sword [figs. 1, 2, 3, and 4].

Take the sword up to a high-level guard posture. Make sure to extend the elbows sufficiently and maintain flexibility in the arms [figs. 5 and 6].

Cut down vertically, doing so with complete coordination of sword, body, and all one's mental and physical energy [figs. 7 and 8].

Perform the blood-shaking maneuver [chiburi] [fig. 9].

Move the right foot back to the left while re-sheathing the blade, and assume the rooted and unwavering posture [figs. 10, 11, 12, and 13].

Finish as for technique one [fig. 14].

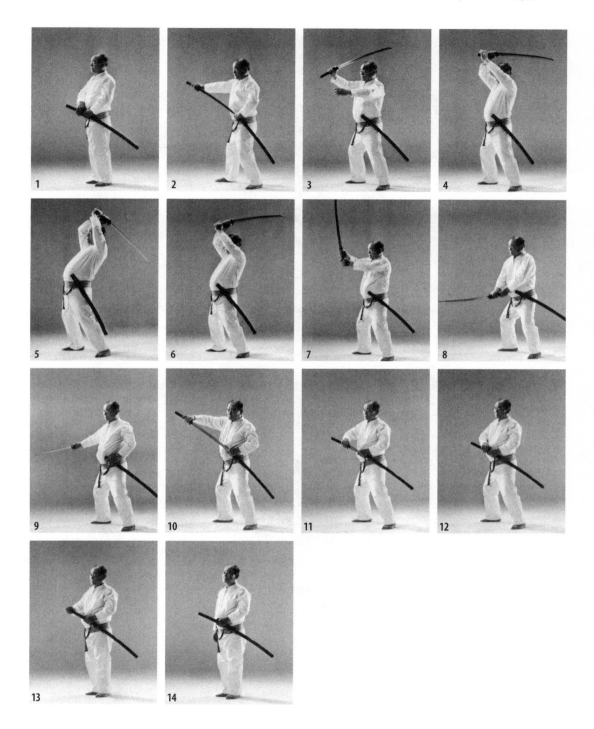

Swordsmen Suganuma Tokinori and Ozonoe Sadahisa perform kumitachi.

The young swordswomen of the Chiba branch dojo perform the first technique from the Toyama ryu kumitachi.

CHAPTER 9

TOYAMA RYU KUMITACHI (KATA)

Characteristics of the Toyama Ryu's Kumitachi Kata

The Toyama ryu is the military sword-handling methods (gunto no soho) that were formulated at the former Imperial Army Toyama Military Academy before the War, a set of fundamental sword techniques executed from a standing position.

The major characteristic of this system is that its paired kumitachi kata were formulated using kesagiri as their primary method, and this technique appears far more often by comparison than it does in the various classical schools. This is because kesagiri is the most natural and instinctive technique for practical, combat-focused martial arts.

The author (uchidachi) and swordsman Sato Shimeo (shidachi) perform Toyama ryu kumitachi at the Kyoto Butokuden in May 1978.

Formalities

Uchidachi: Nakamura Taisaburo (black jacket)
Shidachi: Tanabe Tetsundo (white jacket)

Bowing to express respect to the kami and to the joseki

Bowing to express respect to each other

To perform the salutation toward the sword, raise it as far as the center of the face with both hands.

Bowing to express reverence for the sword [torei]

Fixing the sword into the belt [taito]

First Technique: Both Opponents Start with Swords Sheathed

UCHIDACHI (BLACK JACKET)

This technique relates to the shohatto motion—the initial drawing cut of iaido.

Advance three steps forward with the sword still sheathed [figs. 1, 2, and 3].

Upon entering combative distance with shidachi, draw your sword into an initial horizontal cut [figs. 4 and 5].

The cut is evaded by shidachi as he withdraws by a single step. Stay in place and receive his counter, a diagonal descending cut [fig. 6].

Both sides take up a midlevel ready posture [chudan no kamae], and perform the blood-shaking maneuver [chiburi] [figs. 7 and 8].

Both sides sheathe their swords [figs. 9, 10, and 11].

Starting with the left leg, withdraw five small steps back to the starting positions [figs. 12 and 13].

SHIDACHI (WHITE JACKET)

Advance three steps forward with the sword still sheathed [figs. 1, 2, and 3].

Upon entering combative distance, uchidachi will attack you by drawing his sword into a horizontal cut [figs. 4 and 5].

Evade the cut by withdrawing a single step, and counter by drawing your own sword and cutting down from the upper right with a right descending diagonal cut [fig. 6].

Take up a midlevel ready posture [chudan no kamae], and maintain correct situational awareness [fig. 7].

Both sides take up a midlevel ready posture [chudan no kamae] and perform the blood-shaking maneuver [chiburi] [fig. 8].

Both sides sheathe their swords [figs. 9, 10, and 11].

Starting with the left leg, withdraw five small steps back to the starting positions [figs. 12 and 13].

Second Technique: Both Opponents Start in the Midlevel Ready Posture

UCHIDACHI (BLACK JACKET)

[This kata and all others up to the sixth technique begin after both participants have drawn their swords.]

Draw your sword and advance into combative distance, looking for an opening [figs. 1 and 2].

At the moment you raise your sword to a high-guard position to cut down into shidachi, he thrusts toward your chest [figs. 3, 4, and 5].

As shidachi raises his sword into a high-level guard posture and demonstrates correct awareness, assume a lower guard posture and withdraw, taking three small steps backward [fig. 6].

As shidachi moves into a midlevel ready posture, advance three small steps forward to intercept and cross sword tips in a mutual midlevel guard [fig. 7].

Mutually disengage and come out of the ready posture [fig. 8].

The sequence finishes in the same manner as the first technique [fig. 9].

SHIDACHI (WHITE JACKET)

Draw your sword and advance into combative distance [figs. 1 and 2].

At the moment that uchidachi raises his sword to a high-guard position to cut down into you, thrust toward his chest [figs. 3 and 4].

Withdraw by taking a big step from the left leg and pull out the blade [fig. 5].

Raise the sword into a left-side forward, high-level guard posture and demonstrate correct situational awareness [fig. 6].

Pull the left leg back and assume a midlevel ready posture [fig. 7].

Mutually disengage and come out of the ready posture [fig. 8].

The sequence finishes in the same manner as the first technique [fig. 9].

Third Technique: Both Opponents Start in the Midlevel Ready Posture

UCHIDACHI (BLACK JACKET)

Advance into combative distance in the midlevel ready posture [fig. 1].

Upon reaching the correct distance, step in one step and perform a thrusting stab toward shidachi's chest [fig. 2].

The thrust is evaded and countered with a left descending diagonal cut [figs. 3, 4, and 5].

Both practitioners assume a midlevel ready posture [figs. 6 and 7].

The sequence finishes in the same manner as the first technique [figs. 8 and 9].

SHIDACHI (WHITE JACKET)

Advance into combative distance in the midlevel ready posture [fig. 1].

Upon reaching the correct distance uchidachi will make a thrusting attack [fig. 2].

Deflect uchidachi's thrust at your chest to the left, using the side of the blade; then take your sword up to the diagonal upper left and rotate it round to the upper right before cutting down with a left descending diagonal cut [figs. 3, 4, and 5].

Assume a midlevel ready posture while displaying correct situational awareness, and withdraw one step from the left leg [fig. 6].

Both practitioners assume a midlevel ready posture [fig. 7].

The sequence finishes in the same manner as the first technique [figs. 8 and 9].

Fourth Technique: Left-Side-Forward High-Level Guard versus Horizontal Midlevel Guard

UCHIDACHI (BLACK JACKET)

Advance into combative distance in the high-level guard posture [fig. 1].

Upon reaching the correct distance, step in one step with the right leg and perform a spirited descending cut directly toward shidachi [figs. 2, 3, and 4].

The thrust is evaded by shidachi moving his body to your right and countered with a right descending diagonal cut [figs. 5, 6, and 7].

Both practitioners assume a midlevel ready posture [fig. 8].

The sequence finishes in the same manner as the first technique [figs. 9 and 10].

SHIDACHI (WHITE JACKET)

Advance into combative distance in the horizontal midlevel ready posture and, upon reaching the correct distance, uchidachi will make a descending cutting attack from a high guard [figs. 1 and 2].

Open your body out to the left and raise your sword up to the diagonal upper right. Do not make contact with the side of the blade [figs. 3, 4, and 5].

Perform a right descending diagonal cut [fig. 6].

Assume a midlevel ready posture while displaying correct situational awareness [fig. 7].

Both practitioners assume a midlevel ready posture [fig. 8].

The sequence finishes in the same manner as the first technique [figs. 9 and 10].

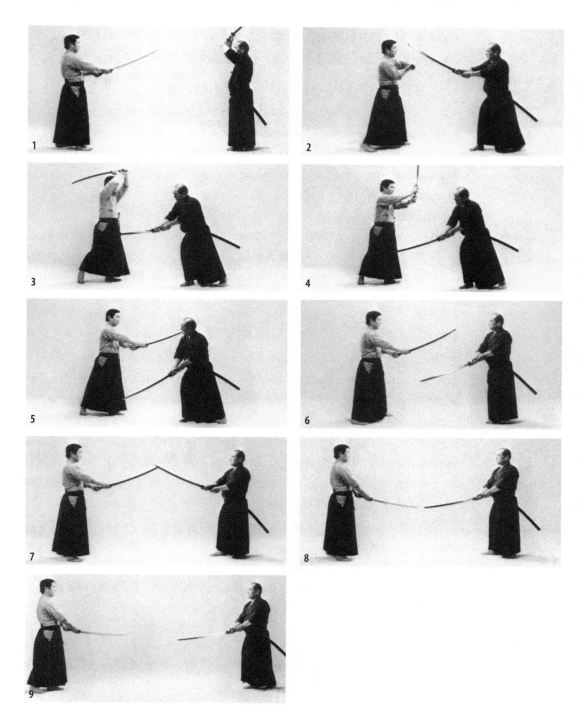

Fifth Technique: Right All Directions Ready Posture versus Horizontal Midlevel Guard

UCHIDACHI (BLACK JACKET)

Advance into combative distance in the right all directions ready posture [migi hasso no kamae] [fig. 1].

Upon reaching the correct distance, step in one step with the right leg and perform a right descending diagonal cut at shidachi from the diagonal upper right [figs. 2 and 3].

The cut is deflected to the right [fig. 4].

Shidachi counters with a left descending diagonal cut [figs. 5 and 6].

Both practitioners assume a midlevel ready posture [figs. 7 and 8].

The sequence finishes in the same manner as the first technique [fig. 9].

SHIDACHI (WHITE JACKET)

Advance into combative distance in the horizontal midlevel ready posture and, upon reaching the correct distance, uchidachi will make a left diagonal descending cut from a right all directions ready posture [migi hasso no kamae] [figs. 1 and 2].

Deflect uchidachi's attack diagonally to the left, using the side of your blade, and then rotate it around, up, and to the right [figs. 3 and 4].

From a right-side forward high-guard position, advance a step forward and deliver a left descending diagonal cut [figs. 5 and 6].

Assume a midlevel ready posture while displaying correct situational awareness [fig. 7].

Both practitioners assume a midlevel ready posture [fig. 8].

The sequence finishes in the same manner as the first technique [fig. 9].

Sixth Technique: Right-Side-Forward, High-Level Guard versus Horizontal Midlevel Guard

UCHIDACHI (BLACK JACKET)

Advance in the high-level guard posture and, when reaching engagement distance, step in with the right foot [figs. 1 and 2].

Perform a descending vertical cut directly at shidachi [fig. 3].

The attack is evaded by shidachi moving his body to your left and countered with a left descending diagonal cut [figs. 4 and 5].

As shidachi assumes a high-level guard position while displaying situational awareness, uchidachi assumes a low-level ready posture and withdraws three small steps, beginning from the left leg [figs. 6, 7, and 8].

As shidachi moves into a midlevel ready posture, advance three small steps forward, beginning from the right leg, to intercept and cross sword tips in a mutual midlevel guard [fig. 9].

The sequence finishes in the same manner as the first technique [figs. 10 and 11].

SHIDACHI (WHITE JACKET)

Advance into combative distance in the horizontal midlevel ready posture [fig. 1].

Upon reaching the correct distance uchidachi will make a descending cutting attack from a high guard. Evade by moving your body off to the right [figs. 2 and 3].

Raise your sword to the diagonal upper right. Do not make contact with the side of the blade [fig. 4].

Deliver a left descending diagonal cut [fig. 5].

Assume a midlevel ready posture [fig. 6].

From there assume a left-side forward high-guard posture and maintain correct situational awareness [figs. 7 and 8].

Both practitioners assume a midlevel ready posture [fig. 9].

The sequence finishes in the same manner as the first technique [figs. 10 and 11].

Public martial arts demonstration on the occasion of an official visit
by the American Army Chief of Staff in 1977

CHAPTER 10

NAKAMURA RYU BATTOJUTSU (KATA)

About the Nakamura Ryu Battojutsu

During the War I was assigned to the Second Yamashita Army Group Southern Special Attack Unit, in the northeast of China, as a special instructor of practical battlefield martial arts. There I taught the Toyama ryu iaido system of military sword-handling techniques (gunto no soho) and also integrated tameshigiri into the training.

During this period there was an incident in which I was demonstrating a bayonet versus a short-sword kata[63] for the trainees (with me using the short sword and Sergeant Honma using the bayonet). I made an error and was stabbed straight through the inside of the thumb on my right hand. With my right hand out of action for a while, I spent some time thereafter practicing cutting through a simulated target using the sword single handedly in my left hand.

Given that I had not sufficiently developed the correct intuition for how to grip the hilt one handed, at first I experienced many failures that led to the bending or chipping of my blades. After going through many failures in this way, I finally realized that making a truly decisive cut single handedly is impossible. I did, however, learn through intuitive experience that the objectives of tameshigiri can still be achieved single handedly if one employs the left and right kesagiri techniques, or in undertaking the dai giri exercise.

---

63. The modern martial discipline of *jukendo* [the way of the bayonet] was, unsurprisingly, developed by the Japanese military during the early twentieth century. Before becoming completely sportified, the kata covered how to use the bayonet when detached from the rifle as a short sword.

Even after my injury had completely healed, I actively continued to build up my experience of cutting at all kinds of angles and, receiving inspiration from the eiji happo exercise that forms the basis of learning calligraphy, I invented the happo giri eight-way cutting exercise.

It is noted that the number eight has a certain universality running through all things, and so it was that I changed the five fundamental stances of swordsmanship to eight, and also systemized the eight different methods of re-sheathing the blade. What I formulated from my logical and scientific research was the core of the Nakamura ryu.

Our forefathers put their whole being and all their efforts into leaving us the densho and gokuisho scrolls of transmission and secret knowledge, and the spiritual aspects of this are completely understandable to me. However, when looking at the sword methods they record objectively and divorced from the reverence and respect they are due as part of our culture and traditions, we can find many technical points that are imprecisely explained or that have been deliberately left unclear. This applies to both the stances used in the kata and in the detailed handling methods themselves. It goes without saying that we must never criticize our forebears' training, be it in the spiritual or the technical aspects of the art, but given the ideals of sword handling we are beholden to improve on their techniques in a logical manner.

One example of this is the iai syllabus of the Omori ryu, which has not a single kata covering the most natural and instinctive techniques of left and right kesagiri among its eleven forms. On this matter we have no choice but to say that the study and research behind the system was insufficient. Other classical schools also follow this example and feature few kata based on the practical sword technique of kesagiri. This is an undesirable state of affairs for the sword arts.

In the current era, demonstrations of the classical kobudo arts are overly obsessed with the kata of the classical schools, impeding the demonstration of effective technique.

The Nakamura ryu's approach to the sword arts takes the nature of the times into full consideration and does not place importance on the "meaning" or "significance" behind the techniques for cutting down an enemy. It places theory as a secondary concern after the trainee's personal experience and aims for a logical and scientific training in the methods of sword handing.

The Practical Techniques of the Nakamura Ryu

The modern martial art of aikido logically applies rounded, circular movements in all aspects of its technique, from throwing to receiving a foe's attack. For the sword techniques of the Nakamura ryu too, an effective circular motion using correct blade angle and cutting trajectory is a defining characteristic.

Another unique feature of the discipline is the logical nature of how the blade is stopped or realigned after making a cut, utilizing the momentum of the blade to flow into an attack against the next enemy.

Furthermore, in the Nakamura ryu we train not only in solo kata against the air but also in tameshigiri against straw, bamboo, and other simulated targets, aiming to polish technique to avoid errors in the cutting angle. We also aim to unify the student's heart and mind with his ki and all his physical and mental powers, and to foster and nourish the spiritual aspects of his training.

Beyond teaching the basic motions of sword handling, the Nakamura ryu does not particularly fixate on the formal kata, and encourages the practice and perfection of freestyle sword technique, allowing the practitioner to judge the correct cutting trajectory and distancing in a logical way, whether indoors or out. This is the Nakamura ryu, a devoted study of the methods of the sword.

What follows is a breakdown and explanation of the happo giri [eight-directional cutting], created with inspiration from the eiji happo exercise that forms the basis of learning calligraphy. All directions for cutting to the left or right are always given from the perspective of the direction the sword is facing.

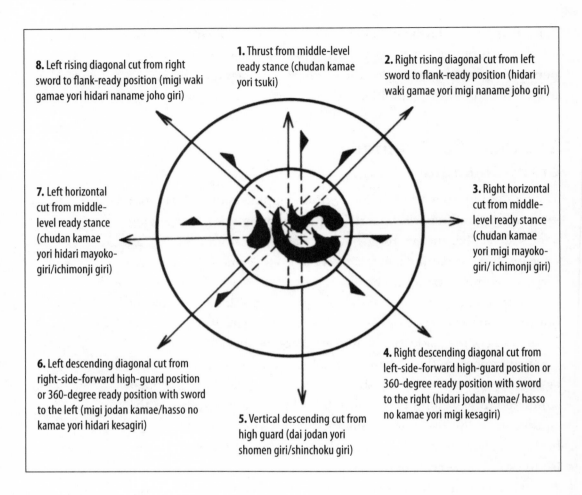

8. Left rising diagonal cut from right sword to flank-ready position (migi waki gamae yori hidari naname joho giri)

1. Thrust from middle-level ready stance (chudan kamae yori tsuki)

2. Right rising diagonal cut from left sword to flank-ready position (hidari waki gamae yori migi naname joho giri)

7. Left horizontal cut from middle-level ready stance (chudan kamae yori hidari mayoko-giri/ichimonji giri)

3. Right horizontal cut from middle-level ready stance (chudan kamae yori migi mayoko-giri/ ichimonji giri)

6. Left descending diagonal cut from right-side-forward high-guard position or 360-degree ready position with sword to the left (migi jodan kamae/hasso no kamae yori hidari kesagiri)

5. Vertical descending cut from high guard (dai jodan yori shomen giri/shinchoku giri)

4. Right descending diagonal cut from left-side-forward high-guard position or 360-degree ready position with sword to the right (hidari jodan kamae/ hasso no kamae yori migi kesagiri)

1. The Eight Stances (Happo No Kamae)	2. The Eight Cuts (Happo Giri)	3. The Eight Sheathing Methods (Hasshu No Noto)
1 Chudan kamae (midlevel ready posture)	Morote zuki (two-handed thrust)	From natural sword-wearing posture
2 Gedan kamae (low-level ready posture)	Hidari mayokogiri/hidari ichimonji giri (left horizontal cut)	From horizontal sword-carrying posture
3 Hidari jodan kamae (left-side-forward high-guard position)	Migi mayokogiri/migi ichimonji giri (right horizontal cut)	From chudan kamae (midlevel ready posture)
4 Migi jodan kamae (right-side-forward high-guard position)	Shinchoku giri/ karatakewari/ suemonogiri (vertical descending cut/ bamboo splitter/fixed-target cutting)	From left kesagiri
5 Hidari hasso no kamae (sword to the left eight aspects position)	Hidari kesagiri (left diagonal descending cut)	From right kesagiri
6 Migi hasso no kamae (sword to the right eight aspects position)	Migi naname joho giri (right diagonal rising cut)	From left reversed-sword position
7 Hidari waki gamae (left sword out to the flank ready position)	Migi kesagiri (right diagonal descending cut)	From right reversed-sword position
8 Migi waki gamae (right sword out to the flank ready position)	Hidari naname joho giri (left diagonal rising cut)	From facing the blade edge forward

Formalities

Bowing to show respect to the kami and to the joseki is a practice common to all martial arts, and so details of how to perform these essential formalities have been omitted here.

Bowing to the sword

Fixing the sword into the belt

The Eight Stances [Happo No Kamae]

1. Chudan kamae
   [midlevel ready posture]

Front view   Side view

2. Gedan kamae
   [low-level ready posture]

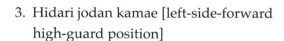

Front view   Side view

3. Hidari jodan kamae [left-side-forward high-guard position]

Front view   Side view

Front view   Side view

4. Migi jodan kamae [right-side-forward high-guard position]

Front view   Side view

5. Hidari hasso no kamae [sword to the left eight aspects position]

Front view   Side view

6. Migi hasso no kamae [sword to the right eight aspects position]

7. Hidari waki gamae [left sword out
   to the flank ready position]

Front view · Side view

8. Migi waki gamae [right sword out
   to the flank ready position]

Front view · Side view

Front view   Side view

The Eight Cuts [Happo Giri]

1. Morote zuki [two-handed thrust]

2. Hidari mayokogiri/hidari ichimonji giri [left horizontal cut]

3. Migi mayokogiri/migi ichimonji giri [right horizontal cut]

4. Shinchoku giri [vertical descending cut]

5. Hidari kesagiri [left diagonal descending cut]

6. Migi naname joho giri/
migi naname gyaku giri
[right diagonal rising cut]

7. Migi kesagiri [right diagonal descending cut]

8. Hidari naname joho giri/
hidari naname gyaku giri
[left diagonal rising cut]

The Eight Sheathing Methods [Hasshu No Noto]

1. From natural sword-wearing posture, raise the right hand and sheathe the blade (from the Toyama ryu).

2. From horizontal sword-carrying posture (taken from the Omori ryu).

3. From chudan kamae [midlevel ready posture], remove the right hand from the hilt while in chudan kamae; then take a reverse grip on the hilt with it and sheathe the blade.

4. From left kesagiri, with both hands to the diagonal lower left, change the grip of the right hand from above the hilt, and then spin the blade up and round from below to sheathe it.

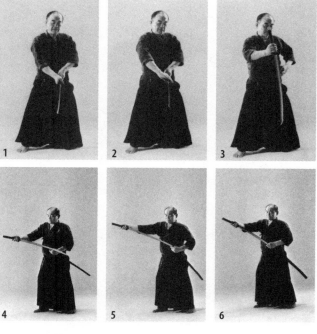

5. From right or left kesagiri, with both hands to the diagonal lower right, change the grip of the right hand from above the hilt; then sheathe the blade.

6. From left reversed-sword position, turn the hilt round to the left and rest the back of the blade on the right knee. Then change the grip of the right hand from above the hilt and sheathe (based on the Omori ryu).

7. From right reversed-sword position, turn the hilt round to the right and rest the back of the blade on the left knee. Then change the grip of the right hand from above the hilt and sheathe.

8. From facing the blade edge forward, raise the right hand from below to sheathe.

First Technique

Right horizontal cut going into a left descending diagonal cut [migi mayokogiri, hidari kesagiri]

ORDER

Step forward with the right foot and draw the sword, making a single-handed horizontal cut [figs. 1, 2, and 3].

Step forward with the left leg and then the right, making a left descending diagonal cut with both hands [figs. 4, 5, and 6].

Place the left hand at the mouth of the scabbard and perform the blood-shaking maneuver [chiburi] [fig. 7].

Grip the scabbard, pull the back leg up to be parallel with the front leg, and sheathe the sword [figs. 8 and 9].

Assume the rooted and unmoving posture [fudo no shisei], and return to the start position [fig. 10].

[See next page for photographs.]

Second Technique

Right rising diagonal cut going into a right descending diagonal cut [migi kiriage, migi kesagiri]

ORDER

Step forward with the right foot and draw your sword, making a right rising diagonal cut [figs. 1, 2, 3, and 4].

Turn the blade round from the upper right to the upper left, step in with the right foot, and deliver a right descending diagonal cut with both hands [figs. 5, 6, and 7].

The sequence finishes as for the first technique [figs. 7, 8, 9, and 10].

Third Technique

Left descending diagonal cut from a right side 360-degree ready position going into a right sweeping horizontal cut [migi hasso kamae, hidari kesagiri, migi yoko harai giri/mayokogiri]

ORDER

Step forward with the right foot and draw your sword serenely, assuming a 360-degree ready position with the sword to the right side [figs. 1, 2, 3, 4, and 5].

Step forward with the left leg and then the right, making a left descending diagonal cut [figs. 6 and 7].

Make a horizontal sweeping cut from left to right [figs. 8, 9, and 10].

Push the hilt out in front of and to the left of the body, and rest the back of the blade on the right knee (around 5 sun; 15 cm from the tip of the blade). Remove the right hand and switch grips from a standard grip below the hilt to a reverse grip above it in order to sheathe the blade using the left reverse-sheathing method (based on that of the Omori ryu) [figs. 11, 12, 13, and 14].

Pull up the left leg until it is parallel with the right, and then return to the original position [fig. 15].

Fourth Technique

Right descending diagonal cut from a left side 360-degree ready position going into a left sweeping horizontal cut [hidari hasso kamae, migi kesagiri, hidari yoko harai giri/mayokogiri]

ORDER

Step forward with the left foot and draw your sword serenely, assuming a 360-degree ready position with the sword to the left side [figs. 1, 2, and 3].

Step forward with the right leg and then the left, making a right descending diagonal cut [figs. 4 and 5].

Make a horizontal sweeping cut from right to left [figs. 6, 7, and 8].

Push the hilt out in front of and to the right of the body, and rest the back of the blade on the left knee (around 5 sun; 15 cm from the tip of the blade). Remove the right hand and turn it round to the right of the left hand [figs. 9, 10, and 11].

Change grips from below [fig. 12].

Sheathe the blade using the right reverse-sheathing method [figs. 13 and 14].

Pull up the right leg until it is parallel with the left, and then return to the original position [fig. 15].

Fifth Technique

Left rising diagonal cut from a right sword-to-flank ready posture going into a right horizontal sweeping cut and then a right descending diagonal cut [migi waki gamae, hidari naname joho giri, migi yoko harai giri/mayokogiri, migi kesagiri]

ORDER

Take the right leg back and draw your sword, assuming a right sword-to-flank ready posture. Step forward first the right and then the left leg, and perform a left rising diagonal cut [figs. 1, 2, 3, 4, and 5].

Reverse the blade over to the left, and make a right horizontal sweeping cut [figs. 6, 7, 8, and 9].

Reverse the blade and bring it up to the upper left before delivering a right descending diagonal cut [figs. 11, 12, and 13].

Release the right hand and switch it over to a reverse grip on the hilt. Spin the blade over from below and sheathe [figs. 14, 15, 16, and 17].

Pull the rear leg up until it is parallel with the front one, and then return to the original position [figs. 18 and 19].

Sixth Technique

Right rising diagonal cut from a left sword-to-flank ready posture going into a left horizontal sweeping cut and then into a left descending diagonal cut [hidari waki gamae, migi naname joho giri, hidari yoko harai giri/mayokogiri, hidari kesagiri]

ORDER

Take the left leg back and draw your sword, assuming a left sword-to-flank ready posture. Step forward first the left and then right leg, and perform a right rising diagonal cut [figs. 1, 2, 3, 4, 5, and 6].

Reverse the blade over to the right, and make a left horizontal sweeping cut [figs. 7, 8, 9, and 10].

From there, reverse the blade and bring it up to the upper right before delivering a left descending diagonal cut [figs. 11, 12, 13, and 14].

Re-sheathe the blade, and return to the starting position [figs. 15, 16, and 17].

Seventh Technique

Right descending diagonal cut going into a left descending diagonal cut [migi kesagiri, hidari kesagiri]

ORDER

Step forward with the right foot and draw your sword, assuming a left-side-forward high-level guard position [figs. 1, 2, and 3].

Make a right diagonal descending cut while drawing back the left leg [figs. 4 and 5].

From here step forward with the left foot and make a left diagonal descending cut [figs. 6, 7, and 8].

Perform the blood-shaking maneuver [chiburi] [fig. 9].

Re-sheathe the blade [figs. 10, 11, and 12].

Return to the starting position [fig. 13].

Eighth Technique

Left descending diagonal cut from the draw going into a double-handed thrust before taking up a left-side-forward high-level guard posture and expressing correct situational awareness [nukiuchi hidari kesagiri, morote zuki, hidari jodan, zanshin]

ORDER

Step forward with first the right and then left leg, and then pull back the left while drawing your sword into a left descending diagonal cut [figs. 1, 2, 3, 4, and 5].

Step in fully with the right foot and deliver a double-handed thrust [figs. 6, 7, and 8].

Assume a left-side-forward high-level guard posture and express correct situational awareness [figs. 9, 10, and 11].

Perform the blood-shaking maneuver [chiburi] [fig. 12].

Re-sheathe the blade [figs. 13 and 14].

Return to the starting position [fig. 15].

Soga Yoshiharu as uchidachi and Tanaka Tatsuo as shidachi perform Nakamura ryu kumitachi.

CHAPTER 11

NAKAMURA RYU KUMITACHI (KATA)

About the Nakamura Ryu Kumitachi

The Nakamura ryu's kumitachi forms focus on the methods used in the highly logical happo giri exercise, itself based on the teachings of the classical sword schools. They were created with further study and refining of the Nakamura ryu battojutsu kata, making effective use of the methods within them to express the true essence of the martial arts.

The defining characteristic of these forms is how they train the correct cutting trajectory and blade angle for the practically applicable techniques of left and right kesagiri and tsuki, through relating to experiences with tameshigiri.

Performing Tameshigiri before Practicing the Kumitachi Kata

In the Nakamura ryu it is a principle that tameshigiri is always carried out before performing the kumitachi kata, to allow both practitioners to cultivate a suitable level of focus and application of mental energy [kiai] and to internalize the correct blade angle and cutting trajectory.

Uchidachi: Soga Yoshiharu (black jacket)

Shidachi: Tanaka Tatsuo (white jacket)

Uchidachi (black jacket)

Perform a right descending diagonal cut and then reverse the blade [figs. 1, 2, 3, and 4].

Perform a left rising diagonal cut [fig. 5].

Sheathe the sword [fig. 6].

SHIDACHI (WHITE JACKET)

Perform a right descending diagonal cut and then reverse the blade [figs. 7, 8, and 9].

Perform a right rising diagonal cut [figs. 10, 11, 12, and 13].

Sheathe the sword [fig. 14].

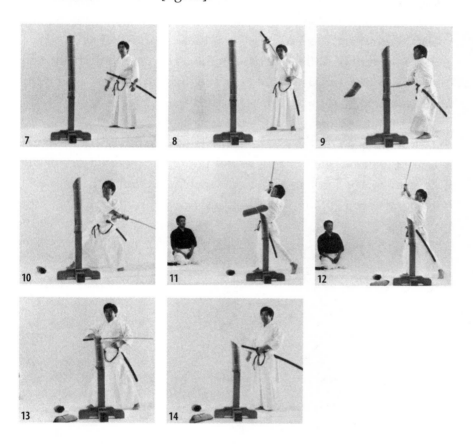

Formalities

Bowing to show respect to the kami and to the joseki is a practice common to all martial arts and so has been omitted here.

However, the bow to salute the sword is specific to the Toyama ryu and Nakamura ryu and is shown in the photographs on this page.

(Uchidachi is wearing a black jacket and shidachi a white jacket.)

First both performers bow to each other.

Grip the mouth of the scabbard in the right hand with the thumb over the sword's guard and hold it at the right hip. Bow to your partner at an angle of approximately fifteen degrees [figs. 1, 2, and 3].

The right hand grips the hilt at the base of the sword guard with the thumb placed on the guard itself. The suspending cord [sageo] is folded over on itself at the central point and inserted under the index finger. The left hand holds the scabbard around the base and both hands are extended out, holding the sword centrally at face height [fig. 4].

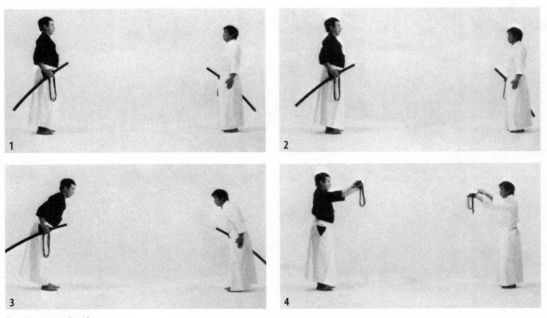

Bowing to each other

Perform the bow toward the sword [figs. 5 and 6].

Fix the sword into your belt. The suspending cord is attached to the belt at the right side of the waist.

Bowing to the sword

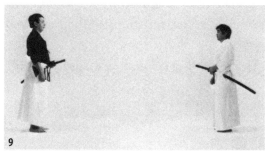

Fixing the sword into the belt

First Technique

ORDER

Both swordsmen begin at a distance of nine paces from each other and advance three paces each, starting from the right foot, to enter into combative distance [maai] [figs. 1 and 2].

As both swordsmen enter combative distance, uchidachi draws his sword and strikes at shidachi with a vertical cut [shinchoku giri] in a single motion [figs. 3 and 4].

Shidachi moves his body one step to the left to avoid the cut and draws his sword, turning the motion straight into a strike at uchidachi's right shoulder with a descending diagonal cut [kesagiri] [figs. 5 and 6].

Both swordsmen take up a midlevel ready posture [chudan kamae]. Shidachi moves his body away to the right while doing this. Both swordsmen withdraw a single step, coming to cross the tips of their swords while displaying proper situational awareness [zanshin] [fig. 7].

Both swordsmen withdraw three steps from each other, and then perform the blood-shaking maneuver [chiburi] [figs. 8, 9, and 10].

Both swordsmen sheathe their blades and assume the rooted and unwavering posture [fudo no shisei] before returning to their original positions [figs. 11 and 12].

All the following techniques up to the seventh are based on this procedure.

Second Technique

ORDER

Both swordsmen approach and enter into combative distance [figs. 1 and 2]

Uchidachi draws his sword and moves straight into a strike at shidachi's left shoulder with a descending diagonal cut [kesagiri]. Shidachi withdraws a single step to avoid the cut and draws his sword [figs. 3 and 4].

Uchidachi reverses his sword for the second attack and strikes at shidachi's right shoulder with another descending diagonal cut [kesagiri] [fig. 5].

Shidachi avoids the second cut by moving his body one step to the right from the right leg, and then stabs toward uchidachi's solar plexus with a double-handed thrust [morote zuki] [fig. 6].

Both swordsmen return to their original positions while taking up a midlevel ready posture [chudan kamae] and displaying proper situational awareness [zanshin] [figs. 7 and 8].

The sequence finishes in the same way as it does for the first technique.

Third Technique

ORDER

As both swordsmen enter into combative distance, uchidachi draws and strikes at shidachi's left shoulder with a descending diagonal cut [kesagiri] [figs. 1, 2, and 3].

Shidachi makes a large withdrawing movement away from uchidachi to avoid the cut while simultaneously drawing his own sword [figs. 4 and 5].

Uchidachi makes another step in toward shidachi and starts to make a thrust at him [fig. 6].

Shidachi rotates his body to the left and strikes at uchidachi's right shoulder with a descending diagonal cut [kesagiri] [fig. 7].

The sequence finishes in the same way as it does for the first technique [figs. 8 and 9].

Fourth Technique

ORDER

Both swordsmen walk toward each other [figs. 1, 2, and 3].

Without stopping, uchidachi draws his sword and strikes at shidachi's left shoulder with a descending diagonal cut [kesagiri] as he passes him by [figs. 4 and 5].

Shidachi rotates his body to the right with a big movement from the right leg while drawing his own sword and cutting toward uchidachi's torso with a single-handed strike [katate nukiuchi] [figs. 6 and 7].

Both swordsmen remain in place and take up a midlevel ready posture [chudan kamae] while displaying proper situational awareness [zanshin] [fig. 8].

Both swordsmen withdraw three steps from each other and assume the rooted and unwavering posture [fudo no shisei] [figs. 9, 10, 11, and 12].

Each swordsman passes by his opponent's right-hand side to return to his original position and then turns to his right. The sequence is finished in the same way as it is for the first technique [figs. 13 and 14].

Fifth Technique

ORDER

Both swordsmen walk toward each other [figs. 1, 2, and 3].

Without stopping, uchidachi spins right to strike at shidachi's torso with a horizontal cut [mayokogiri/ichimonji giri] as he passes by on shidachi's right-hand side. Shidachi rotates his body to the right and withdraws a step to avoid the cut [figs. 4, 5, 6, 7, and 8].

Uchidachi raises his sword from the right, and then steps forward one step with his left foot to deliver a vertical cut [shinchoku giri]. Shidachi steps forward diagonally to the right with his right foot to avoid this second cut [figs. 9 and 10]. Shidachi then draws his own sword into a strike at uchidachi's left shoulder with a descending diagonal cut [kesagiri] [fig. 11].

The sequence finishes in the same way as it does for the first technique [figs. 12 and 13].

Sixth Technique

ORDER

Both swordsmen approach and enter into combative distance [figs. 1 and 2].

Uchidachi draws his sword and immediately strikes at shidachi's right shoulder with a descending diagonal cut [kesagiri] [figs. 3, 4, and 5].

Shidachi withdraws a single step to avoid this, moving from the left leg, and simultaneously draws his sword. Uchidachi reverses his sword, takes up the eight aspects position [hasso no kamae], and then strikes at shidachi's left shoulder with a descending diagonal cut [kesagiri] [figs. 6 and 7].

Shidachi withdraws a single step to the right side to avoid this and strikes uchidachi's left shoulder with a descending diagonal cut [kesagiri] [figs. 8, 9, and 10].

The sequence finishes in the same way as it does for the first technique [figs. 11 and 12].

Seventh Technique

ORDER

Both swordsmen approach and enter into combative distance [figs. 1 and 2].

Uchidachi draws his sword into a strike at shidachi with a one-handed rising diagonal cut to the right [katate migi naname joho giri] [fig. 3].

Shidachi withdraws a single step to avoid this attack [fig. 4], while simultaneously drawing his own sword.

Uchidachi follows up by making a further large step in toward shidachi with his right leg.

Uchidachi attacks shidachi's right shoulder with a descending diagonal cut [kesagiri], and shidachi withdraws a single step from his right leg to further avoid the attack [fig. 5].

Shidachi makes a step in and attacks uchidachi's left shoulder with a descending diagonal cut [kesagiri]. Uchidachi withdraws his right leg to avoid this attack and takes up a high [jodan kamae] guard [figs. 6 and 7].

Uchidachi withdraws his left leg and takes up a midlevel ready posture [chudan kamae] while shidachi assumes a right eight aspects position [migi hasso no kamae] with his left leg forward [figs. 8 and 9].

Uchidachi transitions from the midlevel ready position [chudan kamae] to the eight aspects position [hasso no kamae] and strikes at shidachi's left shoulder with a descending diagonal cut [kesagiri] [figs. 10 and 11].

Shidachi withdraws a single step to avoid the attack while assuming a lower-level guard position [gedan no kamae].

Uchidachi follows up by striking at shidachi with a vertical cut [shinchoku giri] from a left-side-forward high-guard posture [hidari jodan no kamae]. Shidachi comes out of the lower guard position to cut uchidachi's torso with a rising diagonal cut to the right [migi naname joho giri] [figs. 12, 13, 14, and 15].

The sequence finishes in the same way as it does for the first technique [figs. 16 and 17].

CHAPTER 12

HANDLING AND MAINTAINING THE JAPANESE SWORD

Regarding the Appraisal of Japanese Swords

By Tanabe Tetsundo[64]
Iaido kyoshi seventh dan
Jukendo renshi sixth dan
Kendo renshi sixth dan

When appraising a sword, one should first observe the blade in its entirety.

In the two thousand year history of our Yamato race, once known as the nation of a thousand fine glaives,[65] we have been destroyed by the sword and built up again by the sword, and our culture has flourished through the sword. One cannot help but feel that we are a nation of martial endeavor and, throughout the ages, the sword has not only represented and embodied power but also has been the source of that power itself in a quite literal sense.[66]

However, today there are no longer enemies for the power embodied in our swords to be turned against, and the Japanese sword has come to find a most unexpected place in the world as an art object. There is much that feels out of place when in the modern age swords are talked of with an attitude turned entirely to commercial concerns, concerns far removed from their practical use as weapons.

Without exception Japanese swords are, first and foremost, equipment for war and devoted to a singular and solemn purpose. This

---

64. This chapter was written by Tanabe Tetsundo, a senior student of Nakamura, and he is depicted in all the photographs here.

65. 細戈千足国 (*Kuwashihoko chitaru no kuni*). The archaic word *hoko* here was usually used to refer to any kind of pole arm or sometimes to bladed weapons in general.

66. It is enlightening to note the striking similarity of the characters used for power (力; chikara) and the sword (刀; katana) in the Japanese language.

essence must not be forgotten. The gaze of a modern appraiser looks mainly to identify the smith who created the blade, and this kind of appraisal is of course necessary as a basic measure. However, the true appraisal of a sword is made by one who studies the martial ways, and it goes further, looking to evaluate a blade's strengths and deficiencies with regard to whether it is up to practical use.

One must not be taken in and enthralled by surface beauty and needs to look deeper into a blade to assess it and to understand how diligently it was made. Those blades that will warp under even light pressures, those that chip after cutting mere straw, and those that will bend or snap when making contact with bamboo merely imitate the shape and external form of a Japanese sword. They have not inherited its true spirit.

The first step for a novice sword appraiser is to become able to see through to this core inner beauty and not to forget the spirit of patriotism toward our nation's heritage, a spirit that is rapidly fading and becoming lost.

Nomenclature for the Parts of a Sword

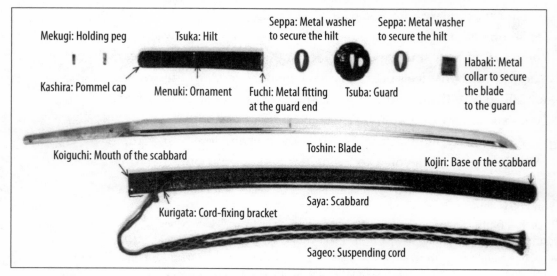

The fittings (*koshirae*) **of the** *uchigatana* **style**

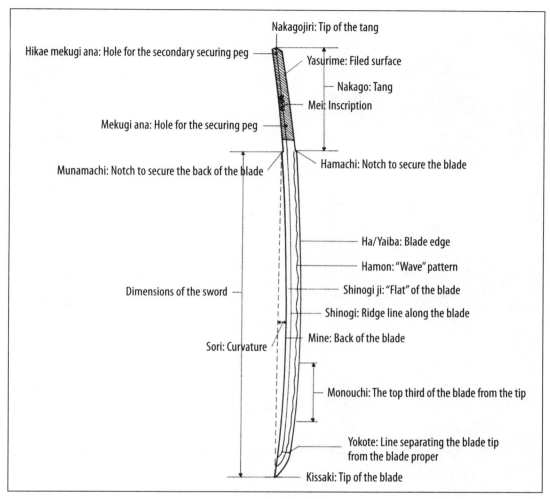

Nakagojiri: Tip of the tang

Hikae mekugi ana: Hole for the secondary securing peg

Yasurime: Filed surface

Nakago: Tang

Mei: Inscription

Mekugi ana: Hole for the securing peg

Hamachi: Notch to secure the blade

Munamachi: Notch to secure the back of the blade

Ha/Yaiba: Blade edge

Hamon: "Wave" pattern

Shinogi ji: "Flat" of the blade

Dimensions of the sword

Shinogi: Ridge line along the blade

Mine: Back of the blade

Sori: Curvature

Monouchi: The top third of the blade from the tip

Yokote: Line separating the blade tip from the blade proper

Kissaki: Tip of the blade

The parts of the blade

How to Appraise a Japanese Sword

1. First perform a bow to the sword to express the due reverence and respect. Raise the sword to head height and perform a single shallow bow. The hilt should be held with the pommel facing to the right and lifted from below using both hands. This gesture expresses respect and courtesy toward the sword itself and to

its owner and ingrains the habit of handling swords in a more careful and diligent manner than other items used in everyday life.

2. Face the blade upward, take a firm grip on the scabbard with the left hand, and secure it on top of the left knee. Grip the hilt from above with the right hand and release the sword from the mouth of the scabbard. Draw the sword serenely from the scabbard in one smooth motion along the line of the back of the blade.

3. It is highly disrespectful and poor etiquette to stop during the draw to look at the hamon, touch the edge of the blade with the hand, or to make a rasping noise by rubbing the back of the blade against the edge of the scabbard while drawing.

4. When appraising a sword one should first observe the whole of the blade in its entirety. Extend the arms forward and hold the sword vertically to view it. One can judge the era in which a sword was forged to a significant extent from its curvature and the overall appearance.

5. When the blade is held up to a soft light source, the hamon pattern will stand out and become clearer. On closer inspection of the hamon one can judge the blade's lineage and the unique characteristics of the smith who made it from various movements of light along the surface. The fall of the light indicates the balance of finer and coarser martensite crystals, the *utsuri* pattern mir-

roring the hamon if there is one, and the darker streaks of crystalline metal that form in its vicinity.

6. The left hand should only contact the blade through a fine silk cloth specifically designed for sword handling, although if there is a suitable alternative permitted by the owner then that may be used instead. Make sure that the cloth only touches the blade along its back surface, avoiding the cutting edge and sides. It is strictly forbidden to use a sweat-wiping cloth or to rest the blade on one's sleeve.

7. One can determine the era and province in which the blade was forged and its lineage from the surface texture of the metal itself and whether it shows a natural wood grain pattern, a more regular, board-like grain pattern, or a straight grain pattern. When looking at swords that undergo practical use one must pay special attention to any scars or blemishes on the blade, looking at and assessing each individual vertical or horizontal notch, air bubble, area of wrinkling or forging imperfection, patch where the hamon has faded, or where other metals have been embedded into the blade. Whatever the quality or renown of the sword, damage to the cutting edge will make it unsuitable for use.

8. The *boshi* line around the tip of the blade is a key feature when appraising a sword. This line reveals the idiosyncrasies and

characteristics of an individual smith or of an inherited school lineage and cannot be viewed in a cursory manor. In days of old a sword with no line along here was said to have "no head." When examining the tip of a blade one must be vigilant for notches known as "crow's beak" [karasuguchi] lines.

9. When removing the tang from the hilt, take a grip around the upper ridge of the pommel with the sword held vertically and the cutting edge facing away. Gently striking the area of the left hand between the thumb and forefinger will cause the blade itself to come free of the hilt. If struck with more force than is necessary some blades will fly out of the hilt with considerable momentum, so caution is required. WARNING: When removing a blade from its hilt make certain to get the permission and acceptance of the sword's owner first.

10. Grip and hold down the metal collar [habaki] with the right hand and pull away the hilt with the left.

11. Observe the whole of the blade including the tang. A blade of renown will have a superb balance between these two elements.

12. When viewing the tang one should come to a conclusion regarding the judgements and deductions made in the appraisal so far. The tang is the only part of the sword that is left in the same state that the smith forged it in and much can be gleaned from its shape, the kind of base it has, and any inscriptions and file marks.

How to Maintain a Japanese Sword

1. When cleaning the sword, first remove the metal collar at the base of the blade [the habaki]. If this is kept in place then oil and uchiko powder can get trapped and build up between it and the blade, becoming a cause of rust. A stiff habaki should be gripped on the flat of both sides and firmly pulled down and away.

2. Thoroughly wipe away any old oil on the blade. *Yoshinogami*[67] should be used to wipe the blade, but any suitable substitute can be used as long as it does not scratch or damage the surface. Hold the paper around the back ridge of the blade and repeatedly wipe up and down the length from the base to the tip.

3. Uchiko powder is applied to further clean away any excess oil. Hold the back of the blade toward you and gently and thoroughly apply powder from the base of the habaki to the tip, gripping the applicator with the thumb on top and making sure to get an even coverage. When the first side is covered, turn the blade over and apply powder back down it from the tip to the base. Finally apply it to the back of the blade too.

---

67. *Yoshinogami* is a special kind of soft traditional paper that was originally manufactured from the pulp of a certain kind of hybrid mulberry tree in the Yoshino area (in the south of what is modern-day Nara prefecture).

4. Use a separate cloth to wipe off the uchiko powder from that used to remove the oil.

5. Hold the back of the blade between the folds of the cloth and lightly wipe up from the base to the tip to avoid the oil pooling or mottling.

6. Wipe the tang down thoroughly, and then clean it well using a cloth with a small amount of oil. Finally reattach the habaki collar and replace the hilt.

7. Take a firm grip close to the top of the hilt where it would meet the scabbard and lightly tap the pommel cap to lock the tang tightly into place.

8. Insert the mekugi holding pin/s.

9. Raise the scabbard firmly with the left hand, making sure that it is stable, and then place a small area at the tip of the sword's blade onto the mouth of the scabbard, pulling back across the back of the blade and serenely sliding the sword in.

10. Make sure not to make a sound when re-sheathing the blade.

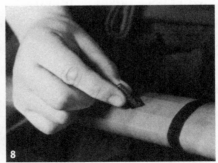

11. Perform a bow to the sword. It is a principle of the sword and of all the martial arts that things should begin and end with courtesy. When passing a sword to someone else, one should keep the blade facing toward oneself and offer the hilt first.

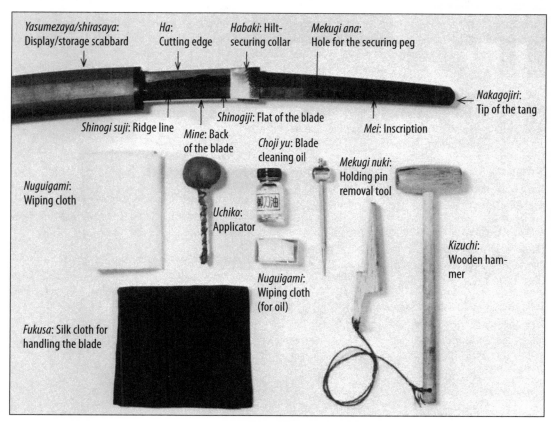

Equipment used in the maintenance of a Japanese sword

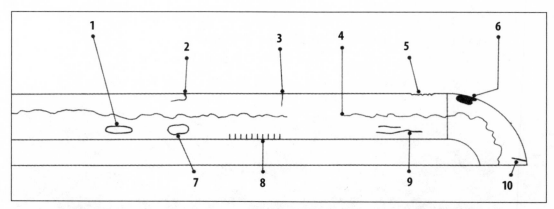

How to identify damage to the blade of a sword used for practical purposes

1. Black rusting (Kurosabi)

Black rust on the cutting edge of a blade can easily eat deeply into the metal and even penetrate through to the other side. This is very dangerous and requires the attention of a specialist polisher.

2. Chipping of the cutting edge (Hakobore)

The metal on brittle blades can flake off in clumps when damaged like this. (Prevents use, but the sword can be returned to use if the balance of the metal is repaired.)

3. Wearing down of the crystalline finish (Nioigire)

This is where the hamon is no longer present. The hamon pattern will fade if intense heat is re-applied after forging.

4. Notches across the blade (Hagire)

Fine lines as if gouged using a needle are visible. When viewed from the opposite side the same line runs all the way through. (Prevents use.)

5. Notches down the blade (Hagarami)

When splits in the layers of metal from forging *[kitae ware]* are present across the cutting edge. This whole area can chip off entirely. (Can prevent use depending on the extent and location of such damage.)

6. Embedded patch of metal (Umegane)

Some pieces of metal embedded in the blade can appear to be the darkened areas of the surface structure known as *sumihada* that are a natural part of forging.

7. Air bubbles (Fukure)

Where specific areas of the metal are raised due to trapped air. Carelessly depressing these can cause the bubble to move around.

8. Wrinkling of the metal (Shinae)

The iron in this area is flawed.

9. Split in the layers of metal (Kitaeware)

Caused when the layers of metal do not fold and merge together properly during forging.

10. "Crow's beak" notch at the tip of the blade (Karasuguchi)

A notch *[hagire]* that falls across the forging line at tip of the blade *[boshi]*.

CHAPTER 13

EXAMPLES OF INSTRUCTING TAMESHIGIRI AND SWORD-RELATED INJURIES

Statistics Regarding Tameshigiri Using Military Swords

In the latter half of the Pacific War the various divisions of the Second Yamashita Army Group Southern Special Attack Unit were formed, and I was assigned as a special swordsmanship instructor to teach the cadets practical battlefield martial arts. In this capacity I carried out instruction based on the syllabus described below.

Hono enbu cutting through five straw bundles at the Hayao Shrine in Shibukawa, Gunma prefecture (January 1978)

Teaching Plan for the Rapid Development of the One-Strike-Kill Ethos with the Military Sword

AREAS OF CONCERN

1. Imparting the spirit and mental fortitude to kill in a single stroke
2. Fostering a vigorous and hardy drive and willpower
3. Polishing and perfecting technical skill

OBJECTIVES

To deepen the trainee's confidence in making cutting and thrusting attacks with his military-issue sword without technical errors in a short time. To bestow upon him a confidence that can be applied to close-quarters combat on the battlefield.

Under the orders of the unit's commander, the regimental adjutant Captain Saito took responsibility for this instruction.

In northern Manchuria (in the northeast of China) there is no green bamboo, so instead we used birch wood and rolled up kamasu-style sacks (see footnote 50 on page 64) to make tameshigiri materials.

Among the officers there were many kendo yudansha, but it goes without saying that handling a live-bladed military sword is something else entirely to using a bamboo shinai.

The results of these first practical tameshigiri exercises, designed to instil in the trainee a confidence in his military sword, are shown in the statistics below.

The exercise was carried out using rolled up straw sacks for targets without wooden "bones" inserted into them, cutting with left and right descending diagonal cuts [kesagiri] from a high-guard position. In total around fifty officers took part.

The results of the test cutting were as follows:

1. Fifteen participants cut through the target.
2. Six participants misjudged the distancing and cutting angle and bent their sword blades.

3. Twelve participants cut through one-third to one-half of the target before the blade stopped.

4. Ten participants cut through one-quarter of the target before the blade stopped.

5. Eight participants cut through one-fifth of the target before the blade stopped.

6. One participant misjudged the distance to the target and only scratched the surface with the tip of his blade. The sword cut through the air but because his grip on the hilt was poor, it flew clean out from his hands due to the momentum behind the strike and, after cutting through his left knee, the sword came to rest seven meters away. This particular officer cadet held a third dan from his university kendo club.

The author (right) and Master Sergeant Yoshii (left) perform bayonet versus military sword kata on the front line at the Manchurian border with the Soviet Union in Heihe province (1945).

As one can see from looking at these statistics, tameshigiri gives immediate feedback on the results of one's technique. This exercise painfully impressed upon me the need to practice it in unison alongside training in kendo and iaido.

A Battalion Commander Cuts His Leg with His Sword

In 1945 I was reassigned from northern Manchuria to the units preparing for the final battle for the homeland and sent to Hakata in Kyushu. Here I was ordered to travel around various areas as a sword teacher, instructing civilian militia units in the *hitori hissatsu* [sure killing of a single enemy] ideology and preparing them for "bamboo spear" patrols.

There was no green bamboo available in northern Manchuria, and so we used birch wood instead as it has comparatively few phloem vessels in its structure. However, there are many bamboo thickets around Hakata in northern Kyushu, so sometimes I would instruct my charges here in bamboo cutting.

The youngest battalion commander in the unit at that time was a Captain Nakai, who practiced the gunto no soho (Toyama ryu iaido) methods while stationed in Manchuria and, since practicing tameshigiri, had gained a confidence in the use of his sword. He always took the initiative when we practiced tameshigiri exercises.

Before instructing in tameshigiri I make certain to give the following warning to the trainees: "The katana is a malevolent entity in its own right, one that will cut you, and so you must take care when handling it. When practicing tameshigiri you must focus your mind and spirit; banish all distracting thoughts; and not let your guard down, making safety the utmost priority in your training."

However, when people start to experience their techniques actually cutting through something, they will often develop a taste and eagerness for tameshigiri and begin to find it interesting. This can lead to a greater and more careless desire to cut things, although it is only human nature.

Commander Nakai started with thinner pieces of bamboo, but after a while spent cutting through these he became more and more confident and wanted to cut thicker ones. However, the thicker the target the more physical power is required to cut through it and so the more one will invest emotionally in trying to generate this power. This in turn means that one's grip manipulation will become rough and inaccurate, and it will be harder to maintain the correct control and stop the blade once the cut has passed through the target. Even in modern iaido demonstrations there are those who do not stop their blade after cutting down and wind up burying the tip in the floorboards. In the same way, when observing tameshigiri we sometimes see swords failing to stop due to the momentum of the circular cutting motion, resulting in performers cutting into their own legs or skimming the tips of the blades across the ground. Commander Nakai had poor grip control and so eventually came to cut down into the kneecap on his left leg. The location of the wound meant that it would soon open up again simply through walking, so he had no choice but to bind the leg with splints.

As far as I recall this incident occurred a mere fifteen days before the end of the War, but it shows clearly that we must take great care when practicing tameshigiri.

My Right Palm Speared Through During a Demonstration

In November of 1943, while stationed in Shenwutun in northern Manchuria, the division I was attached to was assigned just over thirty graduates fresh from the officer-training academy in the homeland. I was ordered to demonstrate model forms to these cadets to cultivate and reinforce in them a confidence in using their military-issue swords. The exercises included the bayonet versus military sabre, bayonet versus short-sword katas, and the gunto no soho syllabus formulated at the Toyama academy, as well as tameshigiri. Once they had seen them demonstrated, I was to go on and instruct the young officers in these forms. The day before the demonstration I practiced going through the kata with Sergeant Honma and successfully completed the military sword versus bayonet sequences. However, during instruction in the short sword versus bayonet forms, there was an unexpected accident. Sergeant Honma was using a real gun with bayonet while I was wielding the short sword (an infantry-issue short sword). We got the order of the sequence wrong and Honma's bayonet thrust pierced straight through my right hand just below the thumb where it was gripping the hilt of the sword. Fortunately the blade did not penetrate through to the bone, and I pulled the bayonet out and went off to the medical room to get it treated. However, the pain when the regimental medic passed gauze through the pierced area was far more agonizing even than when the bayonet went in.

The day after the accident I had to instruct the thirty-plus officer cadets in tameshigiri. To perform the demonstration I borrowed four military-issue swords from various officers and practiced performing left and right diagonal descending cuts [kesagiri] single-handedly, using the left hand. I bent most of the blades, however, and only managed to cut through around half of the simulated targets, being unable to make a single clean stroke. It was this incident that first caused me to learn the proper tenouchi grip control for one-handed cutting, although I was studying and practicing it until midnight that night.

Special martial arts demonstrations at the Martial Flag Festival in Shenwutun in northern Manchuria (1945)

A. Rifle versus short-sword kata (author on the right)

B. Rifle versus rifle kata (author on the left)

When I was still a kendo third or fourth dan, I began my study of the two-sword style and actually took the grading for fourth dan using two swords. I failed on that occasion, but retook it the next time, using the single sword, and passed. In 1940 I went on to take the examination for renshi teaching rank at the Kyoto competition and passed that as well. In 1954 I achieved kyoshi rank at the first All-Japan Kendo Federation kyoshi examinations and, unsurprisingly, this time too used a single sword. I do however still perform using the two-sword style at the annual Kyoto competitions to this day.

Looking back on it now, I see that my studies of the two-sword style have not been in vain. I believe it was thanks to my previous study of Miyamoto Musashi's two-sword style that I was able to succeed in demonstrating a model form to the officer cadets using single-handed left and right kesagiri. Whatever one does, the mental approach and attitude you take on a daily basis is vital.

Falling Down While Demonstrating in Front of a Former General

In 1963 the Tokyo Jukendo Federation's yearly tournament was held in Tokyo's Asakusa. As the first-generation head of the All-Japan

Jukendo Federation, His Excellency the former Imperial Army General Imamura Hitoshi was present at this event and His Excellency Araki Sadao was also invited along as an honored guest, leading to the tournament being held in magnificent style.

Celebratory performance at the Yokosuka Land Self-Defense Force base (1963)

Three days prior to this tournament I had injured my left leg in a car accident and was walking with a pronounced limp. However, I had already promised to give a demonstration of the Toyama ryu battojutsu and tameshigiri, and so I pushed myself to perform.

I managed to show left and right kesagiri and mayokogiri (horizontal and descending diagonal cuts) without a hitch, but when it came to performing a rising gyaku giri from the lower left to the upper right, my body weight floated too far up and I fell over. Fortunately I had managed to cut through the target cleanly. The fall was my own fault as, even though I was carrying a leg injury, I had been lax in preparing for putting the hip into the cut. This shows that it is important to practice daily so that one is able to adapt to and deal with any injury.

Miyamoto Musashi is famous for his two-sword niten ichi ryu style. However, in all sixty or so of his challenge matches and duels to the death, he did not fight a single one using two swords. Musashi trained with two swords daily in this manner so that he could fight effectively using the left hand alone were his right to be injured.

Injury to My Left Hand During a Demonstration

In 1968, at the Yokosuka Naval Self-Defense Force Educational Unit Jukendo competition, I was called upon to perform a model demonstration of the fundamental motions of jukendo alongside drill instructor Tanaka Takeyoshi and then to show the audience the Toyama ryu battojutsu and tameshigiri. However, the fact that the start times for the demonstrations were not put up anywhere became the cause of an avoidable failure.

As we had just finished eating a hearty communal lunch, the officer organizing the competition approached and informed me that "Before the afternoon competitors go on, we will have Nakamura sensei's fundamental motions of jukendo demonstration with instructor Tanaka, continuing to the Toyama ryu demonstration." As I had just eaten, I had a bad premonition about how this was going to go.

I still had a bad feeling about it, but proceeded to don my armor alongside instructor Tanaka anyway and got on with the demonstration. Alas, I was still full after eating, and it did not go as well as could be expected.

Moving on to the Toyama ryu demonstration, I still felt in a very poor condition and could tell that as I proceeded with the techniques there was a laxity in my focus. On the final drawing cut of the sequence, my grip on the mouth of the scabbard was off. I pulled the blade across my left hand in the gap between the thumb and index finger, cutting deep into it. Fortunately the blade was stopped on bone but had it been an area where there was no bone beneath, the whole thumb would have been severed at the base. I can still remember the shock of seeing white bone exposed even now, but at the time only wondered whether I would be able to continue practicing iai sword methods at all.

I tried to press on with the demonstration but I was stopped by four or five members of the audience. I had the base of my left arm bound to stop the bleeding and went to the base infirmary but nothing could be done there. I was sent to the Naval Self-Defense Force base precinct hospital in the commander's car. I had twenty-five stitches, but at that time only the cut itself was treated and not the severed tendon, leaving it paralyzed, and I have not been able to move it since.

I was hospitalized for ten days and had lost a lot of blood, so I had to have a transfusion of around 400 cc. After my discharge rumours began to spread that I could no longer practice iai swordsmanship.

Years later I was performing a demonstration for Television Nihon alongside the famous *rakugo* performer, master Yanagiya Kosan. I was exhibiting the Nakamura ryu tameshigiri and master Yanagiya was showing the Omori ryu. At this time I told master Yanagiya about the incident in which I failed after performing on a full stomach, and it turns out that performing after eating is not good for rakugo performers either.

For kendo or indeed any other sport there are almost certainly no competitors who would ever consider going on straight after eating. When one is full after eating one's mental state becomes torpid, and this will lead to failure in general. Failures while holding a live blade are always especially serious and can cause terrible accidents, as both I and the aforementioned commander Nakai who cut into his own leg are keenly aware. We must learn from this and be aware not to repeat such mistakes.

Injury to the Brow While Performing the Ukenagashi Parrying Technique

Another incident occurred when I performed a demonstration alongside some of Matsuo Kenpu sensei's students at a sword exhibition in the Saikaya department store in Kawasaki city. The demonstration was held in an open-air event hall on the roof of the eighth floor. The weather was fine and bright, but winds of around ten miles per hour were blowing across our allotted area.

I proceeded with the demonstration and performed the ukenagashi parrying maneuver from the Omori ryu. I drew my sword and brought it up above my head in a right diagonal cut, but at that very moment the wind picked up and caught the flat of my blade at the ridgeline, blowing it straight into the left side of my brow. The blade only made a superficial cut, but with blood pouring down my face many of the three hundred or so spectators seemed quite shocked. The cut itself was not particularly deep and only needed two stitches

During the performance at the Saikaya department store, due to strong winds the author received a head injury.

to sort out, but this was indeed a most unexpected injury from the sword.

In a sports hall or dojo such a thing could not possibly have occurred but, depending on place and time, one cannot know exactly what will happen and so must always take great care when practicing with live blades.

The Officer Who Cut into His Groin with a Descending Vertical Cut

During the Sino-Japanese War I was an instructor at the former Toshiba Private Youth Academy. At this time Mr. Uchida Masakichi—a former sergeant in the Imperial Army who worked in the logistics division of the Toshiba Tsurumi factory—was active in the campaigns at Woosung Creek in northern China and was even featured in the newspapers. Mr. Uchida was a friend and colleague of four years my junior, and in 1940 he told me the following story that has left a deep impression.

This solemn tale concerns an officer who attempted to strike down an enemy soldier using a single descending vertical cut. However, this officer misjudged his distancing and either had an insufficiently solid grip on the hilt of his sword or did not manipulate his grip properly while striking, leading him only to cut a line down the enemy's face. The blade did not stop due to the momentum of the cut and carried on through its arc to cut into the officer's own groin, inflicting a serious injury.

Mr. Uchida tells of how he can still picture this quite amazing scene, with blood spraying from the enemy soldier's face and the officer rolling around in agony.

I believe that this incident clearly came about because of the officer's diligent suburi practice; repeatedly swinging bokuto and live blades until he could achieve the correct blade angle for cutting vertically without conscious thought. When it came to an actual live conflict situation and he was consumed by the moment, losing rational thought, it is no surprise that he instinctively went to attack with the same descending cut he had been practicing day in day out, rather than a safer and more practical kesagiri. The officer in question had a third dan in kendo at the time and by all accounts was very proud of this.

At this time I was a fourth dan and learned much from my discussions with Mr. Uchida over the integration of kendo and the skills involved in the use of real swords.

When I teach seminars on the Toyama ryu and tameshigiri, I make sure to use this example to educate my students.

In 1937 I began to train in Omori ryu iai under Tsuchiya Seiichi sensei, head of the Tsurumi Butokukan dojo (Tsuchiya sensei unfortunately passed away in 1944 while I was away on campaign) and continue to practice it to this day. When I teach the Omori ryu to students and members of the organization, I make sure to cover techniques from seiza only after having gone through instruction in standing techniques to a suitable level. I have one particular memory related to this.

On one occasion, sometime around 1938, when I had gone to instruct students at the Nippon University kendo club in Tokyo, there was some time left at the end of the session, so I decided that after demonstrating the Toyama ryu iai I would show them the Omori ryu. However, because the floor of the outer room was made of concrete and not suitable for kneeling on I showed the Omori ryu's seated methods adapted as standing techniques.

The late Haga Junichi sensei (student of Nakayama Hakudo sensei) was present at this session and, upon seeing what I was doing, his expression changed to one of surprise. He turned to me and shouted insistently that "The Omori ryu iai does not contain these techniques!" I was taken aback at this, but he was senior to me so I simply backed down and said "I see . . . "

Haga sensei had a strong attachment to the ways of the classical schools and, indeed, he was correct that the official kata of the Omori ryu do not contain any standing techniques, so on reflection this was not an unforeseeable reaction.

Compared to the other classical schools, the Omori ryu is often thought of as being less embellished and more direct and honest when it comes to methods from seiza but, even so, it does not contain a single kata covering the diagonal kesagiri cut, despite this being the most natural and practical technique for actual combat. We have no choice but to consider this a point for which improvement is needed. In order to further the integration of kendo and iaido I would like to see standing techniques afforded a primary place in training regimes, such that they become the main focus of study and practice.

Injuring My Left Hand at the National Soka Gakkai Martial Arts Tournament

All-Japan Soka Gakkai Martial Arts Tournament (held at the Nippon Budokan in 1973)

In 1969 the Soka Gakkai[68] All-Japan Martial Arts Tournament was held at the Nihon Budokan, and both the kendo and judo tournaments were wildly successful. My acquaintance Ooi Tadao sensei, a sixth dan in kendo, was an official in the Soka Gakkai organization and so on his recommendation I was asked to be a judge at the national tournament and also give a special demonstration of Toyama ryu tameshigiri. Ooi sensei was the mediator at my wedding, and his wife is the daughter of former Imperial Navy kyoshi-level kendo instructor Nabatame sensei and a kyoshi-level instructor of the *naginata* in her own right.

---

68. 創価学会; a lay religious movement based in Nichiren Buddhism that was founded in 1930 and grew to become a substantial organization. The name means "The Value Creation Society."

The Soka Gakkai Martial Arts Tournament is the ultimate model on which all the various national tournaments base themselves and to which they all pay attention. The cavernous space of the Nihon Budokan was filled with what must have been around twenty thousand people, and all the participants and spectators came together with one mind, staying in their seats in the assigned blocks throughout the whole event until they were finally dismissed, with not a single competitor even thinking of packing up and going home when they had lost their match. Everyone's actions were taken together as one, and I was greatly moved by this display of group unity.

In most other tournaments one often sees those who have lost their heats selfishly leave the venue before the awards ceremony, leaving only those teams and individuals who have won medals and their associates at the end for a somewhat lonely presentation. I would like for them to learn from the Soka Gakkai tournament in this respect.

The president of the Soka Gakkai, Ikeda Daisaku sensei himself, even participated in the latter half of the competition and, after a demonstration of the Nippon Kendo kata from the late kendo shihan Mr. Tsurumi, I was called up to perform Toyama ryu tameshigiri.

As mentioned above I had previously injured my left hand at a Naval Self-Defense Force competition some years earlier, and had severed the tendons in my left thumb, meaning that on occasion I lose feeling in it. As I was the sole performer out on the expansive Budokan floor I put my all into the performance and freely demonstrated my sword techniques. However, after completing the final sequence—which involved cutting through seven simulated straw targets in succession using alternating kesagiri cuts (a method based on the concept of a rapid charging attack)—I injured the thumb and index finger on my left hand with the tip of my blade as I was sheathing it. I managed to conceal the injury from the spectators and finish the performance without them knowing, but the bleeding was seen by an official from the organization headquarters and I was led off to the Kudan Police department hospital where I was given three stitches.

In this case there was no wavering in my spirit as I performed but, after charging around forty meters while cutting down seven simulated targets, I had built up too great a momentum and sheathed the sword too early, resulting in an injury.

The day after the tournament Ikeda sensei graciously sent to my house a large bouquet of roses and a copy of his fine book, via a representative from the Soka Gakkai head office, as a gesture of his condolences to the injured. I was deeply touched and moved and was most embarrassed that I could only return the gesture by humbly offering him a copy of my own book *Iai kendo*.

I later heard from the permanent director of the Budokan, Miura sensei, that Ikeda sensei had apparently remarked on how he "would like to practice iai as it was performed in that demonstration." Miura sensei also gifted President Ikeda with a mogito long sword. I am deeply humbled and moved by Ikeda sensei's kindness and consideration.

CHAPTER 14

A LIFE OF TAMESHIGIRI AND A RECORD OF THE RESTORATION OF THE HAYASHIZAKI IAI SHRINE

A Record of My Experiences with Iai and Tameshigiri

SAVED BY ONE'S ART—FROM CONSCRIPTION TO DEMOBILIZATION

I received the draft order for the second time in July 1941 at the special maneuvers of the Kanto Army and was recruited into the Eighteenth Northern Unit (formerly the Thirty-Second Yamagata Infantry Regiment) of the Imperial Army. As I was joining up, a new regiment was being formed and we were sent to Beian in Manchuria's Heihe province (now Heilongjiang province in China), proceeding to Shenwutun the next year to secure the border between the Soviet Union and Manchuria.

An interdivisional kenjutsu tournament had been held for some years leading up to this time between the Aomori, Akita, and former eighth Yamagata divisions. Alas the Yamagata regiment had already been badly defeated twice.

The author in front of the Hayashizaki Iai Shrine (1972).

The incumbent Yamagata unit commander was a man completely uninterested in swordsmanship, and although I was dissatisfied with the current state of kendo instruction in the unit, I had been discharged after my first period of service and was not directly involved in the military again until my second conscription in 1941. My military rank was only that of lance corporal and there was nothing that could be done.

After my first discharge in 1935 I had become an instructor at a youth academy (teaching kendo and jukendo) and also received instruction at the Toyama Military Academy for such a role. By the time I joined up again I had already been awarded a fifth dan renshi certification in kendo and a fourth dan kyoshi certification in jukendo, but there was not a single senior officer who would accept me for this.

However, things changed suddenly in 1942 when Battalion Commander Shindo Iwao was transferred to the unit, and from then on kenjutsu instruction was widely promoted and encouraged.

I was assigned the rank of lance corporal and assistant kenjutsu instructor and devoted myself to the instruction of the regiment as a whole. I moved between the various units teaching military sword handling to the officers, bayonet drills to the lower-ranked noncommissioned officers, and short-sword techniques to the special companies.

This spurred the various companies to put greater effort into kenjutsu instruction, and the exceptional practitioners from each of them were put forward for grading under the auspices of the regiment, being awarded grades between shodan and fifth dan. The level of enthusiasm and dedication to swordsmanship among the companies was quite something.

At this time there was no other battalion that awarded dan grades within its ranks, and those yudansha were graded based on the rules laid out in the *Kendo kyohan*[69] not only on stance, posture, and attitude but also on the propriety of all their actions before and after donning

---

69. A standard text for the instruction of kendo.

their armor. In particular, attention was paid to how they affixed the mask. This led to great overall improvements in technique. In preparation for the interdivisional tournament in the autumn of 1942, we held numerous company-, battalion-, and regiment-level competitions, and commander Shindo formulated a plan he called the "special strategy for obtaining victory in the divisional tournament."

Putting the commander's plan into action, the whole regiment saw a peak in the fervor of their enthusiasm for kenjutsu and, when the tournament came, none of the other units presented the slightest problem to our competitors. The competition ended in a crushing victory for Yamagata, with a difference of eighty-five points over the closest opposition. The division commander, Lieutenant General Uemura Mikio, gave us the following words of praise: "This difference in scores has not been seen since the army was founded!" This approval magnificently swept away the dishonor of the unit's previous defeats.

At the beginning of 1944 commander Shindo was transferred again, this time to the Hamamatsu Air Squadron's heavy bomber academy, and we bade him farewell.

Battalion commander Shindo Iwao (northern Manchuria 1943)

In Shenwutun in northern Manchuria; the author is at the far right of the front row. The photograph inscription reads," To commemorate victory at the 1944 interdivisional kenjutsu tournament."

念記勝優會大術劍團倒愛年九十和昭

Around that time the situation on the Southern Front was looking uncertain, and so the Second Yamashita Special Attack Unit made a large-scale movement, advancing to the south. I myself was reassigned to the southern advance on no less than three separate occasions in 1944, but on each occasion, when going to report to the unit commander, it was ordered that I be swapped out and someone else be sent in my stead. It was my role as a special swordsmanship instructor that prevented me from going to the Southern Front.

During my service I won the divisional kenjutsu tournament three times and on February 11, 1945, on the occasion of the Empire Day celebrations, I received the honor of being presented with a medal in front of the military standard.

In April of the same year, 1945, the fourth Manchurian Army kenjutsu competition was due to be held, and I trained diligently to prepare for it. However, the tournament was abruptly cancelled during my training. Top-secret orders were sent in preparation for the final battle for the homeland, instructing that we leave just a small garrison in Shenwutun and return to Japan. On March 15, the main unit left our base and traveled from southern Manchuria, through Korea, to the port of Rajin where we boarded freight ships bound for Hakata in northern Kyushu, arriving on April 4.

Soon after arriving around 20 percent of the unit were struck down with dysentery, and I myself was sent to the second Imperial Army hospital and quarantined. I was discharged from the hospital after about a month and at the same time received the order to move around Fukuoka prefecture and instruct the civilian volunteer militia units in sword handling and the *hitori hissatsu* [sure killing of a single enemy] ideology for the bamboo spear patrols. During this period of traveling around the units with my three assistants, I finally saw out the end of the War at the Tatara junior school.

Looking back at these events I come to the conclusion that it was due to my role as a special kenjutsu instructor that I was spared assignment to the southern advance. My art very much saved me when I needed it, and thinking about it now I owe my life to Commander Shindo, who created the opportunity for me to become a swordsmanship instructor.

MEMORIES OF SLAUGHTERING THREE COWS WITH A SWORD AT THE END OF THE WAR

As mentioned above, at the end of March 1945, my unit was reassigned for the final battle for the homeland and traveled in cargo trucks from Heihe province to Rajin in Korea and then on to Kyushu. There were not sufficient cargo ships to transport the whole regiment, so during transit we were packed in at three times the usual crew capacity of the vessels and had to move the men in shifts between the interior of the ship and the deck each day and night. On deck there was driving rain and, when the winds were up, freezing spray from the ocean as well. The Sea of Japan is bitterly cold in March and April, and I felt somewhat less than alive during that voyage.

The captains of the transport vessels were wary of attacks from enemy bombers and submarines, so we did not travel directly across the Genkai Sea and instead used an indirect route that took four days from Rajin until we berthed in northern Kyushu.

I had smuggled a camera on board and took a picture from the top deck showing the overcrowding on the inside of the vessel. In 1974 I submitted this photograph to the *Weekly Asahi* magazine's "Pictures from our home in Meiji, Taisho, and Showa" section, and was even asked by one of the magazine's journalists whether "the deck was carpeted with charcoal."[70] I believe that there will be some readers out there who have seen this picture in *Weekly Asahi*.

---

70. The journalist was perhaps referring to the numerous rounded crops of short-cut black hair on the tightly packed soldiers, which would have looked from above like many lumps of charcoal.

There is one particular story that I would like to share, from that same April [the 28th] concerning events that I witnessed at the end of the War from the Tatara junior school.

At the time our regiment kept three cows, and when the War ended there were calls for us to give these as a gift to the civilian population. One private first class named Sato, who was talented in the preparation of pork and beef dishes, approached me and propositioned that if I could behead the cows, he would cook and prepare them for the men and the civilians to eat.

I made sure he was serious and asked him if he would really be happy with doing all the preparation, and he told me with conviction that he would take full responsibility for preparing the meat and so I should not worry. I resolved to behead the cows there and then.

Captain Ichihara opposed the proposal but despite this, Private First Class Sato, three others and I made our preparations for the slaughter. As cows are large and muscular beasts, I reckoned that it would be problematic if I could not cleanly behead them with a single decisive stroke. We prepared a rope and took the first one up to the mountains, bound its head and torso to a pair of pine trees, and I got ready to make the cut. Using a 2 shaku, 3 sun, and 5 bu Shin Shinto–period sword (a nameless blade) from my personal possessions, I took up a wide stance and raised the blade to a high guard before bringing it down with full commitment and coordination of sword, body, and spirit.

The blade cut through the spine and down to the aorta, cleaving through three-quarters of the neck. Blood gushed out like a waterfall, and the creature expired with less convulsing and thrashing than I had expected. We had some trouble unfastening the head and torso ropes but soon took the carcass back down to ground level before Private First Class Sato set to work processing it.

He started by cutting straight down from the chest area to the stomach and then peeled away just the skin, spreading it out like a towel and leaving the bones laying on top while he sorted the organs to the right and the meat to the left. I was very surprised at how cleanly he had butchered the cow. We wrapped the bone and organs in the skin, dug a hole to bury them in the ground, and then distributed half of the meat to the company and half to the local settlement. At this time beef was very difficult to get hold of, and so the gift was received with much joy from everyone.

That night the meat turned up on my plate as beef stew, but I could not get the image of blood gushing from the severed neck out of my head from when I killed the beast. It still smelled of blood, so I just could not get any down my throat and did not eat in the end.

To kill the second cow I borrowed a military-issue sword from the platoon commander (a Shinto-period blade of just over 2 shaku and 2 sun). This time we did not bind the torso and just tied a shorter string to the pine tree, although the cut itself was made in exactly the same manner as before. After the first blow the cow's front legs snapped and it pitched forward, but I managed to sever the head with a second cut.

Private First Class Sato proceeded to process the carcass of the second beast with help from three other soldiers, and this time we offered the meat up to regimental headquarters, who were also very happy with it.

We went out the next day for the third cow, and I was approached by a junior officer cadet who proffered a newly forged military sword (of 2 shaku, 2 sun, and 3 bu) that he had had sent up from his home-town before the War ended and asked if I could use it to kill the final animal. I agreed and made the cut, which was performed in the same way as for the second cow.

As the sword impacted on bone, I felt my tenouchi going awry and the monouchi of the blade chipped, driving home the brittleness of many modern forged blades.

In this way we successfully slaughtered all three of the cows, although had Private First Class Sato not approached me in the first place I do not think I would ever have considered doing it.

The postwar period has seen an iaido revival, and the art has experienced a big rise in popularity, spreading to a level even greater than before the conflict. However, with regard to the proper handling of the sword, I thoroughly recommend the unification of iai practice with tameshigiri. I would be most pleased if readers would learn from this episode in which I cut down three cows at the end of the War and apply its lessons in their own training.

A Kendo Fanatic and Those Who Supported Him

The Founding of the Tsurumi Shiseikan Dojo

After I was demobilized, the Toshiba Private Youth Academy that employed me was broken up and reorganized. I found myself engaged in cultivating company-owned land for agriculture. I had no previous experience of farm work and was not good at it, so at the end of 1946 I resigned my post and entrusted this task to my comrade in swordsmanship and friend from the same prefecture, Mr. Adachi Kyutaro, who did have agricultural experience. At this juncture I started up the Nakamura Trading Company and began dealing in black market goods, although I very much had an amateurish "warrior's head for business."[71]

In the autumn of 1947 my comrade in swordsmanship, Mr. Nakamura Shigeo, who would later become the headmaster of a primary school, visited my residence, and we decided to train together for the first time in two years since the end of the War. We decided to practice

---

71. 武士商法 (Bushi no shoho); literally "warrior business management." A Japanese saying that originates in the late Edo and early Meiji period when samurai families lost their stipends and hereditary class privileges and had to take up regular employment. As they had been provided for by the state for centuries, it is unsurprising that most had little aptitude for business, making this a byword for poor and inexperienced management.

in the earthen-floored room inside the Inari shrine just in front of my home, but as we went to get out my old armor we were shocked to find that it was being used as a mouse's nest. Four mice jumped out from inside the breastplate and scurried away.

This armor was a special, finest-quality set that I had acquired from the Shobudo kendo shop in Tokyo's Itabashi during my time as an instructor at the youth academy before the War. I had not maintained this set of armor for two years since demobilization and had largely forgotten about kendo while I was absorbed in the everyday business of buying up rice and potatoes.

While it was fortuitous that I had managed to restart kendo training with my comrade Nakamura, the armor was alas worn out and rendered useless within two or three months.

Using that training as a springboard I borrowed space at a nearby warehouse and began teaching again with seven or eight students. We were mentioned in the Communist Party's news posters, but I paid this no heed. After a while of training once or twice a week, we had a successful group going.

There was a group of four or five large houses nestled between the Tokaido and Keihin express lines at what is now the Keihin express Kagetsuenmae Station, and in 1949 one of these houses was destroyed in an outbreak of fire. The owners had problems getting together insurance money and so eventually the courts repossessed the property. I negotiated with the courts and convinced them to sell me the land, coming to own 265 square meters of burned-out ruins.

Soon after buying that land, Japan was hit by Typhoon Kitty and much damage was caused in various regions. I bought up two trucks' worth of timber from the housing that was blown down and from old stock in warehouses and, supplementing it with some new timber, built a dojo of around 106 square meters and a house of 66 square meters.

At this time the new Kagetsuen Cycle Race Arena was under construction nearby, and so I came up with the idea of making money from the spectators who would come to the track. I closed down

Nakamura Trading and started up a sushi restaurant, although I had no experience with running such a business. Japan had been defeated in the War but was trying to push on and rebuild, with the spirit of the nation symbolized by the national flag, the *hinomaru*, so I decided to name my shop Hinomaru Sushi. My dojo I named the Tsurumi Shiseikan Dojo.

Soon after this the Zen Nihon Shinai Kyogi Renmei [All-Japan Competitive Shinai Fencing Federation] was founded, with Sasamori Junzo sensei as its head and, in October 1950, the first All-Japan Competitive Shinai Fencing Tournament was held in the city of Nagoya. I participated in this competition representing Kanagawa prefecture, and it was particularly memorable for me as the first tournament I had entered since the end of the War.

The Shiseikan was the first dojo founded postwar, and training there flourished with visits from many august instructors and masters. First and foremost was Nakamura Hakudo sensei; followed by five or six masters from Tokyo, such as Ono Jussei sensei, Shibata Mansaku sensei, Kono Magosaburo sensei, and Haga Junichi sensei; several from Yokohama, such as Yokomatsu Katsusaburo sensei, Ono Seizo sensei, Ono Otosaburo sensei, Konakazawa Tatsuo sensei, and Kono Takeshi sensei; and also many others from Yokosuka and Hiratsuka.

In 1950 the Mito Tobukan dojo (headed by Kono Takeshi sensei) was created as a judicial foundation. Continuing from there, in the next year of 1951, the first kendo tournament to be held in Kanagawa prefecture since the end of the War took place at my Shiseikan dojo, with the Mayor of Yokohama, Hiranuma Ryozo, as chairman. Thanks to the cooperation and efforts of the various sensei who lent their support, the tournament was very successful.

SELLING MY DOJO FROM BEING A GUARANTOR ON A LOAN

In 1952, just as preparations were underway for the founding of the All-Japan Kendo Federation, I was hit by a most unfortunate event.

Back in 1948, Mr. Hayashi Seiichi had borrowed one million yen from Mr. Sano Namio as capital to found his small business, the limited company he named Hayashi Industries, and I agreed to be the guarantor on that loan. Due to poor luck the company folded within a year, and Mr. Hayashi disappeared and was not seen again. As guarantor it fell to me to repay the money, and in 1952 I had no choice but to sell the Shiseikan and Hinomaru Sushi to settle the debts. However, soon after that a demand for the payment of capital gains tax arrived. I stormed into the Tsurumi ward tax office and demanded to know what was meant by being charged tax on top of having lost everything as a guarantor. There followed many hours of negotiations but in the end the law is the law and, after my wife had repeatedly submitted numerous petitions, the period of limitation was set for 1956. This whole incident really did put my wife through a lot of stress and trouble.

Nakamura Trading had closed down and in order to make sure my family had somewhere to live, make ends meet, and repay all the debts, we had to move house within Tsurumi ward seven times between the founding of my dojo in 1949 and 1970. This upheaval put a massive burden on my wife, and I am greatly ashamed that this was all because of my clumsy "warrior's head for business."

I thanked my wife every day for her commitment and support during this period, but my life was secretly dedicated to the sword. In 1958 I won the individual event at the second All-Japan Jukendo Championships. (The kendo championships that same year saw the victory of Mr. Nakamura Taro for the second time in a row.). The situation at home with my family was poor and times harsh, but we kept firmly in mind the virtue of enduring and putting up with hardship. Thanks to this, I was able to follow through and dedicate myself wholly to the martial spirit, something that was possible only because I had support from those around me.

In the May 1979 edition of *Kendo Nihon* there was published a photograph of my comrade in swordsmanship, Mr. Asakawa Haruo (chairman of the Dojo Federation), entitled "a kendo fanatic." This

The author along-
side his wife, Chieko,
at the celebrations
for his award of
the hanshi title in
jukendo (1973)

picture was taken to commemorate his victory at the All-Japan Championships and showed Asakawa posing next to his wife. When I saw
this photograph on the pages of the magazine, I strongly felt that it
was the support from his wife that had allowed Asakawa to achieve
what he did.

I believe that there are many sensei among the martial artists of
Japan who live their lives dedicated wholly to kendo while neglecting their wives. Police department kendo shihan and their assistant
instructors make their living from kendo, so this is somewhat understandable for them, but for the majority of regular kendo enthusiasts
I observe many who, due to their fanaticism for the art, are surely
given grief by wives who do not understand their passion.

That Japan's traditional way of the sword has spread out to all
nations of the world is something for which we owe great thanks to
the unseen support of our wives.

A Record of the Restoration of the Hayashizaki Iai Shrine

THE ORIGINATOR OF IAI, LORD HAYASHIZAKU JINSUKE SHIGENOBU

In the Hayashizaki district of the town of Murayama in Yamagata
prefecture stands the Hayashizaki Iai Shrine, one of Japan's regis-
tered places of Shinto worship. Iaido [battojutsu] enthusiasts from
all around the nation come to this shrine to petition the kami for
improvements in their technique. Before the Meiji era this shrine was
dedicated to Hayashizaki Myoshin and combined with the Kumano
Shrine, but in 1961 was renamed with its current title.

According to one theory, over four hundred years and many
decades ago, Lord Hayashizaki Jinsuke Shigenobu, known as the
originator of iai, witnessed his father being slain. At the time he was
only six years old and still bore his childhood name of Tamijimaru.

The Hayashizaki Iai Shrine building (completed in 1961)

The young man petitioned Hayashizaki Myoshin for his revenge on the killer, three times a day for a thousand days, and on the night of a full moon received divine wisdom in a dream and was bestowed with the sword-drawing techniques of battojutsu. Another theory from the time says that he was not gifted with techniques suitable for the modern sword hilt but with advantageous methods for using long-handled swords. At that time it was said that longer-handled swords gave an advantage from the point of view of combative distance and were thus better suited to actual combat.

From this divine revelation Lord Shigenobu received inspiration for the techniques of iai and, through his own efforts and experimentation, founded his school of *iaijutsu*, naming it Hayashizaki Muso ryu and thus becoming the originator of the art.

The story as told then has it that at age eighteen, Lord Shigenobu used the techniques of iai that were bestowed upon him by the kami to achieve his revenge.

After succeeding in his vengeance, Lord Shigenobu went to give thanks to Hayashizaki Myoshin and offered up a sword forged by the renowned smith Nobukuni, which he had used to settle the vendetta. From then on he wandered the various provinces of the country on a pilgrimage of warrior training and spread his iai swordsmanship far and wide.

The following poem remains engraved on the shrine to this day:

A thousand swings in practice; I receive the merit of the deity,
To be passed down for ten thousand generations.

By Hayashizaki Shigenobu,
fourth year of Eiroku [1558–1570].

The verse dedicated to the shrine's kami.

The shrine also has a grand plaque dedicated to the kami, with the inscription "Warrior of Mito prefecture and fourth-generation head of the Muso ryu Hasegawa Takusuke, August, fourteenth year of Genroku [1688–1704]."

With regard to Lord Shigenobu's later years we have records of him in the third year of Genwa [1615–1624] at the age of seventy-three, leaving the house of Takamatsu Kanbei in Musashi province's Kawagoe before heading for Oushu,[72] but after that it is unclear where he went or where he died. There are many historical references to the life and activities of Lord Shigenobu, but I will not go into them here.

The teachings of iaido in the modern era have split and branched into many different ryuha, such as the Shinmyo Muso ryu, the Muso Jikiden Eishin ryu, the Hayashizaki ryu, the Shigenobu ryu, the Tamiya

---

72. A province that includes modern-day Fukushima, Miyagi, Iwate, Aomori, and Akita prefectures.

ryu, the Omori ryu, and the Hoki ryu, alongside many others that are still extant today.

YAMADA SABURO SENSEI AND THE FIRST CALL TO RESTORE THE SHRINE

Between the Edo period and the abolition of sword wearing in Meiji, the Hayashizaki Iai Shrine covered an area of around 6,620 square meters and was prosperous, thanks to the visits made by daimyo and warriors training in iai who petitioned the kami for improvements in their technique and made offerings.

When the *haitorei* edict forbidding the wearing of swords was passed [in 1876], everyone got caught up in the feeling that the age of the sword had ended. Because the incumbent chief priest[73] at the time was not sufficiently aware of the importance of the Hayashizaki Iai Shrine, its land was sold off. On top of that the treasured Nobukuni sword used by lord Hayashizaki Shigenobu to extract his revenge was sold for a mere twenty yen to one Sawaguchi Matazo from the Tateoka district. For a while the blade passed through the hands of many antique dealers, but its whereabouts were soon lost.

That the treasured Nobukuni blade, symbol of the Iai Shrine, was exchanged for the living costs of a single head priest is an insult to the kami, and I cannot contain my anger at this sacrilege. After the War the incumbent head priest, Oshikiri, tried determinedly to locate the blade's whereabouts, and I hear that he traveled from Hokkaido to Kyushu to follow up on any information.

My own first encounter with this shrine goes back to the spring of 1944. While stationed in Shenwutun in northern Manchuria's Heihe province, I braved the biting Manchurian cold and recklessly continued to instruct my students in swordsmanship. As a result of these exertions I developed a hernia and was hospitalized in the regimental infirmary. While recovering I chanced upon a copy of the book *Nihon*

---

73. The office of *guji* [宮司].

kendo shi (*A History of Japanese Kendo*, written by Imperial Navy kendo shihan Hori Masahira and published in 1934) and saw in its pages a photograph captioned "The originator of iai's Iai Shrine in Akita province's Higashine." At the time I thought to myself that this was strange as Higashine is in Yamagata prefecture and not neighbouring Akita, but as I was currently on duty in the Imperial Army the matter was put aside for the time being.

After demobilization I remembered the book and, after looking further into the matter, I discovered that the shrine was not in Yamagata's Higashine but actually in the neighbouring town of Tateoka (part of the modern-day town of Murayama). As I am a native of that prefecture and also an iai practitioner, I decided to visit the shrine. I also wished to show my devotion to the deity venerated by the shrine at my Shiseikan dojo. I made my visit in June of 1951. (In the published version of my book *Iai kendo,* this visit is dated as 1952, but that is incorrect.) When I arrived the shrine looked to be in a state of disrepair, as if it were being used as a store cupboard, and the kami was being treated as though it were little more than a minor village deity.

The head priest at that time, the late Oshikiri, was still lively and hale despite his more than seventy years, and he graciously put me up for a night when I asked him about the state of the shrine.

During my discussions with Oshikiri we talked about finding a way to restore the shrine, and it was posited that we should perhaps put off seeking the return of the treasured Nobukuni sword for the time being and concentrate instead on restoring the shrine building itself to its deserved glory. I made an important decision to aid in the restoration project however I could and became the elderly priest's right-hand man. With the words "to be passed down for ten thousand generations" from the verse by Lord Hayashizaki Shigenobu, my exalted senior predecessor and kinsman from the same prefecture, firmly in my mind, I set off to begin the campaign.

I first went to discuss the matter with the prefectural governor and headed to the prefectural government offices. It was at this point that I discovered that Yamada Saburo sensei, one of Yamagata's town councillors, was originally from Shikoku[74] and a veteran practitioner of the Tanimura branch of the Muso Jikiden ryu of iai. The very next day at around noon, I performed a demonstration of iai, battojutsu, and tameshigiri in the plaza in front of the prefectural offices after an initial speech from Yamada sensei, and this marked the beginning of the campaign to restore the Hayashizaki Iai Shrine.

From then on, every year I returned to demonstrate at the prefectural offices alongside the priest Oshikiri, and also performed public martial arts demonstrations at the Kamiyama Agricultural College Middle School and other venues, as well as lecturing in many places.

In the next year, 1952, my senior colleague, Matsuo Kenpu sensei, organized and held the All-Japan Iaido Tournament at the Matsuzakaya department store in Tokyo. This event was attended by over fifty august dignitaries, starting with Prime Minister Ikeda and including Oono Kumao sensei, Kouno Hyakuren sensei, Sano Shigenori sensei, and Ikeda Kojun sensei, and was the largest tournament since the end of the War. After staying a night at the Kudan Kaikan, those dignitaries that wished to made a visit to the Hayashizaki Iai Shrine on the way home, and to this day I can still picture the joy that this interest brought out in head priest Oshikiri.

After the visit to the shrine everyone stayed a night in the Zaimokusakaeya *ryokan*[75] at the Kamiyama hot springs complex and then dispersed before the gathering dragged on too long.

Over a decade later Matsuo sensei dedicated a stone plaque to the shrine, written by the first-generation head of the All-Japan Iaido Federation, Ikeda Hayato sensei and bearing the inscription *shinken* [心剣; sword of the heart and mind]. Being involved in such momentous events gave me many cherished memories.

---

74. Shikoku is noted for an abundance of iai practitioners and dojo.
75. A traditional kind of Japanese travelers' accomodation.

In 1961, ten years after the first voices in the shrine restoration campaign were raised at the Yamagata prefectural offices, a new steel-reinforced shrine building was finally completed thanks to the efforts and cooperation of iaido practitioners from around the nation. However, there is no sadness that can compare to the passing of head priest Oshikiri a mere three years prior to that completion.

DEDICATION OF A PLAQUE TO THE SHRINE BY FORMER IMPERIAL ARMY GENERAL HIS EXCELLENCY THE LATE ARAKAWA SADAO

In 1964, the *beiju* [eighty-eighth birthday] celebrations for the late Arakawa Sadao sensei were held in Tokyo's Chinzanso hall, with around one thousand celebrated dignitaries in attendance, headed by the late former prime minister Sato Eisaku. (He later died aged ninety-three while on a lecturing trip to Nara.)

Arakawa sensei had seen my Toyama ryu tameshigiri twice before on video, and so I was requested to perform a demonstration at the celebrations.

I was later graciously gifted with a plaque bearing my own name and the inscription *shinsei kenchoku* [心正剣直; righteous heart made straight and true through the sword] from Arakawa sensei, and I humbly requested that he do me the great honor of writing another

The author at the home of Araki Sadao sensei (1963)

to dedicate to the kami at the Hayashizaki Iai Shrine.

Arakawa sensei wrote the motto *Shinken hyakuja wo harau* [神剣百邪拂; the divine sword sweeps away a hundred evils] on a piece of embellished card and promised to write the calligraphy on a large plaque and dedicate it to the shrine at a later date, but alas he passed away before this could be done. There is a plaque bearing this inscription currently enshrined at the Hayashizaki Iai Shrine, but I penned it myself in Arakawa sensei's place. In the near future I intend to get a proper one carved from wood and dedicate it to the kami there.

Araki Sadao sensei's *beiju* (eighty-eighth birthday) celebrations in 1964. The central figure is Prime Minister Sato.

Araki Sadao sensei's plaque, reads *Shinken hyakuja wo harau* [神剣百邪払 the divine sword sweeps away a hundred evils], penned in Araki sensei's stead by the author.

THE DEDICATION OF THE DIVINE VESSEL

To celebrate the passing of my sixtieth birthday in 1973, I published the sister volumes of *Iaido* and *Iai kendo*. I am not skilled in letters and this was the first time I had published a book, so I decided to simply collect together my life experiences and let them tell their tale.

When I came to publish my books Hatta Ichiro sensei, chairman of the Zen Nihon Jukendo Renmei, and Shoji Munemitsu sensei, first-generation chairman of the Zen Nihon Kendo Renmei, graciously wrote recommendations for me, and I cannot express my gratitude at the honor that this brought me.

Event commemorating the publishing of the author's previous works, *Iaido* and *Iai kendo* (1973 at the Tsurumi Kaikan).

The divine vessel, portrait of Lord Hayashizaki Jinsuke

On April 14 that year a celebration was held to mark the publication, and it was supported by many fine masters. The dignitaries were headed by Inoue Seiichiro sensei and included Nomura Noboru sensei (chairman of the Tsurumi ward kendo federation and its chief executive of the board), Hatta Ichiro sensei (chairman of the Zen Nihon Jukendo Renmei), Sasaki Kiyoo sensei (chief secretary of the Zen Nihon Jukendo Renmei), and Tabata Shigeyoshi sensei. During the celebrations I came upon the idea of dedicating a divine vessel to the Hayashizaki Iai Shrine and requested a piece from the renowned sculptor Kawabe Hidekuni.

The form the vessel would take was copied from the venerated figure shown in a portrait depicting the originator of iai, Lord Hayashizaki Jinsuke Shigenobu, in his later years and has him holding a jewel to symbolize his enlightenment through the way of budo. It was dedicated to the Rinzenji Temple in Hayashizaki at the end of the Edo era. The sculpting of the divine vessel was a work that Kawabe sensei put his heart and soul into.

Finally, on August 18, 1973, over two hundred local people gathered for the dedication ceremony, which was led by mayor Yuuki of Murayama. The ceremony for the interment of the divine spirit was carried out with ritual prayer from the Hayashizaki Iai Shrine's new head priest Iida, and afterward I performed a hono enbu dedicated to the shrine's kami. The event was a great success.

Thanks to the success of the dedication ceremony and the support of the Murayama Office of Industry and Tourism, I was featured

The author's appearance on Yamagata Television Broadcasting's "Saturday Wide Yamagata" in 1973, marking the enshrinement of the divine vessel at the Hayashizaki Iai Shrine. The person second from the left is the shrine's head priest Iida.

on Yamagata Television Broadcasting's "Saturday Wide Yamagata" program alongside head priest Iida. I believe that this exposure has doubtlessly spread awareness of the Hayashizaki Iai Shrine among the people of the prefecture.

THE COMPLETION OF THE IAI SHINBUKAN INC. BUILDING AND THE ERECTION OF THE STONE TABLET

On November 4, 1979, as part of the memorial celebrations marking the 450 years since the birth of Lord Hayashizaki Shigenobu, originator of iai, a ceremony marking the completion of the Iai Shinbukan foundation building was carried out.

The creation of this building was conceived when the former head of the shrine support association, Okuyama Hirasaburo sensei, passed away and Mr. Osao Nobuharu became the head priest. At this time 1,324 square meters of land to the eastern side of the complex was dedicated to the shrine. Mayor Ooto of Murayama took command and organized the building work, showing great dedication and giving much valued support to the cause. It is thanks to him and to the support of many iai and kendo organizations from around the country that we finally came to see the dojo building's completion.

As well as its value for educating our youth and raising them in the principles of the martial spirit, the efforts in establishing the shinbukan are also a reassuring bulwark for the fostering and promotion of iai and battojutsu and the spirit of the Japanese sword.

Furthermore, to mark the completion of the shinbukan building, it was decided that a stone plaque marked with the motto *hyakuren jitoku* [long and constant practice leads to one's mastery] should be commissioned and dedicated to the shrine under the name of the speaker of the House of Representatives, Kouno Kenzo sensei. This was done to petition the kami for the continued development and promulgation of the sword arts and for the glory and prosperity of the shrine itself, and was made possible through the cooperation and support of all

The calligraphy *hyakuren jitoku* (long and constant practice leads to one's mastery) is engraved on the stone plaque to commemorate the completion of the shinbukan dojo at the Hayashizaki Iai Shrine (Spring 1980).

members of the All-Japan Toyama ryu Iaido Federation.

The warrior's first and most fundamental art is the use of a sharp-bladed sword to decide between life and death, and so all theory and reason are of no use to him, continuous forging of the martial spirit being his foremost concern.

This principle is not limited to iaido or kendo, and in academic study or any other endeavor the four characters of *hyakuren jitoku* represent the true path of learning and personal improvement. I would be most glad if this lesson were to be passed down and taken to heart by future generations. The unveiling ceremony for the stone plaque is scheduled for March 1, 1980.

THE NOBUKUNI BLADE IS FINALLY FOUND

After the treasured sword that Lord Shigenobu used to avenge his father was sold off, all knowledge of its whereabouts was lost. I have already mentioned above how the head priest Oshikiri searched for it with a dedication so great he even sought the blade in his dreams.

In his last years Oshikiri gave up on finding the sword but, through a strange twist of fate, its whereabouts became known while I was preparing my books *Iaido* and *Iai kendo* for publication. I was sent a picture of the Nobukuni blade and later displayed this same picture in a magazine. The sword turned out to be in the possession of the Zen priest Okuyama Kan (resident in Akamatsu in Okura village of Yamagata prefecture's Saijo district), a master in the Hayashizaki ryu of Konno Nenosuke sensei (resident in Murayama city's Hon Iita) who is the father of my comrade in swordsmanship and fellow son of Yamagata, Takashashi Mitsuo (resident in Tokyo's Suginami ward).

These three things—not only the restoration of the shrine but also the rediscovery of the relic sword, and the fact that it was still in the safe keeping of a fellow son of Yamagata—must have delighted the late head priest Oshikiri as he watched on from beneath the grass.

It is said that the Nobukuni sword was a gift from the Ashikaga Shogun and was a treasured heirloom passed down in the Hayashizaki family.

When Jinsuke used it to achieve his vengeance, the length of the Nobukuni forged sword was 3 shaku and 3 sun with the tang at 8 sun. It was also said at the time that the sword had an especially long hilt of 1 shaku and 5 sun.

After he got his revenge, Lord Hayashizaki went on a long warrior pilgrimage across the country and, through his training and practice of swordsmanship, came to shorten the blade to 2 shaku, 9 sun, and 2 bu in the second year of Keicho [1591]. He is said to have finally dedicated the sword to the shrine in the second or third year of Genwa [1616 or 1617], and it is for this reason that the Nobukuni blade currently bears no inscription. (This information was taken from the personal library of Yamagata prefecture's Konno Nenosuke sensei).

The author in Nara

CHAPTER 15

VARIOUS ANECDOTES CONCERNING TAMESHIGIRI

Musashi and Kojiro's Duel on Ganryu Island

Yoshikawa Eiji's novelization of the life of "sword saint" Miyamoto Musashi is exceptionally famous and well known.

Musashi was the founder of the Niten Ichi ryu of swordsmanship and author of works such as *Gorin no sho* [The Book of Five Rings] and *Dokkodo* [The Book of Individual Action]. He also left to the world many fine artifacts such as paintings, sculptures, and the *namako* style of sword guard.

However, I have some reservations about his words in *Gorin no sho* that "through being able to defeat one man or ten men it is possible to defeat one thousand or ten thousand men" and personally believe these words to be fanciful.

It may be presumptuous for me to write critically about a revered legend such as Musashi here, and in doing so I may well have to bear the anger of those dedicated to him and his depiction in Yoshikawa's novel—but novels are, after all, just novels. Fiction writers try to capture an audience's imagination, dramatizing the events the story is modelled on and writing them as if they were fact. Accordingly, novels are not fact in and of themselves.

Around 1952 or 1953 I discovered an extensive collection of documents in my hometown relating to the life of Lord Hayashizaki Jinsuke Shigenobu. Many of the popular tales of the lives of master swordsmen were largely based on novels or other stories, and so I asked the three greatest writers of epic swordsmanship novels, Yoshikawa Eiji sensei,

Nakayama Yoshihide sensei, and Shibata Renzaburo sensei, if they would adapt these documents into a novel about Lord Hayashizaki. Nakayama sensei always said to me that "As one would expect, an honest historical document will not make for a good novel." Although, having said that, in April 1956 he did publish an adaptation of it under the title *Zokushin kengoden [Continuing New Tales of Master Swordsmen]*, through Shinchosha Publishing, that changed some of the historical details. Yoshikawa Eiji sensei also produced a work based on that same documentation entitled *Ken no shikunshi [Four Virtuous Men of the Sword]*, published under Togensha Publishing.

It is apparently also true in Miyamoto Musashi's case that the events of his life are not represented in the novels about him exactly as they occurred in reality. In 1951 I attended the National All-Schools Martial Arts Tournament held in the outer gardens of the Meiji Shrine for the first time since the end of the War. On this occasion I was joined in discussion by many august martial arts masters, including the eighteenth inheritor of Miyamoto Musashi's Niten Ichi ryu, Aoki sensei (a native of Kumamoto prefecture and kendo instructor to the Taiwanese police department before the War) and Kunii sensei of the Kashima shinryu. The main focus of this conversation was the famous duel to the death on Ganryu Island between Miyamoto Musashi and Sasaki Kojiro.

According to what Aoki sensei said, the duel itself did actually happen, but what is not often mentioned is that there was a considerable age gap between Musashi and Kojiro when they fought, with Musashi being in his prime at twenty-eight years old and Kojiro, who by this time was known as Sasaki Ganryu, being a venerable seventy-one.

Aoki sensei laughed at how Yoshikawa Eiji sensei had ignored these facts and dramatized the events in his novel, and this brings to mind many points in the story as it is widely told that do not quite sit right with me.

I shall put aside the claim that Musashi did not honor the appointed time set for the duel and deliberately turned up late to infuriate Kojiro. When considering this duel from the perspective of using swords in actual combat, the main point that I am skeptical about is the story that in preparation for the fight Musashi used his short sword to carve a bokuto from a red oak boat oar, in order to create a weapon that was 2 or 3 sun longer than even Kojiro's famously long sword and thus gain an advantage in terms of controlling the combative distance.

The duel at Ganryu Island depicted in a playhouse picture (from the archives of the Tokyo Central Library)

I have drawn up a list below of all the points that I am skeptical about, based on everything I have seen in films, plays, and novelizations that portray the duel scene.[76]

1. It would be impossible to carve up a red oak oar (a tool used to row a Japanese-style boat) using a short sword.[77]
2. There is no way that a veteran of over sixty previous duels like Musashi would even temporarily have relied on an ad-hoc weapon such as a hand-carved bokuto he made himself from an oar.
3. Such a wooden weapon made from an oar would have had considerable weight and thus would have presented problems to the user from a technical perspective.
4. Kojiro would be well used to wielding his long blade and would certainly have had an advantage in a duel over Musashi were he using such an ersatz bokuto.
5. It is reasonable that a wooden sword 2 to 3 sun [6.6 to 9.9 cm] longer than Kojiro's long sword would be advantageous in

---

76. Although the details of the scene vary between works, the most popular and well-known version has Musashi spend several hours after the designated time of the duel carving a wooden sword from an oar before heading out to the island in a boat and leaping straight out to attack Kojiro with the sun behind him, narrowly avoiding Kojiro's first strike and felling him in return.

77. The blade of a *wakizashi* is not designed for carving or whittling and would doubtless be damaged by using it for such an endeavor.

such a confrontation, but if the reach of that weapon could be avoided, then the duel would be decided in short order.

6. The idea that Kojiro would have walked around with such a long sword rested over his shoulder in the Edo period is also highly dubious.[78]

7. It would not have been a good idea from a tactical perspective for Musashi to have jumped from his boat into the shallows of the water and conducted the duel there. On a sandy surface like the beach on the island footing would have been poor and neither combatant could jump up if knocked down.

8. Kojiro would have understood that fighting while staring into the glare of the sun while Musashi had his back to it would place him at a disadvantage.

9. It is said that Kojiro's first strike cut through the knot of Musashi's reddish brown headband, sending it flying off, but in the next instant he was struck on the head by Musashi's weapon and knocked down dead. However, even if the headband were actually sliced off, then it would have been impossible for just the cloth to be cut with no damage at all to the head beneath.

Looking down a list of all the problems with the popular story in this way, one can clearly see how it has been written to capture the imagination of the masses and depict the duel in a way that makes it sound feasible.

Aside from the duel at Ganryu Island there is also the famous tale of how Musashi faced off against Tsukuhara Bokuden,[79] himself wielding twin bokuto while Tsukuhara fought with a pan lid. This story is widely known and has even been depicted in art works, but if one looks at the facts it is clear that it is another fictional tale, as Musashi had not even been born at this time.

---

78. As it was no longer the fashion to do so at this time.

79. 塚原朴伝 [1489–1571]. A renowned sword master and founder of the bokuden ryu who also has many legends and stories associated with him.

The Chujo ryu that Sasaki Kojiro was an exponent of has a link to the sword techniques from seiza seen in the koryu iai practiced today, so I would like to touch on it further here.

Even in the time of Sasaki Kojiro warriors have absolutely never worn a long sword at their hip while inside a house. They would have worn only the kodachi short sword on such occasions and would have considered methods of dealing with an enemy using that instead.

Sasaki Kojiro was a student of Chujo ryu master Toda Seigen, an expert in using the short sword [kodachi/wakizashi].

The main reason for warriors to train in the short sword was due to a custom of the time dictating that, when inside a castle or when entering a house, they could wear only the shorter of their two blades in their belt; they would remove the longer one and carry it in the left or right hand. It is said that Seigen believed the true mark of a martial artist was the ability to triumph over an opponent's long sword using only one's own shorter blade. He made a personal decision to train and master such methods.

It is thought that the seiza-based techniques in modern iaido originated with such indoor short-sword methods, and I surmise that over time techniques intended for the short sword may have changed to become kata for the longer blade.

Additionally, Kojiro founded the Ganryu lineage and was skilled in the decisive and lethally focused tactics of the *kosetsuto* (literally "the tiger cutting sword," also known as *tsubamegaeshi* or "swallow reverse"). Although he was a nominally a student of Seigen's short-sword style, Kojiro pretty much ignored these teachings and instead focused his studies and training on longer swords, leading to his attracting much criticism from his fellow students and ultimately being expelled from the Chujo ryu.

The True Nature of *Fudoshin,* an Unwavering Mind Capable of Subduing a Fierce Tiger

The martial arts are a path of training and dedication to deciding between life and death, and so at their core is the fundamental principle of *fudoshin,* a mind and spirit that is dauntless and unwavering.

Of particular note are the teachings of the *shikai* [four cautions] taught in kendo, which stress that a swordsman should not be surprised, afraid, doubtful, or uncertain. These four cautions against varying forms of distraction sum up the essence of fudoshin: to move away from the boundaries of attachment to physical things, exceed material desire, and come to a place in which the fundamental self is not moved by any and all possible outcomes.

In the solo practice of iaido using a live blade, it is essential to approach training with the same mental state as if a real foe were before you, or the exercise will be no more than a sword dance. The same attitude is required in kendo competitions. The mental state of fudoshin sweeps away all obstructive and wicked thoughts and finds harmony with the grand flow of nature and the universe, like the clear and mirrored surface of still water, endlessly spreading out across the vastness of existence without end. Whatever is undertaken once this state is achieved will see no failure and cannot be rivalled. Mastering the way of the sword will reveal the essence of all the many arts and can become the source and wellspring of all human endeavor.

The true principle behind the way of the sword is not the functional combative ethos of *jutsu* but closer to the path of self-perfection that is *do.* The realms of fudoshin cannot be understood by simply teaching about them using words; one can be enlightened to them only through many long years of forging the self and training the mind and body. Only once such a state has been reached will it be possible to polish and perfect one's personal character.

As shown in the teachings of the "four cautions of the sword" [*ken no shikai*] mentioned above, if one thinks something in their heart and mind then it will without fail be manifested in their actions.

Fudoshin means that if one studies the way of the sword and arrives at an unwavering mental state, then no enemy will be able to draw near, but such a state is born only from endless polishing and forging of the spirit with all of one's being.

In short, none can rival or pose serious opposition against one who ignores concerns of life and death and has no conscious emotion or desire.

The sword methods starting in seiza seen in iaido practice express the teachings of movement in stillness [静中動; *sei chu do*], with the act of sitting serenely in seiza and slowly drawing the sword while adopting a state of no conscious thought or emotion being the aspect of stillness [*sei*].

All actions after the draw belong to the movement [*do*] aspect, as do kendo competition and all parts of kendo training, although before and after kendo the student always sits in seiza and again adopts the aspect of stillness [*sei*]. Meditating in this way is part of the customs of the martial arts and should always be done.

The treatise *Fudochi shinmyoroku*,[80] written by Zen priest Takuan Soho, is undeniably famous among martial arts enthusiasts, but there is one tale in the work regarding fudoshin that is recounted particularly often. Putting aside concerns of whether the tale is true, I would like to look further into it here.

The tale concerns the third-generation Tokugawa Shogun Iemitsu, who ordered the Yagyu lord of Tajima to subdue a fierce and terrible tiger that had been captured on the Korean Peninsula using the inner secrets of his swordsmanship.

The lord of Tajima responded to this order and stepped into the cage bearing a metal war fan. The tiger was driven mad with rage

---

80. 不動智神妙録; literally "divine record of unwavering knowledge." Thought to have been written between 1624 and 1645.

and poised itself to launch a fierce attack, but lord Tajima showed not the slightest fear or surprise and struck the tiger on the head with his iron fan. Upon being struck like this the tiger became like a common house cat and shrank its neck back in submission, although its eyes were still filled with anger.

Unsurprisingly the line of warriors who sat observing this feat rolled their tongues in disbelief. However, the priest Takuan, who was also present, laughed heartily and said to the lord, "My lord Tajima, you cannot call that the true ultimate secret of the martial arts; take a good look at this." Entering the cage the tiger rose up again in bestial anger and made to attack the priest. Takuan carried no weapons at all but spat into the palm of his hand and calmly walked over to place it by the tiger's nose. At this the tiger licked at the hand while wagging its tail excitedly, rolling on its back like a dog being indulged by its master. Takuan leisurely straddled the tiger and addressed the lord again saying, "You see, Lord Tajima: this is the true ultimate expression of the martial arts." The story tells of how Iemitsu and the assembled warriors were agape with awe at this feat, and it clearly expresses the teachings of fudoshin.

Contrasted with the active, moving *[do]* fudoshin of lord Tajima stemming from his *kiai* [conscious focusing of all physical and mental energies into one action], the priest exhibited the fudoshin of stillness *[sei]*. This unwavering mental state that subdued a fierce tiger was born of long training and dedication to the path of maintaining the everyday mind *[heijoshin]* and is surely a fundamental and inviolable rule of mortal combat in martial arts.

In Honor of the Spirit of Ishida Kazuto Sensei

On August 24, 1978, the headquarters of the All-Japan Toyama ryu Battojutsu Federation, the Shoshizankai Shubukan dojo, located at the residence of Mr. Tokutomi Tasaburo in the city of Izu in the Izu area was graced with a visit from the head of the All-Japan Kendo Federation, Ishida Kazuto sensei.

Ishida sensei's visit was because he was "wanting to observe the kata and tameshigiri of the Toyama ryu battojutsu."

Ishida sensei was ushered to the joseki position for honored guests, but he would not go with this and instead sat in a corner of the dojo in seiza before even a cushion could be laid down for him. As Ishida sensei observed with a stern aspect and bearing all assembled, including Mr. Tokutomi, were most shamed and embarrassed at this display of humility.

Once the demonstrations had concluded Ishida sensei declared to us that he "would like to have all those who reach fifth dan in kendo made to possess a Japanese sword and, through kendo, to learn the methods of its use and its noble spirit," and we were brought to feel a deep admiration for chairman Ishida's respect toward the Japanese sword.

Around this time Ishida sensei also gifted me a copy of the book *Nihon kobudo no zenyo [All Aspects of the Classical Martial Arts of Japan]* that was specially published to commemorate the inaugural All-Japan Kobudo Exhibition Event (published as a supplement by Gekkan Budo). In that publication the great Ishida sensei discussed the teachings of Yamaoka Tesshu sensei's Itto Seiden Muto ryu, wisely expounding on how "The sword of no sword *[muto]* is to have no sword on the outside of your heart. This means that when facing down a foe, you do not rely on the sword and instead use your heart and mind to strike at that of the opponent and makes the constant forging of one's spirit vitally important." Ishida sensei was the exalted fifth-generation inheritor of the Muto ryu, and reading his words I came to feel as though I had unconsciously had a lesson imparted to me, explaining that the act of cutting with the Japanese sword or spear is really the cutting of one's own heart and mind.

As a gesture of thanks for Ishida sensei's most magnanimous gift of the book, I humbly sent him some soba noodles that were a famed delicacy from my native prefecture of Yamagata. For this I received a most polite letter and was shamed and embarrassed at this act of generosity. Ishida sensei's noble character, showing his deep understanding of bushido and all due propriety, emanated from the page, bringing me low with admiration and respect.

Furthermore, in 1978 at the second Toyama ryu tameshigiri tournament I humbly asked Ishida sensei if he would accept the role of most senior advisor to our federation. To this I received a response saying that "Ishida is personally delighted at this and will humbly accept the position," and I was overcome at the great honor he did us in accepting.

Later, in October of that year, the film *Eien naru budo [Budo: The Art of Killing]*, which depicted the essence of Japan's martial arts and ways, basked in the glory of winning two gold medals for the Best Picture award and the Best Editing award at the first Miami International Film Festival, and so I sent Ishida sensei a copy of the All-Japan Toyama ryu Iaido Renmei magazine that reported this triumph. Ishida sensei called me on the telephone and congratulated me, saying "It seems that your film showing the martial arts of Japan has taken the

石田和外会長を偲ぶ会

A gathering to remember the late Ishida Kazuto sensei (held at Tokyo's Kudan Kaikan in 1979)

highest accolade at the world film festival. I congratulate you for this and I am looking forward to the picture's unveiling in Japan."

The film was unveiled in Japan in early October 1979 but, just as everyone was looking forward to seeing it, on May 9, an article was published reporting that Ishida sensei had honorably passed away. I was surprised and saddened at this grave news and with the newspaper in hand I telephoned Mr. Tokutomi, but we were both at a loss for words with shock.

Ishida sensei was the chairman of both the All-Japan Kendo Federation and the Yasukuni Shrine Welcoming of the Heroic Souls Society, and under his auspices I had intended that all the officials appointed by these organizations should view the film together, inviting them to a private screening before all others. That this was not now possible was most regrettable.

I would like to introduce here one of the classical poems that Ishida sensei was fond of in his daily life.

Shingi isshi [Heart and Skill Originate as One]
BY THE ZEN PRIEST IKKYU

1. (Absence of thought or emotion)
   Think not of the moon as it reflects on the waters of lake Hirosawa, nor think of the waters as they reflect it.
2. (The movements of the heart and mind as they flow without stagnation)
   The water bird leaves no trace as it comes and goes, forget not the path once it is gone.
3. (The ascetic training to achieve such a state)
   The white heron has hidden itself from the world in the unseen snow-covered fields of winter grass.
4. (The heart and mind)
   What manner of thing is spoken of when we speak of the heart?
   The sound of the wind in the pine trees, rendered in an ink painting.

This poem encapsulates the unspoken teachings of Ishida sensei and was written on a *fusuma* sliding screen in the matted guest room at his home. On occasion I was allowed to read these insightful words.

I sincerely pray for Ishida sensei's peaceful rest and happiness in the next world.

Recollections of the Practical Swordsmanship of Takayama Masakichi Sensei

Soon after the end of the War in 1949, after I had established the Tsurumi Shiseikan dojo, I had former Imperial Naval Academy swordsmanship instructor Kuramochi Matao (kyoshi sixth dan) become my assistant and right hand man. Kuramochi would continue to assist and cooperate with me in instructing swordsmanship for another twenty-seven years, even after the shiseikan had closed down, hiring out schools and other open spaces in which to conduct training. However, in 1971 he died of cancer.

Before passing away, Kuramochi commented to me that "Nakamura sensei's swordsmanship is the same as the battojutsu of Takayama sensei, who promoted practical battlefield sword methods to the naval officers while I was at the Imperial Naval Academy." Intrigued by this I made investigations and found that one of my seniors at the Toyama Military Academy knew of him. This led to Takayama sensei and I meeting a total of three times.

One of these occasions was when I was involved in making the NHK[81] program *Ryoma ga yuku* [In the Footsteps of Sakamoto Ryoma] and instructed and performed as a stand-in for Mr. Kitaoji, who was playing Ryoma. They had Takayama sensei come along to the studio, and we trained together in the Nakamura ryu and Takayama ryu styles. I also personally received instruction from Takayama sensei.

---

81. Nippon Hoso Kyoku (日本放送局): The Japan Broadcasting Company, Japan's public television network.

It turns out that during the Sino-Japanese War Takayama sensei built up a great deal of experience in actual combat using the sword on the battlefield, and using this he studied and developed his own practical cutting methods. There was nobody like him in the kendo world at that time, and I myself am as nothing when compared to such efforts and dedication.

After the War, when the occupying forces came ashore on the homeland, Takayama sensei was indicted as a war criminal for his slaying of several score Chinese soldiers during the earlier Sino-Japanese War. However, I hear that he was spared investigation.

The late Takayama Masakichi sensei, instructor of practical battlefield swordsmanship in his prime.

The essence of martial arts is dedication to training for one's whole life, as long as you have breath left in you. Takayama continued in his martial studies right up until he passed away and managed to collate the publication *Nihon budo taikei (A Survey of Japan's Martial Ways)* and write "Takayama ryu toho iai" ["Takayama Ryu Iai Swordsmanship"]. On the occasion of my visit to lecture at the Ground Self Defense Force Officer Candidate Training College in Kurume in 1978, I was gifted with copies of these publications. I shall refrain from touching on their content here however, and instead would like to illustrate Takayama sensei's great and exalted practical martial arts research and his enthusiasm and respect for the budo by introducing an extract of his other fine work, *Takayama ryu toho saiko shuisho (A Prospectus for the Resurrection of Takayama Ryu Swordsmanship)* that was written after the War. May it be of value to all my readers.

From *Takayama ryu toho saiko shuisho [A Prospectus for the Resurrection of Takayama Ryu Swordsmanship]* (Original text)

The Takayama ryu was founded in the Maizuru army regiments and the Maizuru Police Department and is grounded in the local area of the town of Maizuru, with the support of the Maizuru Middle School and the other Maizuru educational institutions of the municipal area of Kyoto. Its teachings have been refined and perfected under the decisive resolutions of the Imperial army, navy, and air force and assessed and promoted within the Imperial Army Toyama Military Academy. It has become a part of the educational syllabus for the army and navy and is taught in all Imperial Army academies as well as Imperial Navy educational institutions, military schools, in aviation preparatory training, and in the education of supplementary students and warrant officer cadets from the various naval branches. It is employed in the battles of the Imperial Army and Navy and has been further developed on the battlefield. The Takayama ryu is supported and perfected by the warm enthusiasm of the entire town of Maizuru and will ultimately protect

Japan as its final defense. It is the sole and unique ultimate way of the Japanese sword in Japan.

Thus at this critical moment, on the brink of the destruction of the Japanese people, the Takayama ryu will become the people's way of the sword for combat. Bearing the affectionate name of Takayama ryu battojutsu, it will be used faithfully by all soldiers, bureaucrats, and the common people of our nation, and will be greatly trusted and valued highly by all in the final conflict to defend Japan from dissolution. It will also be valued thus in education as a means to forge the spirit. On August 15, 1945, we failed to gain victory in our battles and must now endure shame and insult, forced to capitulate beneath the knees of the enemy by swearing unconditional surrender. The Takayama ryu has endured through this crushing fate and the destined end of the Great Japanese Empire alongside the nation and its people. The axis of enemy forces escalate their pressure and persecution of Takayama ryu swordsmanship, getting harsher each day, and see us as the sole party responsible for all of Japan's kendo. I, Takayama Masakichi, have now done all that I can and all that must be done and taken on the full burden of responsibility. Having discarded the rank equivalent to general that was bestowed upon me by the Imperial military, as well as the recognition from the military for my Takayama ryu and my tenth dan hanshi rankings for kendo, iai and jukendo, I have returned to the unadorned and undecorated state into which I was born. I have resigned myself to the indelible shame and dishonour left in the history of Japan's martial arts of seeing out our defeat as an instructor of said marital arts to the nation during the War. I had taken on the whole responsibility for Japan's kendo, deciding to take my own life to atone for our ingnominous defeat. However, I was ordered from above to desist in my suicide to atone and have been left with the destiny of passing on the Takayama ryu that has shone as an example of greatness in contributing to our nation in its time of crisis and protecting Japan from dissolution. Japan shall most certainly rise again. In preparation for such a time I have come to the realisation that I must now retreat to live in the mountains around Kuju in Kyushu as little more than a beggar and endure the unendurable. Based on my unshakeable faith that, despite Japan's having been broken, the martial arts of Japan will always remain unchanging, I now dedicate myself to showing my humble support for those who died and praying for the safety and protection of their spirits. I am emboldened by the fact that there will be a day when I can see all of the honored dead again and have lived on in the warmth of the town of Kuju for twenty-six long years, watching with a heavy heart as the world beneath the heavens of Japan changes, like the light of a revolving lantern. Knowing not where I should live to be granted the reunion with my comrades that is my only reason for living, the emotions of my whole life are the tears of an old man that flow endlessly like a fountain. I feel this sorrow deeply in my liver and seeping into my bones, and I have no words to express my respect. I can only cry at the weight of emotion in these tragedies. The Takayama ryu that had nobly defended Japan to the last was destroyed by those in control, who were engulfed in the bitter ideologies of defeat prevalent after the War was lost, while conversely sports kendo using bamboo shinai was placed on a pedestal of honor as physical education. This created the new foundations for the development of Japanese kendo and resigned the Takyama ryu to the fate of being ousted for all time. However, in such a dire situation one's sincerity can move heaven and earth, and a path to salvation was opened with discussions and examinations of the worth of the Takayama ryu being made in the nation's highest institutions of physical education for national defense. The Takayama ryu was once again acknowledged, with full permission to teach it being given, and the Takayama Research Dojo has also received extensive support. I have dedicated the remaining time I have in my life, however short this may be, to using the Takayama ryu to contribute to Japan's kendo world. As a single man of the sword, I cannot begin to express my joy at this opportunity, an opportunity that I had given up on even in my dreams. I am also keenly aware of the weight of this great responsibility that I have again been given.

I shall continue to use the essence of kendo as a practical martial art—to teach kendo for spiritual training in these times of peace. Now, as an old man, I humbly and sincerely ask that you understand my devotion and give the Takayama kenkyukai the same warm and spirited support and encouragement that it received during the War. Alongside my declaration to restore the glory of kendo, I would humbly request your support and assistance for the reemergent Takayama ryu swordsmanship with all my heart from here in the mountains of Kuju.

—Takayama Masakichi, former martial arts instructor to Japan during the war years and representative for Takayama Ryu Toho

I would also like to express my great and heartfelt appreciation and thanks to Mr. Chihara Yoshio, a graduate of the former Imperial Navy Military Academy and native of Kyoto; Mr. Oike Shotaro, also from Kyoto; Mr. Ukizu Masaya from Wakayama; Mr. Nakamura Nobuhiro from Ibaraki; and Koyama Isami sensei from Maizuru for their assistance when, in 1977, I requested materials from the research of the Takayama ryu for publication in the pages of the magazine *Nihon budo*.

Appearing in the Film *Eien Naru Budo* (*Budo: The Art of Killing*)

In order to get this film made, producer Masuda Hisao and director Nemoto Masayoshi, two men both born after the War but with a burning passion for Japan's martial arts, presented the idea to every film company in the country. However, not a single one would take on such a project or fund it. Fortunately, American producer Mr. Arthur Davis, himself a great expert on Japan, was willing to donate over a hundred million yen of his own funds for the sake of the martial arts. It is thanks to him that the film finally saw completion.

The theme of the film was the philosophy from the *Hagakure kikigaki* treatise on Japan's code of bushido, the tenet central to budo that one is "to live always as though one is already a dead man." It showcased the various disciplines of Japan's martial arts, but it also looked at subjects from the work of swordsmiths to Noh theatre and Zen Buddhism, all in front of the backdrop provided by the great natural beauty of Japan's four seasons and different regions. This picture was a unique documentary made to transmit correctly the essence of Japan's martial arts, contrasting motion and stillness, life and death.

The martial arts also contain spiritual and religious aspects, and those who follow the ways will drill their techniques with daily training, staking everything on defeating the enemy. At the same time, the ultimate purpose is found in aiming to polish the self and perfect one's character.

Furthermore, in this age of peace, the martial arts have become a kind of artistic expression, fighting to polish the self in order to get closer and closer to perfection.

This film that approaches the true essence of Japan's martial arts and tells of their history took around three years to make, and in November of 1978 it was showcased at the first Miami International Film Festival in the United States where, out of more than eighty pictures submitted from all around the globe, it took two gold medals for the Best Picture award and Best Editing award.

However, I cannot help but feel regret about the production of this fine film. Were such a picture about the martial arts of Japan to have been made and funded by Japanese hands and Japanese money, then I would have no complaints at all. But is it not a great shame and embarrassment to a lover of the martial arts, nay to a Japanese person who is a martial arts enthusiast, that it was the personal money of a single American that made the film?

Today Japan's political sphere and economy are in turmoil. Looking at the current state of Japan's film industry, with its rampant overabundance of romance pictures, pornography, and comic book films, I cannot help but feel there has been a drop in the Japanese people's overall levels of education. I lament the future of the nation.

It does not follow for all, but among people who dedicate themselves to the martial arts there are many who aim for proper philosophical guidance and strive toward fostering a patriotic spirit. In particular, at the core of the martial arts is the tenet that one should value courtesy and respect, the most important things for humanity.

Thus I would like for the government and politicians in general to gain a fresh awareness and appreciation of the martial arts. We have come to a period in history when the whole of the Japanese population is awakening and, for the sake of educating those young men who will support the future of our nation, I would hope for all to gain a fresh recognition of the importance of forging the martial arts spirit through this film.

A scene from the film *Eien naru budo (Budo: The Art of Killing)*.

Matsumoto Koshiro Is Instructed in Killing

In spring of 1952, as part of the promotions for the opening of a new Shinkokugeki[82] production of Miyamoto Musashi, the late Kurihara sensei from Tokyo's Taito ward borrowed space in the Miyagi Mae plaza to set up a temporary dojo facility and hold a kendo tournament in the hopes of resurrecting kendo after the War. The winner of this tournament would be presented with a "Miyamoto Musashi prize," and the runner up awarded a "Sasaki Kojiro prize." Many kendoka from Tokyo and the surrounding prefectures gathered, and an epic contest was held that centered mainly on the renshi-level competitors.

I myself competed in this tournament using the two-sword style but came to face off against the late Nakamura Taro in the semifinals. (Nakamura would later go on to become the kendo instructor for the Kanagawa prefectural police department and win the third and seventh All-Japan Kendo Federation national tournaments.) The referee officiating this match was Nakamura's own father, the late Nakamura Tokichi sensei (later to be awarded hanshi rank). The Nakamura family really were a dedicated kendo family, with the father Tokichi opening up the Taigijuku dojo as one of the first new dojos after the War and working hard toward the resurgence of kendo. The second son, Fujio, also currently holds the rank of kyoshi. Alas it is most unfortunate that Taro died of cancer at the age of forty-seven. He will be missed. I myself have visited the Taigijuku dojo to train on three separate occasions, and it brings back fond memories.

At the time of the tournament Nakamura Taro was a kendo fourth dan and was the youngest competitor on the mats that day. His footwork was excellent and his two-level strike highly regarded, making him a kendoka of outstanding skill. Although I managed to score a single point against him in the three-point match, I was soundly defeated and Taro went on to the final. At the same time Mr. Murata

---

82. Literally "new national drama." A stage production troupe founded in 1917 by Sawada Shojiro and renowned for its realistic sword fight choreography.

Shigeru (currently ranked eighth dan) also went through and would be his opponent for the deciding match. Murata was my junior and would occasionally come to my dojo for training, but his skill was outstanding.

The final between Murata and Nakamura was a solid match that saw both competitors making effective use of their techniques from chudan kamae, although in the end Nakamura secured victory and took the Miyamoto Musashi prize while Murata got the Sasaki Kojiro prize. This magnificent tournament at Miyagi Mae was held in the days before the foundation of the All-Japan Kendo Federation and was a fresh and memorable experience for all at the time.

The Shinkokugeki production that the tournament was held to promote received critical acclaim and achieved wild popularity, with Tatsumi Ryutaro playing Musashi and Shimada Shogo as Kojiro.

Around the same time the actor Matsumoto Koshiro was due to start filming on the Toho Studio's production of Araki Matauemon. It turns out that I had been noticed for my use of two swords at the aforementioned Miyagi Mae tournament, and I was approached by Kurihara sensei and requested to instruct Matsumoto for choreographing the bloody battle scene at the Kagiya crossroads that used the two-sword style. I taught Koshiro the basic stances of the two-sword style and tameshigiri using left and right kesagiri at the Shinbashi Enbujo with the late Nakamura Kichiuemon Jo in attendance. I was surprised to find that in the next day's edition of the *San* newspaper, there were reports of the Miyagi Mae tournament including pictures of the moment when Nakamura Taro and Murata Shigeru were awarded the Miyamoto Musashi and Sasaki Kojiro prizes at the Shinkoku theater and continuing to an extensive report entitled "Matsumoto Koshiro is instructed in killing" with a photograph of Kurihara sensei, Kichiuemon Jo, Koshiro, and myself cutting bundles of straw. (This would become a major stimulus for the resurgence of kendo.)

At that time the postwar Act for the Prohibition of Kendo was still in force, and due to this the media and journalists were wont to roll their eyes at talk of things like the resurgence of kendo or tameshigiri with the Japanese sword. This reminded me very much of the period at the beginning of the Meiji era when, after the *haitorei* edict banning the wearing of swords was passed, Sakakibara Kenkichi sensei's kendo shows achieved popularity for a time and opened the way for a similar resurgence of the sword arts.

"Yes, just like that!" Sixth dan Nakamura (second from the right) instructs Matsumoto Koshiro (far right). In the center is Nakamura Kichiuemon Jo.

CONCLUSION

There will be some out there who think it undesireable and backward to stress the essential value found in test cutting with the Japanese sword in this age of civilization that we live in today.

However, I personally believe that in touching upon the spirit of the Japanese sword, which is steeped in tradition, and by continuously training in kendo, iaido, and tameshigiri, one has as his objective the training of the spirit, the nurturing and development of one's personal character, and the forging of one's mind and body. These are pursuits that resonate through the here-and-now practicality of our everyday lives and cannot be explained by mere reason or logic.

The grand traditions of the Yamato race are those of a nation that values martial endeavor in particular. The spirit of bushido is not simply that of lauding military might for the sake of conflict with others but actually has at its core the Japanese spirit of harmony. This is clearly reflected in the first character used to write bushido, "武" [bu; military, martial], which is made up of radicles meaning, "To stop the glaive." Accordingly, it is precisely these methods of spiritual training and enhancement found in one's everyday life that foster the true spirit of the Japanese martial arts. Furthermore, I firmly believe that for these arts to have value they must be experienced firsthand, by actually taking up the Japanese sword and undergoing its trials.

The spiritual teachings of the martial arts, philosophies, and mental states such as munen muso, fudoshin, heijoshin, kendo no shikai, shinkiryoku, kigurai, hoshin, shishin, zanshin, and so forth are all ways of spiritual training derived from physically and mentally experiencing the martial arts—arts that deal in life and death—for oneself. The ultimate value in such training is not found in theory but in going out and engaging in it.

It is not completely pointless to try and explain concepts such as these to novices through theory, but true understanding will only come naturally through gradual mastery and training by unquestioningly following the example set before you. Simply put, life itself is training to be done unto death.

Kendo competitions embody the spirit of endless and constant forging of the self, with victory or defeat being decided long before the event in each competitor's daily trials. We must unite the arts of kendo, iaido, and in particular tameshigiri together into one discipline, avoiding getting caught up in concerns over the various classical kata and penetrating through to the essence of all swordsmanship to touch upon the soul of the Japanese sword itself. Once such a feat has been achieved we will surely be able to taste the true spirit of the martial arts!

I shall continue to work ceaselessly to exhort the value in the essence of test cutting with the Japanese sword to all sword enthusiasts of character and devotion.

NAKAMURA TAISABURO
Spring 1980

ALL-JAPAN TOYAMA RYU TAMESHIGIRI TOURNAMENT

On September 16, 1979, a tournament was held in the Tsurumi Kaikan, Yokohama, to decide the greatest practitioner of tameshigiri in Japan. More than two hundred participants from all over the country gathered, regardless of style, to show their skills. The following photographs are of the swordsmen and swordswomen who achieved success in the finals for the individual and team events.

The judging panel watches a spirited performance of dodangiri.

Swordsman Obata from the Toyama ryu entertainment-industry branch wins the individual event. His poise and presence radiate like the journeymen warriors of old.

Swordsman Yamanaka, representing the Japan Self-Defense Force, demonstrates *suihei giri* in the semifinals of the individual event.

Swordsman Shirai from Yokohama achieves success in the team event.

Swordsman Shinoda performs a rising cut.

Swordsman Kojima from Totsuka performs a diagonal rising cut to the right.

Swordswoman Ms. Terajima from Yamanashi

Swordsman Aoyagi performs hidari kesagiri. Here we see the very moment he is about to cut.

Swordsman Yoshida performs dodangiri.

Swordsman Nakano performs dodangiri.

APPENDIX 1:
ORIGINAL FOREWORDS

The original Japanese publication of this book in 1980 contained the following five forewords. They have been included here to give the reader a better idea of the importance and impact of Nakamura's work on the Japanese martial arts and sword community at the time.

Introduction

By Kouno Kenzo
Chairman of the Nihon Taiiku Kyokai (Japan Sports Association) and former Speaker of the House of Councillors

There is a saying from the old days: "One who forges on through the tribulations of youth in pursuit of a life of value will be able to lead a life of even greater value." This philosophy is exemplified by my good friend, Nakamura Taisaburo, who is without doubt a hero of swordsmanship in Japan's martial arts world.

This book, *The Essence of Test Cutting with the Japanese Sword* [Original Japanese title], has been written based on Nakamura's immensely valuable experience of martial arts as applied in real conflict and on the teachings of the classical schools to which he has dedicated his whole life. Furthermore, it manages to express, in its entirety, the spirit of the Japanese sword—the soul of the proud Yamato warrior. I would like to express my deepest admiration and respect regarding the publication of this work.

Nakamura is truly a martial artist who represents the best of modern Japan, and his most uncommon level of study into what lies at the heart of swordsmanship has produced the *happo giri*—an exceedingly logical method of sword handling of great value to pass on to future generations. I hear that this method was formulated taking inspiration from the eiji happo that forms the basis of teaching calligraphy. The numerous unique photos in this book are worth looking at as they illustrate, break down, and analyze the happo giri and many other sword techniques in great detail.

During the War Nakamura was assigned to northern Manchuria (in the northeast of China) to teach swordsmanship to various unit officers in the Imperial Japanese Army, and in this role as a sword instructor he implemented real combat-based test cutting training based on techniques that integrated both iai and kendo practices. Nakamura posesses a wonderfully frank and openhearted character, and his honest and unpretentious life has truly been colorful and filled with all the glories of a martial artist.

In my opinion Nakamura's martial arts philosophy, as expressed through his sword, is something rare and special. His spirited activities have always come from a firm and unyielding view of life and show a constant effort in struggling to achieve his duty and ideals.

I am a firm believer that the promotion of the Japanese martial spirit among the nation's youth, those destined to rise in turn to lead the next generation, is of great importance and intimately tied to their moral and intellectual education. As such I devote myself continuously to the promulgation of martial arts and sports.

I was once affectionately called the "marathon speaker," and nowadays I am the chairman of the Japan Sports Association. In the same spirit that Nakamura approaches his budo, even now, if I have a spare minute, you will find me running and breaking a sweat. The marathon is a battle with loneliness and a struggle against oneself, and this highlights the important truth that both sports and the martial arts are more than simply ways of training the body; they are also a foundation for mental and spiritual growth and a valuable friend.

As we welcome in the 1980s, politics and the economy are threatened by the three dark spectres of inflation, recession, and rising prices. But it is exactly at times like this that I feel we need a healthy and robust sporting mindset alongside the martial arts.

I am overcome with nothing but admiration at "the Showa era's martial artist of the true battlefield," Nakamura Taisaburo, a master of the Japanese sword, steeped in the traditions of the Yamato people, and can thoroughly recommend this book to all enthusiasts of the martial arts, lovers of the Japanese sword, and those with an appreciation of its fine and noble spirit.

A Sense of Power That Comes Only from the Battlefield

By Hatta Ichiro
Chairman of the Zen Nihon Jukendo Renmei
[All-Japan Jukendo Federation]
and former Member of the House of Councillors

Since the War Nakamura Taisaburo sensei has consistently endeavored to spread the military sword-handling methods that were formulated at the former Toyama Academy (now Toyama ryu iaido) and the practice of tameshigiri far and wide, and in recent years has formed the Zen Nihon Toyama ryu Iaido Renmei. This fine organization has unashamedly brought out the essence of the Japanese sword with its thorough research into the techniques of actual cutting with sharpened swords, as relevant to the sister disciplines of iaido and kendo, and I must express my deepest respect and admiration toward the fighting spirit of its members.

Nakamura sensei is a true master of both kendo and iaido, with vast experience, and he was also an all-Japan jukendo champion. During the War he was assigned to the Second Yamashita Army Group Southern Special Attack Unit as an instructor of practical battlefield martial arts and taught combat-focused military sword handling to the military officers of the day in a most realistic manner.

I have seen Nakamura sensei appear on the television many times, and the tameshigiri technique he displays at various martial arts events is already in the realm of *kamiwaza* [literally "divine skill"]. The sheer power and presence that he radiates as he cuts down the green bamboo and straw targets like a raging gale is something that can only come from practical experience on the battlefield and cannot be impersonated.

On top of this, the Nakamura ryu happo giri exercise that Nakamura sensei formulated based on his own experience with tameshigiri capitalizes fully on the strengths of the Toyama ryu iaido and is an eminently logical sword-handling method that elicits from me nothing but awe.

Nakamura sensei is a peerless representative of the Yamato people and has integrated kendo, iaido, and tameshigiri in his ceaseless endeavors in research into perfection of the spirit of the Japanese sword. I can widely recommend this book to all who share his passion and interest.

The International Promotion and Development of Japanese Martial Arts

By Kiyoura Sueo
Chairman of the Kokusai Budoin Renmei
(International Martial Arts Federation)

The International Martial Arts Federation has set working toward the international proliferation and development of Japan's martial arts and contributing to peace and goodwill around the world as its goals. We have been honored by having former prince Higashikuni Naruhiko (Japan's first postwar prime minister) take on its presidency.

Until recently the Federation promoted nine distinct martial disciplines, but it has now set up a new division devoted to battojutsu, making a total of ten arts, and in the interests of fostering the spirit of the Japanese sword Mr. Nakamura Taisaburo, shihan of the Toyama ryu and of hanshi ninth dan rank, has agreed to become our first battojutsu representative. Mr. Nakamura was recently (January 20, 1980) presented with the certificate of recognition for leadership of the battojutsu division at the Higashikuni Manor by the prince himself.

I have had the fortune to read Mr. Nakamura's previous publications *Iaido* and *Iai kendo,* and not only do they cover a substantial amount of theory on iaido and kendo but are written based on his long years of experience with the Japanese sword, both before and after the War, and bring together these disciplines alongside tameshigiri into one holistic whole.

During the War Mr. Nakamura was apparently stationed in Manchuria (the northern part of China) as a special swordsmanship instructor, carrying out training for officers of the Imperial Army divisions, making good use of the gunto no soho methods (a system created at the Toyama Military Academy from actual battlefield experiences and now referred to as Toyama ryu iaido), and including tameshigiri test cutting exercises practical for actual combat. I hear that during the second half of the War in the Pacific he was assigned to the ranks of the Second Yamashita Army Group Southern Special Attack Unit on no fewer than three separate occasions, but each time he was always ordered by the unit commanders to be exchanged out for someone else so that he could continue with his swordsmanship instruction. Finally, four months before the conflict ended, Nakamura's unit was ordered to return from northern Manchuria and transferred to Fukuoka in northern Kyushu to prepare for the final battle for the homeland. Nakamura's commanding officer ordered him to instruct civilian militia units in the *hitori hissatsu* [sure killing of a single enemy] ideology as related to sword handling and to prepare "bamboo spear" patrols in readiness for an American Army invasion. It was doing this that he saw out the end of the War.

After the War Mr. Nakamura expressed his feelings that "My art has saved me; my role as a sword instructor has saved my life," and told of how "bearing this in mind I shall push on along the path of the sword with unceasing thanks toward it." This is exactly what he has put into practice.

Since then he has continued to perfect what he has learned from those priceless experiences, and I must express my utmost admiration and respect at his publication of this new book, *The Essence of Test Cutting with the Japanese Sword.*

Mr. Nakamura has formulated the excellent happo giri sword-training method based on all his experiences with test cutting using the Japanese sword and even now continues with his research into the sword as the first-generation soke of Nakamura ryu battojutsu. I believe that this book will become a must read for all kendo and iaido enthusiasts and, joining with the president of our federation, former prince Higashikuni Naruhiko, I would like to thoroughly and widely recommend this volume to all practitioners of the Japanese sword arts.

In Commemoration of the Publication of Nakamura Shihan's *The Essence of Test Cutting with the Japanese Sword*

By Fushimi Ryu
Chief Executive Officer of the Zen Nihon Toyama ryu
Iaido Renmei (All-Japan Toyama ryu Iaido Federation)

Nakamura Taisaburo sensei has spent his life so far dedicated to pursuing the essence of the Japanese sword—the spiritual heritage of the Japanese people—and has encouraged an ethos of all-or-nothing dedication among martial arts enthusiasts. The publication of this book, which correctly communicates the heart and soul of the Japanese sword, is a momentous occasion and for sword enthusiasts is in no uncertain terms akin to the cutting of the Gordian knot. I would like to recommend this book as a text that all who study the martial arts and the way of the sword should own.

It is said that the bushi comes to the realm of egolessness through constantly facing down and coming to terms with their own death at the end of much arduous contemplation and meditation, and achieves the inner masteries of the oneness of sword and zen, expressed as *ken zen ichinyo*.

This book is the consummation of a process of practical and ideological maturation and perfection in much the same way that the martial arts of Japan emerged from the ideology of bushido, and even attempts to examine the psychological and spiritual makeup of the Japanese people. I hope that it will encourage much reflection and self-improvement as a wise and scholarly text on the Japanese spirit, extolling the appeal and enthralling charm of the Japanese sword, pride of the Yamato people, and that it will become a foundation for physical, intellectual, and moral education through the medium of the Japanese sword.

Former Supreme Court judge, chairman of the Zen Nihon Kendo Renmei [All-Japan Kendo Federation] and a fifth-generation master of Yamaoka Tesshu's Muto ryu school, the late Ishida Kazuto sensei came to know Nakamura shihan through his television activities and other channels. They got together to practice and talk on many occasions. It is said that Ishida sensei expressed great approval of Nakamura, saying of him, "He is someone to whom others are drawn, a rare sword master of the Showa period and possessed of immense natural ability, a rare and seldom-seen talent." It is in no doubt that Nakamura sensei is a towering and influential figure in the world of Japanese martial arts.

In recent years the refinement and polish in Nakamura shihan's technique is something that can only be described as magnificent and should be beheld by a wider audience, his skill deepening as he increases in age. I thoroughly recommend this book, which illustrates and breaks down that technique with modern photography, as a must-read volume for all modern warriors dedicated to practice with sharpened swords.

Nakamura Ryu Happo Giri and Its Value in Fight Choreography

By Hayashi Kunishiro
Chairman of the Nihon Bugeki Kai
[Japan Martial Film Association]

In creating sword-fighting scenes for Japanese period drama you cannot just make do with perfunctory and careless movement and choreography because "it is only acting." Over many years I have adopted the sword-handling methods of the koryu schools into my work and have experienced and researched all kinds of martial arts and sports that have relevance to creating period fight scenes. All these disciplines have some value, but above all it is a lethal sword technique that is most required by the *jidaigeki* fight choreographer's craft. The happo giri of Nakamura ryu battojutsu is a most logical sword-handling method the like of which cannot be found in other koryu schools. It does not get caught up in a rigid fixation on the formal kata of iaido or kendo and in its eminent practicality for actual combat touches on the true warrior spirit of budo.

Modern kendo has become very sportified in its nature, and although the technical perfection within it exceeds the kendo of the past, it has visibly moved away from the realities of the battlefield. On the other hand, mainstream iaido has become fixated on the old style sword methods of the koryu. The drawing methods from seiza that it promotes are a technique that would be unthinkable from the perspective of real sword fighting with sharpened blades, so neither of these disciplines have a great deal of use as reference for period-fight choreography. Compared to these the logicality of the Nakamura ryu happo giri live-bladed sword-handling method, linked to the purely practical, standing technique–only curriculum of Toyama ryu iaido, runs through the essence of iai, kendo, and tameshigiri and in my opinion is of great value in researching sword-fight choreography.

Nakamura sensei has more experience of the essence of test cutting with the Japanese sword than anyone alive, and I can thoroughly and widely recommend this book based on that experience to enthusiasts everywhere.

APPENDIX 2:
THE TRUTH BEHIND THE SCHISM
IN THE ZEN NIHON IAIDO RENMEI

This passage was included in the "anecdotes" section of the original edition and gives Nakamura's opinion on the organizational politics in the Zen Nihon Iaido Renmei around the time of publishing in 1980. Although perhaps of little interest to the modern reader, it has been included out of completeness and to give further insight into the man himself.

The Truth behind the Schism in the Zen Nihon Iaido Renmei

Five years ago Kouno Hyakuren sensei, twentieth-generation inheritor of the Muso Jikiden Eishin ryu and chairman of the All-Japan Iaido Federation [Zen Nihon Iaido Renmei] passed away, causing a crisis surrounding the sucession of the twenty-first generation inheritor. The All-Japan Iaido Federation, which should rightly unite all the different ryuha of iaido together under one body, was caught up in this affair and, as a result split in schism, a development that in all truth I find most exceedingly lamentable.

At the time I was an advisor to the Federation and sincerely desired that it remained united, so I sent a letter to the various senior instructors urging them to work toward keeping it together. However, it appears that my efforts were in vain. I would like to go into the truth behind this event—the splitting asunder of the organization that was the All-Japan Iaido Federation, due to a confusion of public and private matters regarding but a single ryuha—and to ask whether this is really an acceptable precedent for future individual ryuha issues.

In May of this past year of 1975, at the All-Japan Iaido Federation's Kyoto tournament, I was surprised and shocked when I came to look at the list of federation officials in the program for the event.

Thanks to the efforts of Oono Kumao sensei, the All-Japan Iaido Federation has been honored with fittingly august figureheads from its inception right through today, such as its first and second heads, former Prime Minister Ikeda Hayato and His Royal Majesty, the former Kaninnomiya prince, and vice heads such as Genda Minoru, Takaki Sakuyuki, and Oono Kumao. It was unbelievably reckless and selfish for a small group to completely reconstitute the whole register of officials without the permission of the head or vice head of the organization, in the mere three months since the passing of chairman Kouno.

I see this lamentable outcome as resulting from the unauthorized actions of a core of federation officials, originating in the succession disputes of a single school, the Muso Jikiden Eishin ryu.

Some time later I received a letter from Oono Kumao sensei and various officials representing the different local branches, entitled "The dissolution of the All-Japan Iaido Federation" and after that, one entitled "The founding of the Greater Japan Iaido Federation" and a memorandum from Hatajima sensei announcing his resignation and taking on responsibility for the standing down of his majesty as the head of the organization. All of these were put out by officials who were wound up in the succession disputes. In my opinion they were most miserable undertakings.

Currently the former All-Japan Iaido Federation has split into three organizations: one that bears the original name, the Greater Japan Iaido Federation [Dai Nippon Iaido Renmei], and the National Iaido Federation [Zenkoku Iaido Renmei]. The sucession disputes of a single ryuha should at most affect the creation of cliques within that school, and it is truly regrettable that such an occurrence has caused the swordsmen dedicated to iaido in such an important federation to become split and separated. I humbly request that all the officials of the old federation take responsibility for this tragedy and consider the future.

Looking back over its history, the All-Japan Iaido Federation started out when Oono Kumao sensei and a number of other Iaido representatives approached the All-Japan Kendo Federation [AJKF], hoping to have them integrate iaido under their auspices. However, as the kendo federation was founded purely around sports kendo using a shinai, they turned down the art of iaido that uses a real sword as not being compatible. Ono sensei had no choice but to found his own separate organization of dedicated iaido enthusiasts and, using his connections, managed to get his junior from Kyoto university, the then Prime Minister Ikeda Hayato (now deceased) to become its head. However, four years later, seeing that the practice of iaido had flourished and was growing in popularity, the AJKF set up an iaido division, despite at first having denied the art of iaido.

This was also an attempt to oppose Oono sensei and his associates' campaign to ressurect the Dai Nippon Butokukai, and it is due to this kind of politicking that today's All-Japan Iaido Federation cannot help falling behind.

For many years I and a number of other iaido enthusiasts have called for the unification of the All-Japan Kendo Federation's Iaido division and the All-Japan Iaido Federation, but alas as both groups are too caught up with attachments to their ryuha such unification has still not been realized to this day. I personally express my admiration and respect to the All-Japan Kendo Federation's Iaido division for its contribution to the promotion and popularization of iaido, but I cannot help but find the situation regrettable.

These actions, which led to the schism in the All-Japan Iaido Federation while overall leadership of the art was in such a quandry, can be nothing but the unauthorized and selfish undertakings of people who have forgotten the true spirit of the martial arts. As long as they hold to the name of the All-Japan Iaido Federation, those in charge should suppress their petty, private concerns and adopt an attitude that prioritizes the public communal good, embodying the Japanese way of harmony in their actions during these trying times, helping each other out while holding their own opinions, and managing the organization without getting caught up in individual lineages' succession problems.

The schism that split the All-Japan Iaido Federation makes it a laughingstock when viewed by the All-Japan Kendo Federation's Iaido division and is of great detriment to its reputation. To redeem the organization, we must bring back the true spirit of the martial arts and thoroughly revise our approach and understanding.

Struggles for power and influence are not limited to the political sphere but are an inevitability in all things. However, for a group that is, even in the smallest sense, dedicated to the art of iaido, based on the spirit of the martial arts, all members should come together in unity and work for the benefit of the art, aiming toward the lofty goal of fostering the spirit of the Japanese sword.

How many different martial arts organizations and governing bodies must exist today? Far too many, that is for sure. I sincerely hope and wish for the unification of all martial arts groups and federations into one integrated organization under the auspices of a government body, as it was in the prewar days with the Dai Nippon Butokukai, in order that correct education in the martial spirit can be carried out without interference.

ABOUT THE AUTHOR
NAKAMURA TAISABURO (1912–2003)

Nakamura Taisaburo began his study of the martial arts at the age of fifteen, and when he joined the Japanese Army in 1932 held the rank of third dan in both kendo and judo. He taught kendo within the army and at a junior military academy and served in Manchuria in the elite Yamashita Special Attack Force, later being assigned to the Toyama Military Academy in Tokyo where he became an instructor of combat swordsmanship, bayonet, and knife fighting. Nakamura was convinced that his special skills with the sword were what resulted in his returning to Japan as an instructor and saved him from the fate of many of his sword instructor comrades. He therefore dedicated his life to the study and teaching of the life-giving sword—katsujinken—but was adamant that practice remain rooted in the realities of combat. To maintain the tradition of Toyama Academy swordsmanship, he founded the All-Japan Toyama Ryu Iaido Federation and continued his lifelong research into the practices of Japanese swordsmanship. The outcome of these efforts was the founding of Nakamura Ryu Battodo in 1952. Among his numerous titles and ranks, he was awarded tenth dan hanshi in battodo, seventh dan kyoshi from the All-Japan Kendo Federation, eighth dan hanshi jukendo, and eighth dan hanshi tankendo. He continued to study, practice, teach, and inspire until his death in Tsurumi on May 13, 2003.

ABOUT THE TRANSLATOR

GAVIN J. POFFLEY is a professional Japanese translator and a dedicated martial artist. He has extensively trained in both the classical and modern forms of budo, holding dan grades in Okinawan karate and koryu jujutsu. Poffley earned a bachelor's degree in Japanese language and culture and a master's degree in Japanese translation from the School of Oriental and African Studies in London and has also earned qualifications from Tokyo University of Foreign Studies and Hiroshima University.

CONTRIBUTORS

The following people are gratefully acknowledged for their contributions toward the cost of translation and photographic reproduction.

U.S.A.

Dave Drawdy
Carl McClafferty
Carl Jenkins
Joshua Badgley
Viet Nguyen
Alfred S. McLaren, Jr.
Raymond A. Sosnowski
Tom Wadlow
Katka Davitaia
Patrick Bannister
Chris Treichel
RJ Oak
Jason Lee A. Hatcher
Christopher Durr
L. Kent Jensen
Kristian Ryan T. Estacio
Joe Ortiz
Emily Bannister
Marta Beck
Dillon Heh
Andre Gomes
Yoshi Satoh

U.K.

John Evans
Karen Watson
Matthew Simpson
Chris Barron
Meryl Wade
Gareth Huw Davies
Sanya Weber
Szymon Chobrak
Piotr Kwiecien
Tillmann Pape

Australia

Shandor Remete
Gordon Armstrong
Mat Rous

Canada

Darko Gedelovski

Indonesia

Ary Ginanjar Agustian

Serbia

Dejan Damnjanovic
Bojan Ivkovic

Japan

Kakuseikai (鶴誠会)

Kagawa Battoudou (香川抜刀道)

Kindai Taiikukai Iaido Bu (近畿大学体育会居合道部)

Itsue Otsuka (大塚 乙衞)

Naotsugu Hitotsuyanagi (一柳 直嗣)

Masao Inoue (井上 雅雄)

Kouji Tsutsumi (堤 光司)

Kenji Hidaka (日高 健治)

Masataka Iwahashi (岩橋 正貴)

Akifusa Suganuma (菅沼 昭房)

Kotaro Nakamura (中村 宏太郎)

Yutaka Tsuzuki (都築 裕)

Tsutomu Ishikawa (石川 務)

Kenzo Nakamura (中村 憲三)

Itsuo Imamura (今村 逸夫)

Yoshitaka Nomura (野村 義隆)

Seiji Sato (佐藤 征二)

Hiromitsu Takano (高野 弘光)

Takeo Maeda (前田 武郎)

Junji Kida (喜田 純二)

Yuuichiro Shoguchi (将口 裕一郎)

Koichi Iseki (井石 広一)

Shuichi Kitamura (北村 秀一)

Teruaki Kubo (久保 輝明)

Masatoshi Kyokuyama (曲山 正敏)

Osamu Tomioka (富岡 修)

Ayato Suzuki (鈴木 彩斗)